MW00581549

Interests and Opportunities

Pittsburgh Series in Composition,
Literacy, and Culture

David Bartholomae and Jean Ferguson Carr, Editors

Interests and Opportunities

Race, Racism, and University Writing Instruction in the Post–Civil Rights Era

STEVE LAMOS

UNIVERSITY OF PITTSBURGH PRESS

All archival materials listed as obtained from the University of Illinois archives appear courtesy of the University of Illinois at Urbana–Champaign Archives. All archival materials listed as obtained from the University of Illinois English Department archives appear courtesy of the University of Illinois at Urbana–Champaign English Department.   .

A version of chapter 2 appeared as "Literacy and the Institutional Dynamics of Racism: Late-1960s Writing Instruction for 'High-Risk' African American Undergraduate Students at One Predominantly White University," *CCC* 60.1 (2008): 46–81. Copyright 2008, National Council of Teachers of English. Reprinted by permission.

A version of chapter 3 appeared as "Literacy Crisis and Color-Blindness: The Problematic Racial Dynamics of Mid-70s Language and Literacy Instruction for 'High-Risk' Minority Students," *CCC* 61.2 (2009): 373; W126–48. Copyright 2009, National Council of Teachers of English. Reprinted by permission.

Library of Congress Cataloging-in-Publication Data
Lamos, Steve.
 Interests and opportunities : race, racism, and university writing instruction in the post-civil rights era / Steve Lamos.
   p. cm. — (Pittsburgh series in composition, literacy, and culture)
 Includes bibliographical references and index.
 ISBN 978-0-8229-6173-4 (pbk. : alk. paper)
 1. English language—Composition and exercises—Study and teaching—United States.
 2. Racism—United States. I. Title.
 PE1405.U6.L323 2011
 808'.0420711—dc23   2011020851

CONTENTS

Chapter 1. The Development and Evolution of High-Risk
            Writing Instruction   1

Chapter 2. The Late 1960s and Early 1970s: Coming to Terms
            with Racial Crisis   21

Chapter 3. The Mid-1970s: Literacy Crisis Meets Color Blindness   56

Chapter 4. The Late 1970s and Early 1980s: Competence Concerns
            in the Age of *Bakke*   86

Chapter 5. The Late 1980s and Early 1990s: Culture Wars and
            the Politics of Identity   117

Chapter 6. The Late 1990s to the Present: The End of an Era?   151

Notes   179

Works Cited   193

Index   213

Interests and Opportunities

The Development and Evolution of
High-Risk Writing Instruction

THE 1960s FOUND U.S. mainstream colleges and universities presiding over an overwhelmingly white student body. Studies from the time period reveal that mainstream four-year institutions had an African American population of roughly 2 percent (Egerton, *State Universities* 6) and a combined population of "other" races and ethnicities (i.e., Latinos, Native Americans, and Asian Americans) that was even smaller (Karen 229–30). As the 1960s progressed, however, activists involved in the Civil Rights Movement increasingly demanded through demonstrations, rallies, and protests that predominantly white campuses be desegregated. Ethnic studies scholars Thomas J. LaBelle and Christopher R. Ward recount that "charges of racism, sexism, and elitism were clearly part of the student outcry against the status quo [during this time]. These criticisms, in turn, led to the occupation of administrative offices, and in certain cases campus violence, to demand change in higher education through greater representation of the minority experience in the curriculum" (71).

In response to these activist demands, predominantly white four-year institutions across the United States began to develop "high-risk" educational programs that were explicitly designed to recruit, admit, and graduate "low-income and minority-group students who lack the credentials—but not the qualities—to succeed in college" (Egerton, *Higher Education* 7). Buttressed by large-scale federal support, high-risk programs were rapidly developed on campuses throughout the late 1960s and early 1970s in the form of TRIO programs, educational opportunity programs (EOP), open admissions programs, and other related efforts—all designed to offer "assistance in meeting basic college requirements, opportunities for academic development, and motivation [for students] to successfully complete their postsecondary education" (McElroy and Armesto 375).[1] One 1971 study of approximately twelve hundred predominantly white institutions found six hundred four-year campuses reporting one or more full-scale high-risk programs, along with another three hundred or so programs featuring at least some new form of support (McDaniel and McKee 1). Another 1977 study found that over 60 percent of all "senior colleges" in the United States, along with 80 percent of all community colleges, had some sort of high-risk program (Roueche and Snow 30). Even in the present day, a large number of high-risk programs continue to operate at significant cost: the current federal TRIO program, which serves a range of underrepresented students, encompasses more than 2,850 programs at a cost of nearly $880 million (U.S.D.E., Office of Postsecondary Information n.p.). Meanwhile, its Student Support Services (SSS) program, geared specifically toward supporting disadvantaged college students, comprised 947 programs in 2009, with a budget of just over $300 million (U.S.D.E., "Student Support" par. 1).

The proliferation of high-risk programs in turn prompted the widespread development of high-risk writing programs—which, since the mid-1970s, have been most commonly known as basic writing (BW) programs—designed to meet the purported language and literacy needs of these students. Geneva Smitherman describes this widespread development: "Programs and policies such as Upward Bound, open enrollment, Educational Opportunity Programs (EOPs), preferential/affirmative action admissions, and the development of special academic courses ('basic' writing) brought a new and different brand of student into the college composition classroom. Unlike the returning military veterans and other working class white students of the 1950s and early 60s, this new student spoke a different language which not only reflected a different class, but also a different race, culture, and historical experience" ("CCCC's Role" 354). During the last four decades of their operation, high-risk/BW programs have prompted a range of important disciplinary and institutional discussions among compositionists and high-risk/BW scholars.[2] At the level of the discipline, these programs have occasioned the Conference on College Composition and Communication's (CCCC's) "Students' Right to Their Own Language" resolution and statement; the authorship of books like Mina Shaughnessy's *Errors and Expectations* and Smitherman's *Talkin' and Testifyin';* the development of the *Journal of Basic Writing* and the larger high-risk/BW movement that this journal helped to launch; various discussions of high-risk/BW testing and assessment, including specific discussions of assessment programs such as the City University of New York's (CUNY's) Writing Assessment Test (WAT) and Cal State's English Placement Test (EPT); and lively debates regarding the need for high-risk/BW "mainstreaming" and other efforts at reconfiguring programs. Furthermore, high-risk/BW programs operating within specific college and university contexts, especially well-known university systems such as CUNY, have prompted countless institutional discussions, debates, and decisions concerning how best to meet the purported language and literacy needs of particular student populations.

My goal in this book is to theorize key ways in which, during the last four decades, these disciplinary and institutional discussions of high-risk/BW programs have been shaped directly by various ideologies of race, racism, language, and literacy. More specifically, I aim to analyze how scholars in composition and high-risk/BW writing within the professional literature have theorized and debated the needs of students who possess "a different race, culture, and historical experience" (Smitherman, "CCCC's Role" 354) at key historical junctures since the late 1960s. I further aim to analyze how such disciplinary discussion has directly influenced administrative decision-making and program-building within one particular high-risk writing program, the EOP Rhetoric program at the University of Illinois at Urbana–Champaign (UIUC), Illinois's predominantly white flagship public university located about two hours south of Chicago. EOP Rhetoric was one of the larger and more widely known high-risk writing programs of the era, but it has not yet been the subject of extensive analysis.

The need for historical analysis of high-risk/BW discussion and activity is especially urgent in light of our troubling contemporary educational and political climate. As many of us know only too well, the last decade has witnessed widespread attacks both on high-risk programs in general and on their high-risk/BW writing program components in particular. For instance, CUNY's Open Admissions program was dismantled in 1999 with the justification that the program was "adrift. . . . Academic standards are loose and confused, and CUNY lacks the basic information necessary to make sound judgments about the quality and effectiveness of its programs" (Schmidt et al. 5). As a result, CUNY decided that all so-called remedial courses, including its famous BW offerings, must be restricted to two-year CUNY campuses or even for-profit remedial centers (7). Similarly, Minnesota's General College program, an open admissions college within the larger University of Minnesota campus that had been operating in one form or another since the 1930s (Detzner, Poch, and Taylor xv), was dismantled in 2005 as part of a larger "strategic repositioning" effort purportedly designed to "elevate the University of Minnesota into one of the top three public research universities in the world within the next decade" (Bruininks 2). Like CUNY, Minnesota required that all "remedial" coursework, including its own BW courses, be relegated to two-year colleges (11–13). Still further, the important recent volume *Basic Writing in America,* edited by Nicole Pipenster Greene and Patricia McAlexander, points out that program dismantling has recently taken place across a range of other four-year campuses, including the University of Cincinnati, the University of Louisiana–Lafayette, Cal State–Fullerton, and others.

It seems clear that contemporary high-risk/BW programs are presently perceived as antithetical to the needs and goals of mainstream four-year institutions. It also seems clear that, as Barbara Gleason has lamented, even remaining high-risk/BW program efforts are being "fatally compromised by the socio-political forces that . . . [gather] around the issue of remediation" ("Evaluating Programs" 582)—a concern echoed by many other high-risk/BW scholars during the last decade as well.[3] By analyzing in some detail the racialized nature of past discussions surrounding these programs, I hope to imagine new ways to address this problematic contemporary situation.

The Capacity for Change and the Limitations
of "Standards" in High-Risk/BW

I will focus repeatedly throughout this book on specific ways in which disciplinary and institutional discussions of high-risk/BW activity have promoted an important level of egalitarian reform and change within mainstream four-year contexts. In this sense, my work reflects Deborah Mutnick's assertion that "basic writing for all its internal contradictions, has played a vital role in increasing access to higher education, in particular for working-class people of color" (71–72). I believe that Mutnick's point is one worth stressing. Many disciplinary and institutional discussions of high-risk/BW philosophies, practices, and structures have in fact attempted to theorize the needs of marginalized students, particularly marginalized minority students, in egalitarian ways. Such work deserves to be recognized, analyzed, and celebrated for the changes that it has prompted.

At the same time, I will also focus repeatedly throughout this book on key ways in which the potential for reform present within these discussions of high-risk/BW activity over time has ultimately been limited, and at times quite profoundly, by appeals to mainstream "standards." In this sense, my work reflects Tom Fox's argument that appeals to standards within the context of high-risk/BW instruction and other egalitarian institutional ventures —especially appeals to the need for students to learn and use "Standard English"—have typically sought to preserve and protect the existing social and educational status quo. These appeals to standards, Fox argues, have attempted to define educational activities and achievements in terms of "essence, not contexts . . . objectivity, not values that are contingent upon historical or material needs" (4). In this sense, they have been aimed at "conserv[ing] and maintain[ing] institutions and language" (3) and ensuring that "the same students who have always gone to college still go" (7). But my work here also recognizes that these appeals to standards have also served in many instances, as Catherine Prendergast points out, to reify a racist status quo rooted in "White property interests, White privilege . . . [and] the conception of America as a White nation" (*Literacy* 7). More specifically, Prendergast argues, these sorts of appeals have been rooted in the notion that "literacy belongs to Whites" (5), thereby serving to preserve the existing racial order under the guise of offering access to it.[4] I believe that these arguments from Fox and Prendergast are also worth stressing directly. Many disciplinary and institutional discussions of high-risk/BW philosophies, practices, and structures have seen their attempts to promote race-based egalitarian change limited, undercut, or even undone with the help of uncritical appeals to standards and Standard English. These problems also deserve to be recognized and thoroughly critiqued.

Of course, I do not want to go so far as to argue that *all* appeals to standards or Standard English are necessarily problematic. High-risk/BW programs that seek to enact race-conscious reforms may well need to stress certain standards at certain times and in certain contexts—a point that Mike Rose stresses explicitly when he asserts that high-risk/BW discussions should embrace standards that are tied to "high expectations," "good teaching," and "democratic ends" (96). But Rose nonetheless insists that would-be reformers must identify and critique those standards that ultimately strive to "shut down rather than foster learning" (95) or otherwise to serve as "a barrier to [students'] development" (95) within high-risk/BW activity.[5] My aim here is similar. I embrace the pursuit of worthwhile standards, but I also seek to identify and critique those problematic standards that promote an unfair social and racial status quo under the guise of serving students' needs.

Theorizing High-Risk/BW

As a framework within which to understand high-risk/BW, I adapt critical race theorist Derrick Bell's argument that attempts to promote racial justice through school desegregation programs (of which high-risk/BW is but one example) have been successful at times, but always to a degree ultimately dictated by the expectations, beliefs, and values of the white mainstream. Specifically, Bell insists that the overall trajectory of post–Civil Rights Era school desegregation "may not actually be determined by the character of harm suffered by blacks or the quantum of liability proved against whites. Racial remedies may instead be the outward manifestations of unspoken and perhaps subconscious judicial conclusions that the remedies, if granted, will secure, advance, or at least not harm the societal interests deemed important by middle- and upper-class whites. Racial justice—or its appearance—may, from time to time, be counted among the interests deemed important by the courts and by society's policy makers" ("*Brown v. Board*" 22).[6] Bell calls this concept "interest convergence," describing it as the phenomenon whereby the "interest of blacks in achieving racial equality will be accommodated only when it converges with the interests of whites" (22). Bell certainly acknowledges that the pursuit of racial justice for its own sake might count among such white interests, arguing that "there were whites for whom recognition of the racial equality principle was sufficient motivation" to enact change (23). But he is also careful to assert that other political, social, and economic interests—which in the case of *Brown v. Board of Education* included Cold War politics, post–World War II treatment of black U.S. soldiers at home, and the need for increased economic development in the U.S. South (23)—typically play a more central role for the white mainstream. Indeed, Bell argues that race-based change occurs at the behest not only of those "whites concerned about the immorality of racial inequality," but of "those whites in policymaking positions able to see the economic and political advances at home and abroad that would follow" such change (22). Interest convergence posits, in short, that efforts to promote racial justice within a given context are typically dictated less by those various groups whom they are ostensibly designed to serve (i.e., underrepresented minority groups vying for equal opportunity) and more by those who hold hegemonic racialized power (i.e., mainstream whites and others who have the power and influence to preserve a racialized status quo that already serves their interests and needs).

I apply Bell's concept of interest convergence here by arguing that disciplinary and institutional discussions of high-risk/BW activity over time reveal a shifting dynamic of convergence and divergence between the interests of two loosely defined groups: (1) scholars, teachers, and administrators (quite often, though certainly not always, members of minority groups) espousing "race-conscious" discourses aimed at promoting egalitarian race-based change to philosophies, practices, and structures of writing instruction within predominantly white environments; and (2) scholars, teachers, and administrators (quite often, though certainly not always, white) espousing status-quo-oriented "mainstream" discourses committed to preserving and perpetuating philosophies, practices, and structures of writing instruction that maintain existing racialized balances of power and privilege. Furthermore, I assert the following:

1. During periods of convergence, a certain amount of racially egalitarian change within disciplinary and institutional discussions did occur, albeit change that was bounded in important ways by mainstream concerns regarding the need to preserve racialized standards, including Standard English.

2. During periods of divergence, such change was thwarted or even undone, often through direct appeals to these same racialized standards.

3. Understanding these past dynamics of convergence and divergence is key to theorizing new strategies for contemporary "story-changing" work, as described by Linda Adler-Kassner, that can be used to reframe discussion about writing instruction and the students that it serves.

By analyzing these dynamics of convergence and divergence within discussions of high-risk/BW activity, alongside the hegemonic standards that regulate them, I certainly do not mean to preach despair or complacency. Instead, I believe that acknowledging the power of these standards constitutes a first step in a larger effort designed, as Bell asserts, to "imagine and implement . . . strategies that can bring fulfillment and even triumph" in the fight for racially egalitarian language and literacy instruction ("Racial Realism" 306). Such imagining and implementation of new strategies should be aided in particular by Adler-Kassner's ideas about story-changing: her work can help us to imagine and develop new forms of race-conscious high-risk/BW activity that highlights its value to a range of interested stakeholders—including white mainstream institutions themselves (see chapter 6).

Understanding Issues of Race and Racism over Time

My attempts here to analyze high-risk/BW activity using the lens of interest convergence and divergence is influenced in a general sense by two bodies of important contemporary scholarship. The first of these is "alternative history" work in composition that seeks, as Gretchen Flesher Moon argues, to "challenge the dominant narrative of composition history," while at the same time "proposing alongside it a complicated and discontinuous array of alternative histories" (12).[7] The second is "institutional critique" work in composition geared toward what Porter et al. describe as "mapping the conflicted frameworks in . . . heterogeneous and contested spaces [within an institution], articulating the hidden and seemingly silent voices of those marginalized by the powerful, and observing how power operates within institutional space" (631) and toward attempts to "expose and interrogate possibilities for institutional change" (631).[8] But in a more specific sense, this project is influenced strongly by a number of recent institutionally focused alternative histories, most of which are book length, that focus simultaneously on the reform potential inherent within specific discussions of high-risk/BW activity and on the ways in which this reform potential has been limited through appeals to standards, including Standard English.

One institutionally focused alternative history with a strong influence on my project is Stephen Parks's 1999 *Class Politics: The Movement for the Students' Right to Their Own Language.* This book analyzes the genesis and evolution of one of the most important disciplinary statements to inform the development of high-risk/BW programs, the famous "Students' Right to Their Own Language" (SRTOL) statement within CCCC. Parks argues that early drafts of the SRTOL were quite progressive in the way that they both demanded "broad-based alliances against class and racial oppression" (5) and critiqued "the corporate economy of the United States and its treatment of working-class citizens of all races and ethnicities" (5). Parks also praises early versions of the SRTOL for the ways in which they tried explicitly to "validate languages other than Standard English" (167)—that is, to contest directly the idea that Standard English is somehow superior to all other forms of English. But Parks ultimately concludes that the potential for change present within early versions of the SRTOL was eventually undermined by the way in which its final 1974 version accepted and even embraced mainstream expectations regarding standards within language and literacy instruction. He concludes that this final version of the SRTOL focused more on "how to expand acceptable dialects within corporate capitalism, not how to use dialects to question [this capitalism]" (184), thereby undermining its important potential for promoting change.

Another of these histories is Mary Soliday's 2002 *The Politics of Remediation: Institutional Student Needs in Higher Education,* which focuses on the genesis and evolution of high-risk/BW activity at the City College of New York (CCNY) in the CUNY system, especially the leadership of visionary administrator Mina Shaughnessy. Soliday argues that BW at CCNY under

Shaughnessy successfully began "transforming the lives of thousands of students" (139) in New York City, contributing directly to a larger Open Admissions effort that helped a significant number of "poor, inner-city whites and people of color to find and keep white collar jobs" (139).[9] Soliday also insists that Shaughnessy was largely successful in interrogating "the conditions of teaching and learning" writing at CCNY and in CUNY more generally in ways that served to "transform teachers and the institution, not just the students" (102). But Soliday nonetheless concludes that many of these positive changes at CUNY have been undermined over time, especially since the end of Open Admissions in 1999, through an increasingly uncritical and problematic contemporary embrace of traditional notions of standards: she asserts that "critics of remediation [and of high-risk/BW have] waved the red flag of declining standards and literacy crisis to justify the need to downsize, privatize, and effectively restratify higher education" (106).

A third history of this type is Nicole Pipenster Greene and Patricia McAlexander's 2008 edited collection *Basic Writing in America: The History of Nine College Programs.* This collection offers a set of historical narratives detailing the ways in which specific high-risk/BW programs within sites across the country have been or are being dismantled in the present day. As they introduce these narratives, Greene and McAlexander insist that high-risk/BW efforts have successfully served as a "means of social reform" (6) within a larger "battle to grant access to groups who had not traditionally been part of academe" (6). They also laud what they describe as the "passionate concern" within many high-risk/BW programs for assuring that "students of all races and backgrounds" ultimately receive "the opportunity to fulfill their human potential" (8). But Greene and McAlexander nonetheless insist that BW-influenced reforms have been increasingly undermined by "those who wished to limit [access to] academe to the traditional student population" (7) through appeals to "standards, cultural literacy, [and] intellectual excellence" (7).

Such book-length discussions offer crucial information regarding disciplinary and institutional discussions of the high-risk/BW movement that is directly relevant to my project.[10] In particular, they stress the potential for reform embedded within various high-risk/BW contexts, including those surrounding the SRTOL, those at CUNY, and those elsewhere across the United States; at the same time, they stress the ways in which such reform was ultimately limited or even undone through various appeals to standards and/or

Standard English. Crucially, however, these particular examples do not typically feature an explicit focus on issues of race and racism: in fact, some of them insist that such an explicit focus may be misguided or problematic.[11] Accordingly, my work here also draws inspiration from a number of other institutionally focused alternative histories, most of which are article- or chapter-length, that focus squarely on issues of race and racism within disciplinary and institutional discussions of high-risk/BW activity. These texts reflect the assertion of race theorists Michael Omi and Howard Winant that "the concept of race continues to play a fundamental role in structuring and representing the social world. The task . . . is to explain this situation. It is to avoid both the utopian framework which sees race as an illusion that we can somehow 'get beyond' and also the essentialist formation which sees race as something objective and fixed, a biological datum. Thus we should think of race as an element of social structure rather than an irregularity within it; we should see race as a dimension of human representation rather than an illusion" (55). These texts also resonate with recent work in composition aimed explicitly at contesting and undoing what Aja Y. Martinez decries as "the empire of force and its historically specific racisms" (594) within contemporary composition instruction.[12]

One example of this type of race-conscious history is Geneva Smitherman's 1999 article "CCCC's Role in the Struggle for Language Rights." In this article, Smitherman praises the SRTOL, a document to which she contributed as one of a group of original authors, for attempting to convey the work of race-conscious "intellectual-activists" in their "struggle for the wider social legitimacy of all languages and dialects and . . . to bring about mainstream recognition and acceptance of the culture, history, and language of those on the margins" (358).[13] Smitherman further argues that the SRTOL prompted crucial disciplinary reforms to thinking about high-risk/BW activity, particularly "1) heighten[ing] consciousness of language attitudes; 2) promot[ing] the value of linguistic diversity; and 3) convey[ing] fact and information about language and language variation that would enable instructors to teach their non-traditional students—and ultimately all students—more effectively" (359). Despite these possibilities for change and reform, however, Smitherman laments that the impact of the SRTOL was ultimately limited by the national and disciplinary invocation of racist standards during what she describes as the "Second Reconstruction" of the early 1980s, a climate in which "the mood of CCCC, like the mood of America, seemed to have shifted from change and promise to stagnation and dreams deferred" (365). Such racism was especially rampant, she says, within articles such as Thomas Farrell's 1983 "IQ and Standard English," which theorized a racialized link between students' ability to reproduce Standard English and their overall cognitive capacity.[14]

Another example of this type of history is Scott Wible's 2006 "Pedagogies of the Students' Right Era," a text analyzing how the race-conscious thinking of the SRTOL was used to promote change by one specific pedagogical collective, the Language Curriculum Research Group (LCRG), operating in CUNY's Brooklyn College and Borough of Manhattan Community College. The LCRG, Wible says, drew direct inspiration from the SRTOL as it "encouraged English language arts educators to see how their practices in linguistically diverse classrooms were shaped by social attitudes concerning linguistic and cultural difference" (455). Wible further argues that the LCRG embraced the critical interrogation of white mainstream standards, especially those related to Standard English, as something of a central philosophical and pedagogical goal—stressing, for instance, the need for "reflection on how, particularly for white SE-speaking teachers, acknowledging BEV [Black English Vernacular] in the classroom necessarily changed the relationship between students and teacher" (455), as well as the need for teachers to learn "from their own students' language practices" (456). Nonetheless, Wible concludes that the promise of the LCRG's activities was ultimately limited by mid-1970s concerns regarding the "literacy crisis" and its rejection of all non–Standard English language use—specifically by what he describes as "public perceptions that BEV's presence in the classroom drained educational resources and hastened academic decline" (464).

Finally, a third example of this type is Nicole Pipenster Greene's own contribution to the 2008 *Basic Writing in America* volume mentioned previously, a chapter titled "Basic Writing, Desegregation, and Open Admissions in Southwestern Louisiana," which focuses in detail on the racialized dynamics of high-risk/BW programmatic activity at what is now known as the University of Louisiana–Lafayette (ULL).[15] Greene highlights the potential for change within the early-1970s version of high-risk/BW at ULL, a program that explicitly encouraged students to utilize their "natural mode of expression" such that they might become skilled in both "'standard' and 'nonstandard' English" (74). She further praises the way in which the writing program administrator (WPA) of this program during the early 1980s strove "to institute a progressive curriculum that would simultaneously value process over product, preserve the instructor's 'creativity' or autonomy, and quell resistance to innovation" (79). But she concludes, ultimately, that appeals to racialized standards at ULL eventually undermined these efforts, specifically through what she characterizes as an "elitist tendency" (90) arising at ULL in the early 1990s that prompted the president of the university to eliminate all courses deemed "remedial" and move toward "selective admissions" in 1993 (90).

These latter three examples (each circulating alongside a number of other contemporary examples) usefully begin to theorize in detail how discussions of high-risk/BW disciplinary and institutional activity have managed to promote at least some level of racialized reform, but they also stress how such reform has been limited by racialized standards.[16] Because I am obviously interested in the racialized dynamics of high-risk/BW discussions, as well as in the important limitations imposed on these discussions by various appeals to standards, my work here is certainly influenced strongly by these latter examples. Nonetheless, I think that my project, especially in its focus on the dynamics of interest convergence and divergence, offers at least three important new insights concerning these discussions that have not yet been theorized at length within this past work.

The Value of an Interest Convergence and Divergence Framework

To begin, the interest convergence and divergence framework that I adopt here promises to provide important and detailed insight into the subtle but nonetheless crucial power of white racism to shape discussions of high-risk/BW activity within each major period that I analyze in this book. It will show, for instance, that during periods of strong interest convergence, in which some degree of race-based change was actually taking place (e.g., the "racial crisis" era of the late 1960s and early 1970s [see chapter 2]; the era of concern with student "competence" during the late 1970s and early 1980s [see chapter 4]), white power and privilege was asserted somewhat subtly through an insistence that mainstream standards be preserved even in the midst of high-risk/BW expansion. This framework will also show that, during periods of strong divergence (e.g., the "literacy crisis" era of the mid-1970s [see chapter 3]; the "culture wars" era of the late 1980s and early 1990s [see chapter 5]; the "excellence" era of the present day [see chapter 6]), white power and privilege was asserted more forcefully and explicitly through various arguments about the need to get "back to basics," to uphold "excellence," and otherwise to ensure that standards were upheld in the face of threat. By revealing the important (albeit shifting and changing) power of white racism over time, this framework of interest convergence and divergence will demonstrate that issues of race and racism within high-risk/BW have always been fundamental determinants of disciplinary and institutional discussions within high-risk/BW—and, in fact, continue to be in the present day.

Somewhat paradoxically, however, this interest convergence and divergence framework will also demonstrate that white racism has never actually been able to extinguish fully the desire for or the possibility of promoting race-based egalitarian change within high-risk/BW. Indeed, it will show that not even the strongest periods of interest divergence to this point—not that of the mid-1970s literacy crisis, nor that of the late 1980s/early 1990s culture wars, nor even that of contemporary concerns about excellence—have been able to eliminate completely egalitarian impulses or activities. The framework will thereby provide those of us interested in theorizing and enacting race-based reform within various disciplinary and institutional discussions of high-risk/BW activity some degree of hope that our desire for reform can endure even during the toughest of times.

Finally, this interest convergence and divergence framework will also prompt us to think both carefully and critically about how we can use our knowledge of the past as a foundation for formulating new race-based reform efforts in the present day. In particular, it will stress that we should explicitly attempt to promote interest convergence as a means both to imagine and to implement contemporary and future high-risk/BW reform efforts. It will also demonstrate that techniques such as Adler-Kassner's story-changing can prove especially helpful in this regard. Accordingly, I will spend a great deal of my final chapter in this book theorizing some of the specific ways in which we can foster just such convergence by telling new stories about race-conscious high-risk/BW activity that stress its value not only to underrepresented minority students, but to mainstream institutions and their stakeholders as well.

Gaining Access to Sites of High-Risk/BW Discussion

In order to identify, theorize, and analyze the kinds of disciplinary and institutional discussions of most interest to this project, I turn to the composition and high-risk/BW literature as it is represented within key journals (especially *College Composition and Communication, College English,* and the *Journal of Basic Writing*), books, and edited collections. In making this choice, I echo Maureen Daly Goggin's assertion that the scholarship of a discipline constitutes one of the "most important vehicles" through which we are able to make sense of the "complex struggles in which scholars and teachers have engaged to stake a ground and construct a professional and disciplinary identity" (xiii). I agree that this scholarship serves as a kind of archival record for the field that allows us to examine and analyze the shape of disciplinary discussion concerning high-risk/BW writing program efforts over time.

In order to access the institutional discussions of most interest here, I turn to the specific context of the EOP Rhetoric program at UIUC, one especially useful for understanding institutional discussions of high-risk/BW. EOP Rhetoric was developed in 1968 as part of a larger campus desegregation effort at UIUC, Illinois's flagship campus in Champaign-Urbana, about two hours south of Chicago. This larger desegregation effort—known initially as "Project 500" for its early goal of recruiting and admitting 500 African American students and known later simply as "EOP"—was designed to help bring racial diversity to the UIUC campus of roughly 25,000 students, 98 percent of whom were white as of 1967 (Williamson 35). In its role within this larger EOP effort, EOP Rhetoric offered writing instruction to anywhere between 150 and 600 underrepresented minority students per year until fall 1994: at this time, it was abolished in favor of a decidedly color-blind BW program called the Academic Writing Program (AWP) that continues to operate.[17]

Throughout its nearly quarter-century history, the EOP Rhetoric program was perceived as a central pillar of language and literacy learning for EOP students. A report written in the mid-1970s asserted directly that "the success of the English Department's EOP Rhetoric program depends primarily on its ability to meet the verbal skills needs of *individuals* in the Program. Both in EOP Rhetoric 103 [the tutorial section] (where there is a one-to-one student-to-instructor ratio) and in EOP Rhetoric 104 and 105 (where the maximum student-to-instructor ratio is 15-to-1), the Program is designed to meet individual needs in ways impossible in the larger, more heterogeneous regular rhetoric sections" (UIUC, "EOP Rhetoric Report" 1).[18] Accordingly, EOP Rhetoric always featured a great deal of teacher-student contact: courses remained capped at fifteen students per section throughout most of EOP Rhetoric's history, and EOP Rhetoric students were also guaranteed one-on-one support in the EOP writing lab. Also notable was the fact that all EOP students were strongly encouraged by their advisors to take EOP Rhetoric whether their test scores deemed them to be "basic writers" or not. This placement scheme was designed to create a community of underrepresented minority student learners with different skills and talents that could support all EOP students as they adapted to the demands of the university during their important first year on campus. Indeed, the original dean of EOP ("Dean A") asserted in a paper that he gave at CCCC in 1969 that these sections were specifically designed to help students grapple with "the many problems that accrue to being a black student with marginal preparation and skills enrolled at a highly-selective white university" ("Role" 7).[19]

EOP Rhetoric as a Site for Institutional Analysis and Critique

One reason that EOP Rhetoric serves as an important site for examining institutional discussions of high-risk/BW program activity is that the larger EOP program was itself so consistently racialized, in both negative and positive ways. UIUC historian Joy Ann Williamson notes, for instance, that a majority of EOP students were from the city of Chicago, generally "considered the most segregated city in the United States" at the time (3). She also asserts that EOP students met with tremendous racial hostility immediately on their arrival at UIUC, a campus that was in many ways "southern in its attitudes toward race" (3). Particularly striking was the fact that over 250 EOP students were arrested en masse during their first week on campus for protesting crowded living conditions in the dorms, an arrest described by the *Chicago Tribune* with the headline "Negroes Riot at U of I; Negroes Go on Rampage after Row" (87). But despite such rampant racism, many race-conscious student activists involved in the EOP program exercised significant power to effect change at UIUC. Not only were these student activists routinely "invited to participate in university recruitment efforts and sit on university committees" (3), as Williamson notes, but they had significant "status and input on such important decision-making bodies" (3). The power afforded to these race-conscious activists was especially evident within documents such as the following letter from the chancellor of UIUC at the time, written in 1968, just before the larger EOP program was developed:

> Sooner or later, and probably sooner rather than later, some group or other will "demand" that we provide courses in African history, Negro history, Negro culture, Negro music, etc. Could I ask you to take the leadership and quietly discuss this matter with the head of the history department, English department, and . . . others you might think would have an interest in the matter to see if we can come forward with an educationally responsible program and anticipate this demand rather than have to respond to it in a crisis situation? Since there is probably some urgency in this matter, I would appreciate your doing what you can. . . . I think it best to keep the matter quiet for a while until we can get our own plans developed. For once it appears that we are attempting to do something quite a few people will want to become involved in. However, before too long, and I would stress fairly soon, I would suggest that . . . we involve the Black Students' Association in our planning rather than have them hear about it from the newspapers or other sources. (letter to dean of Liberal Arts and Sciences, 22 May 1968, 1)

We can see here the degree to which the chancellor at the time regarded race-conscious activists' "demands" as significant and in need of immediate address: he clearly believed that activists in groups like the Black Students' Association needed to be included directly in university decision-making processes if such processes were to be successful.[20]

A second (and related) reason that EOP Rhetoric at UIUC is worth studying is that discussions surrounding writing instruction within the program itself were also consistently racialized over time. For instance, one of the early directors of EOP Rhetoric argued that the goal of the EOP Rhetoric program and its writing lab should be to help students to "express themselves clearly in their indigenous forms and dialects. Only secondarily, if at all, are students expected to write in the middle-class, white tradition" (Director A, "SEOP Proposal" 1). He also used this race-conscious view as the basis for his decisions regarding issues of the writing lab's pedagogy, staffing, and program structure during its first year of operation (see chapter 2). In distinct contrast, one of the later directors of EOP Rhetoric claimed that the way to best meet the needs of minority students in EOP Rhetoric was to avoid talk of race entirely and instead focus on "explaining the structure and function of written Standard English" to them, while at the same time correcting their numerous "errors" (Director C, "To the Rhetoric Teaching Staff" 1). She similarly used this color-blind philosophy as the basis of a number of fundamental pedagogical, budgetary, and structural decisions relevant to the EOP Rhetoric program and its writing lab throughout the mid-1970s (see chapter 3). These two examples, alongside many others that will be analyzed in detail throughout this book, demonstrate that race mattered profoundly to discussions of language and literacy throughout the history of EOP Rhetoric, although in different ways at different times.

Still a third reason that EOP Rhetoric serves as a valuable site for analysis is that so much information regarding racialized institutional discussions at UIUC has survived in various archives in the form of administrative memos and correspondence, committee meeting minutes, program descriptions and philosophies, and course descriptions. (Furthermore, several key program administrators graciously agreed to comment retrospectively on these documents and the contexts that gave rise to them.) Given John Paul Tassoni's assertion that such materials tend to be "absent from [official institutional memory] . . . at least as that memory is represented in the archives and in the minds of those whom the archives represent" (107), the survival of such material is significant. It affords us the sort of glimpse into the "the myriad administrative, institutional, and intellectual conflicts and decisions" (Henze, Selzer, and Sharer 6) that have far too often been lost within the history of high-risk/BW.

Methodological and Ethical Considerations for Analyzing the Archives

My work with the institutional archives has required me to perform extensive work not only within UIUC's public archives but also within what compositionists Brent Henze, Jack Selzer, and Wendy Sharer refer to as key "hidden archives"—that is, "the old file boxes in the attic; the yellowed, handwritten essays in the bottom drawers; the textbooks thankfully overlooked during the last office cleanings; the records of forgotten meetings; and the indispensable memories of departmental personalities upon which [a particular institution's] history could be built" (vi). Such work within the EOP Rhetoric's hidden archive, one located in UIUC's English Department, required me to ask administrators, faculty, and staff about whether they knew of the location of any such "hidden archive"; to obtain the keys to a locked basement room in the English Department filled with old file cabinets and stacks of papers; and ultimately to obtain explicit permission (first oral and later written) from the department to peruse, analyze, and cite from these departmental records—access and permission for which I remain most grateful.

My experiences with the hidden institutional archives have also prompted me to think at length about methodological and ethical issues related to naming and citation in ways that have not typically been discussed at great length within the composition/BW literature. I have viewed my work with EOP Rhetoric as engaged primarily in what composition ethicist Paul V. Andersen describes as a "text-based" critique of public institutional dynamics governed by "the taboos and institutional policies against plagiarism, and socially enforced customs concerning acknowledgement and citation" (63), rather than first and foremost a "person-based" critique (63) governed by the parameters of "informed consent" (68).[21] Nonetheless, I have also felt a need to adhere at some level to CCCCs "Guidelines for the Ethical Conduct of Research in Composition Studies," requiring that research in the field demonstrate a clear "commitment to protecting the rights, privacy, dignity, and well-being" of individuals (par. 1)—especially the administrative actors who occupy such a central place in these discussions. Thus, throughout my analysis, I have felt a strong tension between a desire to offer as much detail as possible about the particular historical, political, social, and economic circumstances surrounding the EOP Rhetoric program and a desire to treat administrators within this context as unnamed institutional actors operating within this specific context.

Accordingly, I adopt throughout this book a focus on the racialized discourses used by disciplinary and institutional actors within a given context, rather than a direct focus on the purported beliefs and values of these individuals themselves. I aim to analyze, in other words, how and why these administrators articulated specific views regarding race, racism, language, and literacy within specific institutional contexts and how these views shaped disciplinary and institutional discussion; I do not want simply to label individuals as "good" or "bad" on the basis of what I read their beliefs to be.[22] Along related lines, I also employ here what I have described elsewhere as a "hybrid-institutional" approach to naming and citation, one that I believe is being adopted increasingly by other contemporary scholars performing similar types of institutionally focused alternative history.[23] In keeping with this hybrid-institutional approach, I speak at great length throughout this text about the specific institutional contexts and situations surrounding EOP Rhetoric at Illinois, but I make reference to all administrative actors by their institutional titles alone—for example, "director of EOP Rhetoric," "dean of LAS," "dean of EOP," and so on—both within the body of my text and within my works cited section. In this manner, I try to do justice to the specific conditions of EOP Rhetoric at Illinois in ways that allow me to get at the situatedness and specificity of this particular context in as much detail as possible, but I try to avoid singling out identifiable individuals for the reasons noted above. Furthermore, in my works cited section, I refer to real documents by name and date, but reference all institutional actors by title alone. In this way, I try to provide some semblance of what the American Historical Association describes as a "paper trail" (par. 9) without dwelling on the identities of individual institutional actors.

The Late 1960s and Early 1970s

COMING TO TERMS WITH RACIAL CRISIS

THE DECADE OF the 1960s found the Civil Rights Movement turning in an increasingly urgent and confrontational direction. Sociologists and CUNY Open Admissions researchers David E. Lavin and David Hyllegard have argued that this period witnessed "increasing militancy [within] the civil rights movement. Across the country, civil disobedience, strident demonstrations, and riots had riveted national attention on various issues of racial inequality. A developing sense of urgency about equal opportunity was expressed in the enactment of such 'great society' programs as Head Start and the 'war on poverty'" (8).[1] Accompanying this larger shift in the intensity and tactics of protest on the part of race-conscious civil rights activists was a focus on college and university campuses as sites of political protests and change: demonstrations and riots on the Columbia campus in 1968 were motivated in large part by dissatisfaction with race relations on the campus and with the surrounding community of Harlem (Boren 36); demonstrations at Cornell University erupted after a long buildup of racial tension punctuated by the burning of a cross in front of a black dormitory (Downs 162); and unrest at South Carolina State College began with dissatisfaction

21

over segregation in higher education and the failure of the institution to develop a black-centered curriculum (Boren 172).

These protests and demonstrations sparked widespread concern across the nation that a "racial crisis" was brewing within U.S. higher education—a point stressed within accounts of high-risk development from the time period. One especially vivid demonstration of this was the 1970 report of the Nixon-appointed President's Commission on Campus Unrest, a commission established "in the wake of the great tragedies at Kent State University in Ohio and Jackson State College in Mississippi" to facilitate "rational discussion of the subject of campus unrest" (i). This report argued that contemporary campus unrest had a number of important causes, including "war, racial injustice, and the [nature of] the university itself" (4). However, it stressed that a root cause of this unrest was racism, "especially against Blacks but in some parts of the country equally cruel in its effect upon Mexican-Americans, Puerto Ricans, and other minorities" (1/26). It claimed, in fact, that student discontent with this white racism had "no parallel in the history of the nation" (1), as it revealed ugly "divisions in American society as deep as any since the Civil War" (1). The report also warned that, in the midst of this crisis, "militants" (1) of many racial backgrounds were directing their discontent against the mainstream university's "admissions policies, its 'white-oriented' curriculum, and its overwhelmingly white teaching staff" (1), while at the same time "asserting the claims of their communities upon the resources, curriculum, admissions policies, and concern of the university" (1/37). The report finally concluded that, given the "gravity of the racial crisis" (3/14) evident at the time, the entire higher-educational status quo had been placed in jeopardy: "what is at stake is the stability of our social order, the fulfillment of the American promise, and the realization of American possibility" (3/5).

Importantly, however, the President's Commission report also argued that steps could be taken by the federal government to address this looming racial crisis directly. One of these steps was to support the important work of predominantly black institutions: "Predominantly Black institutions are regarded by the young Blacks and their leaders as the major resource related to their communities and their people, capable of developing and providing the new programs, new research and knowledge, and new kinds of public services that the nation now needs in coming to grips with its historic race problem" (3/35). Another crucial step was to support the development of high-risk programs within mainstream predominantly white colleges and universities: "We support the continuing efforts of formerly all-white universities to recruit Black, Mexican-American, Puerto Rican, and other minority students, and we urge that adequate government-sponsored student aid be made available to them. We recommend that in the process of becoming more representative of the society at large, universities make the adjustments necessary to permit those from minority backgrounds to take maximum advantage of their university experience" (R-7). Support of these kinds would be fundamental, the report concluded, to ensuring that minority students' interests and needs were being met. While implementing these programs would "not by itself eliminate the developing alienation felt from and disaffection toward the American society felt by increasingly larger numbers of Black students" (3/36), implementation would nonetheless "constitute progress toward marking possible the vital process of healing the social wounds that 350 years of experience have created" (3/36).

The report offered a vivid portrait of racial crisis as it was being imagined during the late 1960s and early 1970s. It acknowledged the power of white racism at this time rather directly, arguing that such racism was prompting activists to demand "full social justice and dignity." It also argued that student activists—particularly student "militants" from various backgrounds—were increasingly committed to protesting racism in ways that could not be ignored: indeed, within this context of significant "gravity," failing to acknowledge such protest was tantamount to risking "the stability of our social order." But the report also asserted that such racial crisis could and should be addressed with the help of federal support, particularly for high-risk programs. Building these programs could help the United States begin "coming to grips with its historic race problem" by helping "universities make the adjustments necessary to permit those from minority backgrounds to take maximum advantage of their university experience." In this way, the President's Commission perceived racial crisis as the central ailment of the late 1960s and early 1970s, but it also perceived high-risk programs as a central cure.

Concern about racial crisis as articulated within this report and elsewhere at the time helped to give birth to a large number of high-risk programs nationwide: as noted in chapter 1, over nine hundred high-risk programs of one sort or another were developed across the United States by 1970, most featuring some sort of "open admissions" policy or other "special adjustments for blacks in admissions requirements" (McDaniel and McKee 1).[2] One especially well-known example of such a program was the Open Admissions program at CUNY. Open Admissions was launched in 1970 in the wake of late-1960s demands from activists for expanded minority student access to CUNY, including "a separate school of Black and Puerto Rican studies"; a "separate orientation program for Black and Puerto Rican students"; and mechanisms to allow for significant black and Puerto Rican student input into admissions, personnel, and curriculum decisions (Lavin and Hyllegard 11). Officially, Open Admissions guaranteed CUNY admission to all students from New York City high schools who either graduated with an 80 percent grade point average or graduated in the top half of their class (15), providing them with "extensive programs of remediation, counseling, and related services that were designed to enhance students' academic chances" (16). But the program was also intended to afford greater minority student access to and support within CUNY, especially its four-year campuses. Lavin and Hyllegard have noted, in fact, that Open Admissions was directly influenced by concerns of minority activists on CUNY's Admissions Commission that more "Black and Puerto Rican students" be provided with "a fair and equal chance to obtain a B.A. degree," such that "the vicious educational cycle" of poverty and racism would be "smashed" (14).

Another important example of high-risk program activity developed during this time period was the Student Support Services (SSS) program, which was launched in 1970 to "facilitate and encourage access to and participation in higher education by providing special interventions to identify, counsel, tutor, and otherwise assist academically able but educationally or financially disadvantaged students to complete high school and persist in college" (Astin et al. 119).[3] SSS was regarded as a de facto support mechanism for minority students, a point stressed by some of the program's earliest evaluators when they wrote that SSS was designed to address the fact that "the nation's poor include disproportionately large numbers of racial or ethnic minorities— the Black, the Chicano, the Puerto Rican, the American Indian, and perhaps others (Cuban, Filipinos, Orientals, etc.). Each of these groups may have unique problems and needs in maintaining themselves in colleges as a reflection of their cultural background, the fact of different degrees of underrepresentation in college, and the state of development of their collective movement for equality of access to education, occupational, and social opportunity" (Davis, Burkheimer, and Borders-Patterson 2-1).[4] The profound importance of SSS as a high-risk programmatic effort was evident in the significant federal support that it received: program funding for SSS grew from under $10 million to just under $23 million between 1970 and 1973, resulting in an increase of SSS programs from 121 to 323 during these three years (Chaney et al. 4-3). Support for students enrolling in SSS programs was further provided through the substantial federal need-based grant aid offered through Basic Educational Opportunity Grants (later renamed Pell Grants) and Supplemental Educational Opportunity Grants: their funding increased dramatically, from $1.6 billion in 1970 to $3.1 billion in 1975 (Duffy and Goldberg 186).[5] And in the immediate wake of such high-risk program growth and support, minority student enrollment expanded considerably. In 1972, the first year in which the *Digest of Educational Statistics* attempted to discern the racial composition of the undergraduate population, 26.4 percent of whites, 18.3 percent of blacks, and 13.4 percent of Hispanics ages eighteen to twenty-four were enrolled in some sort of higher education; by 1976, these figures were 27.6 percent, 22.5 percent, and 20.0 percent respectively (Snyder, Dillow, and Hoffman 296).[6]

Despite such significant growth of high-risk activity, however, many individuals and groups espousing mainstream beliefs and values routinely demanded limits to the kinds of changes being promoted within these newly developed high-risk programs. Indeed, even as these members of the mainstream conceded that high-risk programs constituted a necessary response to racial crisis, they demanded that these new programs not go too far in terms of the changes that they promoted to status quo thinking about student selection, curriculum, or instruction—often appealing to standards of one sort or another as they attempted to make their case.

For example, even as it explicitly supported high-risk activity, the report of the President's Commission on Campus Unrest cautioned that neither high-risk programs nor the institutions housing them should stray too far from what it considered to be standard university activity, what it called the "traditional principles" of teaching and research (6/5). Specifically, it warned that both high-risk programs and their larger institutional sponsors should be wary of neglecting traditional principles in favor of "service" activities, especially those related to issues of "racism, housing, unemployment, crime, water and air pollution, hunger, and overpopulation" (6/12). These service activities, the commission insisted, not only seemed to "bear little natural relation to research and teaching" (6/12) but were perceived as "highly controversial" by "the various constituencies—from students to taxpayers—that are essential to the financial support and academic freedom of universities" (6/12). In this way, the commission warned that if high-risk programs wished to retain the good favor of their mainstream sponsors, they should not stray too far from standard academic activities.

Related appeals to mainstream standards were also being made within the context of Open Admissions at CUNY. For instance, the New York City Board of Higher Education's 1970 policy statement on Open Admissions argued that the program should aspire to promote "ethnic integration" by "offer[ing] admission to some University program to all high school graduates of the city" (qtd. in Horner, "'Birth'" 10). But it also insisted that the Open Admissions program must take particular care to "maintain and enhance the standards of academic excellence of the colleges of the University" while "preserving the educational integrity of the University" (10). Failing to uphold these standards and preserve this integrity, it argued, would be tantamount to "perpetrating a cruel hoax upon all those who desire and deserve an education of true excellence" (10). The board thus granted that while some degree of race-conscious change may have been acceptable within the context of Open Admissions at CUNY, status quo standards must be maintained in the process.[7]

Still further, the power of mainstream appeals to standards was being noted at the time by several researchers responsible for observing national trends in high-risk program formation. For instance, in their 1971 assessment of high-risk program activity, educational researchers Reuben R. McDaniel Jr. and James W. McKee noted that only 48 percent of the roughly nine hundred high-risk programs that they had studied reported making a substantial effort to alter their "regular academic program . . . in light of new data and new understandings involving blacks" (1); the remaining 52 percent, in contrast, had made "no effort to update their programs" (1). This refusal on the part of so many institutions to alter their academic activities prompted McDaniel and McKee to opine that "it is no small wonder that large numbers of black students complain of institutionalized racism and an alien environment in the classroom" (1). John Egerton, a researcher writing about high-risk programs for the Southern Education Reporting Service during the late 1960s, drew similar conclusions regarding the more than one hundred high-risk programs at institutions across the United States that he studied in detail during 1968 and 1969.[8] He argued that the importance of high-risk programs "has been talked about, declared, implied, and assumed to be substantial for several years" (*State Universities* 21), but had proven "largely token" (21) in terms of actual change—especially with respect to standard views regarding student ability, the function of the curriculum, and the traditional work of the faculty (94). Education scholar and high-risk program expert Edmund W. Gordon agreed in his remarks given at a 1970 colloquium on high-risk program activity sponsored by the College Board, concluding that far too many programs had proven "superficially committed to developing heterogeneous populations as long as they are homogenous enough to enable the institution to continue operating without significant change" ("Programs" 114). He further noted that the pressure to retain traditional standards with respect to student "merit" within these programs remained high: "we must conclude that the administrative processes of open admission, like those still prevalent in almost all higher education institutions, are still more influenced by considerations of meritocracy than those of democracy" (114). Clearly, researchers and commentators of the time clearly felt that the changes being promoted by high-risk program development and implementation at hundreds of institutions across the United States were being limited through direct mainstream appeals to and reliance on standards. High-risk programs may have been proliferating at this time, but they were often resistant to changing standard notions of curriculum, of student recruitment and retention, or of merit itself.

Racial Crisis and the Dynamics of Interest Convergence

Widespread late-1960s and early-1970s concerns about racial crisis prompted an important level of race-based change to higher education in the United States in the form of high-risk programmatic activity. Individuals and groups across the political spectrum were strongly concerned with racial crisis, agreeing that some version of this high-risk program activity needed to be developed in order to ensure the future operation of mainstream higher education. And in the wake of this agreement, hundreds of high-risk programs were developed nationally; thousands of underrepresented minority students who had not previously entered mainstream white four-year institutions did so; and numerous new philosophies, policies, and practices were implemented to aid them. The late 1960s and early 1970s were, in this sense, something of a golden age for high-risk instruction, one in which support for high-risk instruction was widespread. Crucially, however, many individuals and institutions espousing mainstream views during this time insisted that these new high-risk programs must nonetheless uphold white mainstream standards related to students, faculty, curriculum, and assessment. These individuals and institutions remained adamant that, while some degree of change within high-risk programmatic activity may have been necessary, such change must not go too far: it should never question or critique traditional standards or their roots in the educational, political, and social status quo. In this way, the mainstream helped to ensure that even such a golden age of high-risk development was guided by mainstream white needs and expectations.

These late-1960s and early-1970s events therefore also indicate an important dynamic of interest convergence emerging within U.S. higher education in response to concerns over racial crisis. Race-conscious activists and mainstream individuals found a fair amount of common interest with regard to the high-risk movement at the time: both saw high-risk instruction as a necessary step toward ensuring that U.S. higher education continued to function. But the development of high-risk programs prompted by this interest convergence was nonetheless tempered by the overarching interests of the white mainstream, especially by its desire to preserve traditional methods of teaching, assessing, and otherwise dealing with students within newly created high-risk programs. This era of racial crisis thereby illustrates one of Bell's central claims: activist and mainstream interests did converge at this time in ways that helped to prompt some level of race-based change and reform; however, such change was not ultimately dictated by an overarching concern for racial justice, but instead by white mainstream concern for preserving status quo higher-educational practices in the face of perceived threat.

Race Consciousness Meets Bidialecticalism

The implementation of the high-risk program movement during the late 1960s and early 1970s proved important not only for U.S. higher education in general but for the fledgling field of composition in particular. This point was made directly within the opening sentences of one of the most well-known disciplinary statements about language and literacy instruction for underrepresented minority students issued at the time, the CCCC's 1974 "Students' Right to Their Own Language": "American schools and colleges have, in the last decade, been forced to take a stand on a basic educational question: what should the schools do about the language habits of students who come from a variety of social, economic, and cultural backgrounds? Differences in language have always existed, and the schools have always wrestled with them, but the social upheavals of the 1960's, and the insistence of submerged minorities on a greater share in American society, have posed the question more insistently and have suggested the need for a shift in providing answers" (1). Embedded within these larger disciplinary questions were a number of smaller ones. Who were these students from "a variety of social, economic, and cultural backgrounds," and where did they come from? What linguistic and literate skills did they already possess—if any? What skills did they need—if any? What new philosophies, practices, and structures of high-risk writing instruction could best meet those needs?

The questions raised by the SRTOL were important for the discipline of composition during the late 1960s and early 1970s for a number of reasons. Freshman composition had long been utilized before the late 1960s as a kind of sorting mechanism for "new" students entering a long-standing elite higher education environment: for example, students from the middle and lower classes entering places like Harvard in the late nineteenth century and the influx of World War II veterans entering U.S. colleges and universities during the late 1940s under the GI Bill.[9] This historical function of freshman composition as gatekeeper rendered it an obvious choice for "sorting" the new non-white and nonmainstream students entering higher education via high-risk programs—although many activist-minded scholars and teachers certainly hoped to see this sorting occur in more egalitarian ways than it had previously. Furthermore, scholars in composition were beginning to study writing processes in a systematic fashion during this period, demonstrated by events such as the famous 1966 "Dartmouth Conference" on composition and the publication of work including Janet Emig's *The Composing Processes of Twelfth Graders* in 1971 and Peter Elbow's *Writing without Teachers* in 1973. The field was thus primed to begin exploring the ways in which writing processes were shaped in particular by various aspects of racial, cultural, and linguistic difference. Still further, composition was closely aligned with a number of other disciplines, especially K–12 education and linguistics, that were likewise concerned with issues of race, racism, language, and literacy.

These questions were especially important to those with an interest in high-risk writing instruction, however, because the scholars and teachers involved with this instruction saw a key opportunity to rethink writing instruction for all students.[10] Many of these scholars and teachers would argue within disciplinary discussions of the time that high-risk programs could and should serve as important race-conscious mechanisms with which to help students develop "a broader understanding of the intricate connection between one's language and his cultural experience, combined with insight into the political nature and social stratification of American dialects" (Smitherman, "English Teacher" 63). Others would insist with equal vehemence that, while issues of race and racism were somewhat important to high-risk instruction, these issues did not trump the fact that "it is necessary to teach standard English to non-standard speakers . . . if they are to become part of the mainstream" (Baratz 26).

The Emergence of Disciplinary Race Consciousness

One especially useful example of the type of race-conscious disciplinary discussion of high-risk writing program activity emerging during the late 1960s and early 1970s was Geneva Smitherman's essay "God Don't Never Change," written for *College English* in 1973. This essay featured arguments that Smitherman would articulate throughout the decade in forums ranging from her regular "Soul N' Style" column in *English Journal* to her groundbreaking 1977 book *Talkin' and Testifyin': The Language of Black America*. But it is especially noteworthy given my purposes here because it prompted a number of important written responses from scholars who disagreed with its arguments, including a written response from Jean M. Hunt that will be analyzed later in this section.[11] In this sense, "God Don't Never Change" served as an important early catalyst for disciplinary discussion and debate about the role of race within high-risk writing instruction.

Smitherman began her article by asserting that any discussion of high-risk writing instruction must take into account "American political reality" (828) by working to "specify educational goals for Blacks [with respect to] considerations about the structure of white American society" (828).[12] Toward this end, Smitherman argued that black students' language and literacy practices must be recognized as possessing inherent and profound value for communication: "To reiterate a point that I've made many times heretofore: it's *style, not language per se,* in which the uniqueness of Black expression lies. This style must be located in the situational context, in the Black Cultural Universe. And anybody who *knows* anythang about BI [Black Idiom] knows that that's where it's at. (Outside thought: emphasis on *knows,* cause like my daddy the preacher say, everybody talking bout Heaven ain't goin there.) . . . Such stylistic/language forms are an indigenous part of the Black historical past and are rooted in the Black Cultural Sensibility. They achieve a dynamism of meaning which emanates from a shared sense of oppression, and they represent, perhaps, the continuity of our new African sensibility in the New World" (832).

Smitherman demanded next that race-conscious recognition of black students' background and linguistic skill be accompanied by a paradigm shift in terms of thinking about high-risk instruction and its relationship to white mainstream linguistic and literate standards—especially those typically associated with Standard English. She wondered, for instance, "Why is it that [the] substantive features of BI are never included in the descriptive monographs of 'Black English'? Why is it that only the superfluous features of usage are extrapolated and dealt with in 'language programs for the disadvantaged?'" (833). She also wondered whether this noticeable absence was part of some "insidious design afoot to cut off Black students from they cultural roots, from, according to Frantz Fanon, 'those they left behind,' to create a new class of super-niggers, nouveau-white Blacks, who will rap in the oppressor's dialect, totally obliterating any knowledge or use of BI—a form of language firmly embedded in the African-American past" (833).

Smitherman finally stressed that instructional practices within high-risk programs must be both reconceived and reconfigured in light of these realizations, using the following excerpt from a student writer at Wayne State to illustrate her point: "I think the war in Viet Nam bad. Because we don't have no business over there. My brother friend been in the war, and he say it's hard and mean. I do not like war because it's bad. And so I don't think we have no business there. The reason the war in China is bad is that American boys is dying over there" (qtd. at 831). Within her analysis of this short example, Smitherman first remarked (rather incredulously) that the only initial comment made by the student's teacher regarding this sample text was "Correct your grammar and resubmit" (831), a comment that she rejected as "sheer and utter nonsense" (831) given its exclusive concern with "matters of sheer mechanical correctness" (831). She also argued that instead of allowing this student to "[get] away with sloppy, irresponsible writing just because it happen to conform to a surface notion of correctness" (832), this student's teacher should have considered helping him or her to revise a text in which "every statement . . . [serves as] a generalized comment without any specific, supporting details," one in which "the same modification structures or sentence patterns [are utilized] . . . with tedious repetition," and one that "uses one simple kernel structure after another instead of combining and condensing" (832). Substantive rhetorical work with students like this one, Smitherman concluded, would have helped to ensure that high-risk instruction moved far past mere attention to "*zero, -s,* and *–ed* morphemes" and toward "involving students in the totality and complexity of the communication process" (832).

We see Smitherman articulating at least three key tenets of race consciousness across these passages. First, she stressed that scholars and teachers must recognize the degree to which black students do possess existing linguistic and literate strengths that can be utilized as a foundation for future learning, rather than disregarded as deficits to be overcome. These skills were both distinct and powerful, she insisted, part of a "Black Cultural Sensibility" that could not be expressed via another linguistic or literate mode. Second, she stressed that scholars and teachers working within high-risk programs must critique the white mainstream standards according to which instruction was typically conducted, especially Standard English, precisely because these standards emanated from those who possessed "the power to define reality; those dialect pace-setters, who in America happen to be white and middle class." Refusing to do so, she insisted, was tantamount to a kind of philosophical, pedagogical, and institutional imperialism, one that served to "cut off Black students from they cultural roots" rather than attempting to educate them in any sort of fundamental way. And third, she demanded that scholars and teachers acknowledge these racialized realities as a part of practices and programs aimed at helping students to grasp the "totality and complexity of the communication process."

Another important example of disciplinary race consciousness circulating at this time was the 1974 full-length version of the SRTOL, a document widely heralded as a watershed moment in terms of thinking about the linguistic and literate diversity of students within high-risk writing programs and within composition programs more generally.[13] Writing retrospectively as one of the original authors of this document, Smitherman described the SRTOL in 1999 as a "pioneer[ing]" document for the large discipline of composition, given its attempts to respond to "a developing crisis in college composition classrooms caused by the cultural and linguistic mismatch between higher education and the non-traditional (by virtue of color and class) students who were making their imprint upon the academic landscape for the first time in their history" ("CCCC's Role" 359). Writing in 2004, Patrick Bruch and Richard Marback similarly praised the SRTOL: "Few moments in the history of composition studies have come close to the hoped-for goals of uniting what we know about teaching with what we know to be for the greater good. Perhaps the most prominent of these moments is [the] ratification of 'Students' Right to Their Own Language'" (viii).[14]

The full-length version of the SRTOL from 1974 began by asserting the value and power of all language and literacy practices of whatever origin: "We affirm the students' right to their own patterns and varieties of language—the dialects of their nurture or whatever dialects in which they find their own identity and style" (2). It further argued that white mainstream standards—again, especially those related to Standard English—could be wielded in problematic ways and thus must be carefully critiqued. At one point, the SRTOL characterized these standards as part of a clear "attempt of one social group to exert its dominance over another" (3). At another, it criticized the kinds of common grammar and style handbooks utilized across many disciplinary efforts to teach writing for their overemphasis on this standard: "By concentrating almost exclusively on EAE [Edited American English] . . . handbooks encourage a restrictive language bias. They thus ignore many situations which require other precise uses of language. We know that American English is pluralistic. We know that our students can and do function in a growing multiplicity of language situations which require different dialects, changing interconnections of dialects, and dynamic uses of language. But many handbooks present only the usage of EAE for both written and spoken communication. . . . By appealing to what is labeled 'proper,' they encourage an elitist attitude. The main values they transmit are stasis, restriction, manners, status, and imitation" (10).

And finally, the SRTOL offered specific recommendations for teaching and learning across the discipline of composition that were also clearly steeped in race consciousness. Regarding the issue of reading, for instance, it insisted that teachers across composition should "structure and select materials geared to complex reading problems and oriented to the experience and sophistication of our students," rather than simply "confin[ing] ourselves to the constricting and ultimately ineffectual dialect readers designed for the 'culturally deprived'" (7). It concluded that "we should not be so much interested in changing our students' dialect as in improving their command of the reading process" (8). Regarding the issue of writing, the SRTOL recommended that "if we name the essential functions of writing as expressing oneself, communicating information and attitudes, and discovering meaning through both logic and metaphor, then we view variety of dialects as an advantage" (8); that "if we can convince our students that spelling, punctuation, and usage are less important than content, we have removed a major obstacle in their developing the ability to write" (8); and that while "we do not condone ill-organized, imprecise, undefined, inappropriate writing in any dialect . . . we are especially distressed to find sloppy writing approved so long as it appears with finicky correctness in 'school standard' while vigorous and thoughtful statements in less prestigious dialects are condemned" (9).[15]

Across each of these recommendations, the SRTOL argued that issues of race and racism mattered profoundly to language and literacy instruction: that is, that reading instruction ought to focus upon "improving [students'] command of the reading process"; that writing instruction should not aim toward stressing "finicky correctness in 'school standard,'" at least not "while vigorous and thoughtful statements in less prestigious dialects are condemned"; and that reading and writing instruction both must be conducted so as to acknowledge and cultivate students' existing strengths rather than dwell exclusively upon their perceived weaknesses. In each of these ways, the SRTOL took race-conscious assertions akin to those of an individual scholar like Smitherman and championed their value more broadly to the larger discipline.

These two brief examples from Smitherman and the SRTOL (both circulating alongside a number of others)[16] demonstrate that a number of decidedly race-conscious disciplinary issues were being discussed during the late 1960s and early 1970s:

- How best to recognize the linguistic and literate skills and abilities that high-risk minority students already possessed as a function of their nonwhite and/or and nonmainstream backgrounds;
- How best to examine, critique, and ultimately alter traditional white mainstream standards of language and literacy in egalitarian ways that reflected students' existing racialized skills and sensibilities;
- How best to develop and implement new practices and structures of language and literacy instruction that would allow scholars and teachers to translate race-based awareness of students' existing skills into institutional practice.

But this widespread disciplinary race consciousness was certainly not without its critics. In fact, in much the same way that individuals and groups espousing mainstream beliefs were calling at this time for clear limits to be placed upon race consciousness within high-risk programs more generally, many individuals and groups within composition began calling for clear limits to be placed on high-risk writing instruction in particular, frequently by appealing to standards and Standard English.

The Emergence of Bidialecticalism and the Limits of Race Consciousness

One especially important means through which many scholars and teachers espousing mainstream views appealed to standards during this time was through the notion of "bidialecticalism," rooted in the idea that students must "make linguistic adjustments to specific social situations. These adjustments in phonology, grammar, and lexicon will range anywhere from the obvious adjustments between adults and small children to the more complicated sociolinguistic switching between school, home, and playground talk" (Fasold and Shuy xi). Proponents of bidialecticalism typically acknowledged the need for at least some degree of attention to issues of race and racism within language and literacy instruction as part of the larger process of making "linguistic adjustments to specific social situations." However, they also typically demanded that Standard English use be recognized and emphasized as the explicit goal of these adjustments. They asserted, in other words, that race might matter at some times and in some instructional contexts, but never in ways that changed the need for students to adhere to white mainstream linguistic standards. Bidialecticalism proved quite popular throughout the late 1960s and early 1970s, forming the theoretical basis for myriad publications in composition, education, and linguistics, including the National Council of Teachers of English's (NCTE's) 1965 volume *Language Programs for the Disadvantaged* and its 1968 volume *Nonstandard Dialect;* a 1969 special issue of the *Florida FL Reporter* (a short-lived but nonetheless influential linguistics journal) titled "Linguistic-Cultural Differences and American Education"; the Center for Applied Linguistics' 1970 volume *Teaching Standard English in the Inner City,* edited by Fasold and Shuy; and a number of articles and editorials written in direct response to race-conscious work such as the SRTOL.

One important example of bidialecticalism from this time period is linguist Virginia Allen's "Teaching Standard English as a Second Dialect," an article that initially appeared in the 1969 special issue of the *Florida FL Reporter* dedicated to bidialecticalism.[17] Allen began her argument by asserting that high-risk programs must operate from the recognition that "[nonstandard] varieties of English have validity for many communication situations profoundly important to . . . students" (124). She also insisted that one kind of language was not inherently better than any other: "the presence or absence of standard forms in a person's speech is not a moral or ethical issue" (123). Allen thus seemed willing to grant that a certain level of attention to students' racialized experience was important to the overall learning process.

Allen nevertheless cautioned that high-risk programs must ultimately recognize and respond to the supposed superiority of white mainstream language and literacy standards—that is, the superiority of Standard English—within the predominantly white college and university environment. In particular, she argued that high-risk programs must acknowledge the fact that the standard dialect must be taught, and it should be learned. Even though there is nothing inherently "wrong" or "bad" about using a nonstandard dialect, there are times when it can harm the person who uses it. . . . Undemocratic and unfair as it may seem, the fact is that Standard English is "front door" English. And American schools are committed to the task of making it possible for every citizen to enter by the front door if he wishes to do so. Just as candor and a clear view of the facts are essential in defining what standard English is, so also one needs to be factual and frank in saying why the standard dialect ought to be learned. The student needs to understand that a command of standard English is vital to any American (particularly any "minority group" American) who aims to associate with speakers of the standard dialect on anything like equal footing. (124)

Accordingly, Allen prescribed a series of instructional practices designed to ensure that students acquired this white mainstream standard as quickly and efficiently as possible. She argued, for instance, that proper bidialectical pedagogy should help to "develop a new set of language *habits*" that would allow students to "utter appropriate responses instantaneously, whenever the need arises, without having to stop and think" (125). Such work, she further stressed, must be carried out via skill-and-drill techniques designed to get students "to *use* the pattern, to say sentences illustrating the pattern, again and again, until that mode of speech begins to sound natural to the students themselves" (126). In these ways, Allen insisted that teaching practices must be developed to help students to learn Standard English—a kind of foreign language, so it would seem—as quickly and efficiently as possible.

In these passages, Allen obviously found some value in recognizing students' non-white and nonmainstream language and literacy practices during the course of instruction. But she also saw clear limits to such value as dictated by the need to teach white mainstream Standard English. She argued that even if the need to learn and use this standard may seem "undemocratic and unfair," such learning constituted the only sure means by which minorities could access the "front door" of the American mainstream. She also insisted that no responsible writing instruction could possibly ignore this social fact, at least not if it wished to help a "'minority group' American" to gain "equal footing" on the tricky terrain of contemporary mainstream life. In this way, Allen conceded that recognizing students' racial backgrounds might play some part in responsible writing instruction, but she remained firm that such recognition could never call into question the importance of white mainstream standards.

Other important examples of bidialectical arguments from this time period offered explicit rebuttals to the sample race-conscious texts discussed earlier. For instance, in her 1974 response to Smitherman's "God Don't Never Change" in *College English,* Jean M. Hunt began by arguing that some level of attention to issues of race and racism was warranted within contemporary language and literacy instruction: "I always urge those who can write BE [Black English] to hold fast to that ability" (724). But Hunt is quick to establish white mainstream Standard English—what she called "White English"—as the benchmark against which students' home languages and literacies must be judged within any responsible education program: "students cannot fully appreciate the uniqueness of their own dialect unless they know how it deviates from WE [White English]" (724). She demanded, therefore, that teachers in high-risk programs explicitly reject Smitherman's race-conscious approach to instruction and develop instead pedagogies and activities designed to engage students in the "juxtaposition" of home and standard language and literacy practices. These practices would "alert students to the richness and complexity of language," but nonetheless reinforce the idea that students must learn Standard English once and for all (724).

Similarly, William G. Clark's 1975 "In Response to the 'Students' Right to Their Own Language,'" published in *CCC,* began with an acknowledgment (albeit a rather sarcastic one) of the ways in which the SRTOL had argued race consciously for the viability of all language and literacy practices: the SRTOL, Clark quipped, "had from the beginning been so logical and so impossible and so noble: other dialects *are* as good [as] Standard English. . . . Teaching dialect speakers that their dialect is as good as any other is a *virtuous* act" (217). But when it came to issues such as employment, Clark insisted that the SRTOL ultimately "self-destructs" (217) in the face of white mainstream standards. As proof of this self-destruction, he referenced the following passage of the SRTOL describing the role of Standard English in the workplace: "The speaker of a minority dialect still will write EAE [Edited American English] in formal situations. . . . Therefore it is necessary that we inform those students who are preparing themselves for occupations that demand formal writing that they will be expected to write EAE" (15). This passage, Clark insisted, proved that the SRTOL could not help but offer an "endorsement of Standard English" (217) in ways that "trade nobility for students' employability" (217). Clark concluded, therefore, that the ultimate message of the SRTOL was simply this: "Be gentle with your students. Encourage them. Be interested in their ideas. But, by God, see to it that they write like white folks!" (217).

Both Hunt and Clark acknowledged in their responses that race might matter (or at least might appear to matter) within some high-risk programmatic contexts. But both also posited clear limits to the ways in which race mattered by insisting that language and literacy instruction remain couched within larger attention to white mainstream standards, especially Standard English. For Hunt, facility with Standard English offered minority students the only means to achieve social and economic stability and the only route for students who expect to achieve success in the "real world." For Clark, the need to adhere to Standard English was unavoidable, even within a document as apparently noble as the SRTOL itself. In these ways, both scholars insisted that any disciplinary changes prompted by high-risk activity be limited through recognition of standards.

The bidialectical appeals to standards and Standard English as articulated by the likes of Allen, Hunt, Clark, and a number of others at the time did not necessarily dominate disciplinary discussion of high-risk activity during the late 1960s and early 1970s.[18] Nonetheless, these appeals did possess an important amount of hegemonic power—power that even many activist-minded individuals acknowledged openly. Smitherman expressed concern in *Talkin' and Testifyin'*, for example, that despite the considerable amount of race-conscious work concerning high-risk activity that was circulating at the time, many high-risk programs of this era remained strongly influenced by bidialectical values rooted in "the norms of the white middle class" (203). James Sledd similarly argued in his provocatively titled article "Bi-Dialecticalism: The Linguistics of White Supremacy" that, despite potential for race-conscious change embedded in some high-risk programs, many programs nonetheless continued to operate from the premise that "the prejudices of middle-class whites cannot be changed but must be accepted and indeed enforced on lesser breeds. Upward mobility, it is assumed, is the end of education, but white power will deny upward mobility to speakers of black English, who must therefore be made to talk white English in their contacts with the white world" (1309). Clearly, then, bidialecticalism possessed an important measure of disciplinary power during the late 1960s and early 1970s that limited the scope of possible disciplinary change and reform.

The Disciplinary Dynamics of Interest Convergence

The aforementioned examples of high-risk writing program scholarship from the late-1960s and early-1970s period of racial crisis concern demonstrate that disciplinary discussions of this time period featured numerous important race-conscious arguments from both individuals such as Smitherman and groups such as the CCCC. These arguments insisted that profound change to writing instruction was both desirable and necessary within the larger educational context of racial crisis; they also demanded that the critical interrogation of white mainstream standards, especially Standard English, be central to the process of promoting such change. Nonetheless, disciplinary discussions also featured a strong bidialectical current insisting that high-risk writing programs ultimately needed to embrace Standard English as the endpoint of instruction. Such bidialecticalism asserted that Standard English was the only real key to the "front door" of the American mainstream, and it further insisted that any attempt to critique or otherwise question this superiority of Standard English was unnecessary at best and educationally irresponsible at worst. And in fact, the hegemonic appeals of bidialecticalism were powerful enough at the time that even activists were compelled to acknowledge their influence explicitly.

These dynamics of disciplinary discussion thereby reveal an important degree of disciplinary interest convergence taking place during the late 1960s and early 1970s. Both activists and members of the mainstream had common interests in promoting at least some level of race consciousness within this larger context of racial crisis. As a result, race-conscious scholarship was widely circulated, statements such as the SRTOL were developed, and some version of a disciplinary golden age was born. Nonetheless, those espousing bidialecticalism ultimately stood firm in their belief that a clear focus on standards and Standard English needed to be maintained. They expressed their views through a variety of means, and they ended up having a strong presence within disciplinary discussions of the time as well. In this way, interests clearly converged to promote some race-conscious disciplinary change, but they only converged to a point ultimately deemed acceptable by the (largely) white disciplinary mainstream.

The EOP Rhetoric Program and Its Writing Lab

The profound racial crisis concerns that were shaping national and disciplinary contexts in the late 1960s and early 1970s were also shaping conditions at UIUC. This point was stressed directly by one UIUC administrator at the time:

> [During early] 1968 there was considerable ferment . . . among students, faculty members, and administrators concerning the question of what immediate, dramatic and significant action might be taken by the University to show its concern in solving the single greatest domestic problem in this country. The Office of Admissions and Records as well as other offices on the campus were besieged with visitors from the Black Students' Association, the Committee on Racial Justice, and the old Committee on Student Affairs concerning what the office was doing in the recruiting of disadvantaged students and what additional plans we had in mind. ("Special Education Opportunity Program Recruitment" 1)

This is not to say that UIUC had done nothing to consider issues of race and racism before 1968. In 1965, individual UIUC departments including education, engineering, and law developed small programs to provide additional support for black students already admitted to their programs (Williamson 60–61); at the same time, the College of Liberal Arts and Sciences developed a "verbal communication" summer support program for 30 black and white students determined to be "disadvantaged" and in need of "remedial . . . [work in] oral or written English" (Williamson 62). In 1966, a small-scale high-risk program was developed for about 130 students already admitted to UIUC, 90 of whom were black, in order to provide them with "academic, counseling, and advisory" support (63). Finally, in 1967, the university outlined plans for developing a proto-EOP program that was designed to admit up to 600 high-risk black students per year, beginning in the early 1970s (Williamson 63). Notably, however, these early efforts tended to be both short-lived and developed in isolation from one another, indicative of what one program observer of the time described as "passive support" for minority students at UIUC rather than evidence of coordinated "active assistance" (Carpenter 24).

By 1968, many minority students on the UIUC campus had grown tired of the slow pace of change on the campus. Accordingly, they staged rallies, demonstrations, and sit-ins to demand more input into UIUC's admissions processes and curricula. As these activist voices grew louder, many administrators on the campus began worrying that "racial riots and demonstrations" were going to "plague the university throughout 1968–1969," especially after Martin Luther King was assassinated in April 1968 (Carpenter 114). Accordingly, on 2 May 1968, UIUC's chancellor announced that the university would commit to designing and implementing the EOP program in fall 1968—less than four months away—as a means to recruit and admit about 550 African American students to the freshman class (Williamson 68). The chancellor also stressed that this rapid development was necessitated by the profound racial crisis facing UIUC: "We have done some things, but not enough. The racial crisis of today demands that we take steps of gigantic proportions" (qtd. in Carpenter 29).

This rapid implementation of the EOP program in 1968 demonstrated the power of racial crisis at UIUC during the late 1960s. Activists were "besieging" the administration; demanding that it take "immediate, dramatic and significant action . . . [to begin solving] the single greatest domestic problem in this country"; and even making clear that they might use "racial riots and demonstrations" to get their point across. In response, the UIUC administration agreed to develop and implement EOP over the course of just a few months—a lightning-fast response by any typical measurement of institutional time—in order to bring a large number of African American students to UIUC. The development of the EOP program thus marked a significant shift toward race-based change on the UIUC campus: change may have been simmering for some time at UIUC, but King's death and other racial crisis concerns brought things to a full boil.

The Emergence of Institutional Race Consciousness

One striking illustration of this shift toward race consciousness taking place at UIUC can be found in the operation of the EOP Rhetoric writing lab of the late 1960s and early 1970s. The lab was by far the most well-documented component of the early EOP Rhetoric program, and its early development and evolution offer an important window into the dynamics of high-risk writing instruction during the late 1960s and early 1970s.[19] The writing lab was initially developed in 1968 as a one-on-one tutorial center designed to help students negotiate the language and literacy demands of the university environment. It was viewed as absolutely central to the success of the overall EOP program: in an early document describing lab activities, UIUC insisted that the lab be assigned the "highest possible priority" ("Special Educational Opportunities Program" 13) because it offered the kind of "individualized assistance" that would ultimately enable EOP students "to achieve proficiency in writing necessary for successful college work" (13). Notably, the lab was projected to be quite expensive, with a budget of about $78,000: in fact, the vice-chancellor for academic affairs (VCAA) in 1969 expressed fear that the campus might be in an "impossible situation in funding the Writing Laboratory" unless it found a significant source of campus support (letter to chair of SCSE, 30 January 1969, 1).[20] But the campus board of trustees was nevertheless committed to funding the lab, and it quickly mandated several important administrative changes at UIUC in order to ensure that it was developed in time for the launch of the larger EOP program in fall 1968.

More specifically, the board of trustees decided during summer 1968 that the lab should be developed in fall 1968 under the supervision of a newly created dual administrative structure. Day-to-day operation of the lab during its first year (including all hiring and tutoring activities) would be overseen by four administrators who were affiliated with the English Department and its larger EOP Rhetoric effort: the director of EOP Rhetoric ("Director A"), an individual who was also the director of the overall rhetoric program in the English Department at the time; the "NCTE liaison," who served as a liaison between the nearby National Council of Teachers of English (NCTE) and the UIUC English Department/EOP Rhetoric program; and two codirectors of the writing lab, both graduate students with significant experience teaching and administering one-on-one writing instruction. In contrast, the long-term shape of lab philosophy, practice, and structure would be overseen by the Senate Committee on Student English (SCSE), an administrative entity that had been supervising literacy gatekeeping at UIUC for nearly thirty years with the help of a yearly budget of roughly $100,000 ("Freshman Rhetoric Staff Bulletin" 5). The trustees' decision to integrate the work of these four administrators with the long-standing SCSE was an incredibly important one: it effectively merged one group of administrators espousing race consciousness with another group of administrators who had long espoused color blindness to create one single lab administration.

Director A, the NCTE liaison, and the two writing lab codirectors were all openly race conscious in their thinking about the lab. In one early description of the lab from 1968, for instance, Director A insisted that the fundamental mission of the lab should be to help students "express themselves clearly in their indigenous forms and dialects. Only secondarily, if at all, are students expected to write in the middle-class, white tradition" ("SEOP Proposal" 1). In another description written soon thereafter, Director A insisted that good practice in the lab involved not the judging of students "by preconceived—and often false and narrow—standards. It [rather] involves recognition of individual perceptions and new, varied ways of communicating them. It involves thinking of [writing] not as autonomous but as interdisciplinary. . . . It involves, above all, giving students the confidence they can express their experience coherently . . . in the forms they elect for its expression; and the ability . . . to compare their experiences and forms, objectively, with those of others" ("Glance" 6). The NCTE liaison similarly argued for race consciousness in the lab while writing on behalf of one SCSE subcommittee charged with hiring a permanent lab director (a subcommittee about which I will have much more to say shortly): "Little will be gained and much will be lost if the entire effort in the Laboratory is aimed at instructing the students in standard forms of public discourse. None of us knows what specific hurdles lie between that goal and the students where they now are. Moreover, where such instruction is successful, we risk driving out the originality and spark that characterize some of their apparently 'untutored' writing now. If all we accomplish is getting these students to write like the typical U. of I. undergraduate at the cost of that originality, we have probably lost far more than we have won. And we risk alienating some of our most original students" ("Meeting of Subcommittee" 3). In a similar vein, both writing lab codirectors argued during one meeting of the SCSE that the lab should focus first and foremost on "major thinking . . . organization and following directions," rather than on drill activities designed to instill white mainstream language and literacy practices into students (Ad

Hoc Committee on the Writing Lab, Minutes, 20 January 1969, 6), particularly since "in drills students are able to supply the answers, [but] then they cannot apply them to composition" (6).

In contrast, the various administrators and faculty serving on the SCSE over the course of three decades had typically emphasized color-blind standards within the writing instruction that they oversaw. Since 1941, the SCSE had supervised two powerful language and literacy gatekeeping and remediation mechanisms at UIUC. The first of these was the English Qualifying Exam (EQE), a first-year composition exit exam comprising a timed essay and a quantitative test of Standard English grammar and usage administered to up to 3,800 students per year (roughly 60 percent of the freshman population at the time) who exited the two-semester freshman rhetoric sequence with a grade of C or lower ("Comments on the English Qualifying Exam" 1). The second of these was the Rhetoric 200 remedial writing course, a course required for up to 1,500 students per year (roughly 25 percent of the freshman population) who had failed to pass the qualifying exam one or more times ("Freshman Rhetoric Staff Bulletin" 5). As it oversaw both of these programs, the SCSE had traditionally emphasized its role as a gatekeeper of literacy standards at UIUC. As late as 1967, for instance, the SCSE stressed that up to 60 percent of freshmen could expect to fail the exam on the first try ("Comments on the English Qualifying Exam" 1); that some may well become "two-, three-, four-, and five-time repeaters" of the exam and/or the remedial course ("Information about the English Qualifying Examination" 3); and, finally, that a few students might be denied their undergraduate degree as a result of their inability to pass the course (3).[21]

With the development of the lab in 1968, however, SCSE membership was forced to rethink its activities considerably. At the behest of the trustees, the SCSE was now required to

- Dismantle immediately both its EQE and its Rhetoric 200 course, while redirecting its entire EQE/Rhetoric 200 budget toward the operation of the EOP writing lab (SCSE, Minutes, 22 October 1968, 3);
- Develop and implement "experimental" philosophies and teaching practices within the lab "in lieu of the prescribed rhetoric for limited numbers of students," forming a new committee called the Ad Hoc Committee on the Writing Lab to help it do so (SCSE, Minutes, 22 October 1968, 2); and

- Include Director A, the NCTE liaison, and the writing lab codirectors in the deliberations of both the larger SCSE and the Ad Hoc Committee on the Writing Lab.

The SCSE was expected, in short, to abandon its three-decade emphasis on literacy gatekeeping and to support directly a new race-conscious high-risk writing instructional effort.

The creation of this dual lab administrative structure indicates a striking level of change taking place at UIUC during the summer and fall semesters of 1968. UIUC had decided to develop a writing lab that would be run on a day-to-day basis by four race-conscious administrators from the English Department/EOP Rhetoric program; meanwhile, its day-to-day operations would be supported by an SCSE that had been required to abandon its long-standing gatekeeping programs and functions and embrace race-conscious student support instead. The UIUC campus was now apparently determined to focus much less on what was *wrong* with mainstream UIUC students' literacy skills and much more upon what was potentially *right* about EOP Rhetoric students' literacy skills.

But not everyone saw this race-conscious lab development in a positive light. In fact, it was questioned openly by a number of administrators and faculty at the time, particularly by the chair of the SCSE. This chair was a full professor in the Economics Department and had served on the SCSE for several years previously as a standards-focused member of the committee: he had gone on record in 1967 as one of the few members of the SCSE who still felt that the EQE system was worth preserving as a means to ensure "the graduate's proficiency in English" (SCSE, Minutes, 7 November 1967, 3). Beginning in 1968, he also began to transfer some of the SCSE's former emphasis on standards to the new EOP Rhetoric writing lab, both by promoting staunchly bidialectical viewpoints in his thinking about the lab and by making a number of crucial administrative decisions designed to ensure that his thinking influenced the shape of the lab in the years to come.

The Limits of Institutional Race Consciousness

Numerous SCSE documents drafted throughout 1968–69 attested to the staunch bidialecticalism of this SCSE chair, especially to the importance that he placed on students' ability to produce Standard English. For instance, in a brief response written to SCSE subcommittee members regarding their thoughts on a permanent SCSE director, this chair insisted that "however unfortunate the situation is, upward mobility within the dominant economy and social structure is tied in some measure to command of standard written English. So, in fact, is the usual form of success in college" (letter to Subcommittee on the Recruitment of a Director, 21 January 1969, 1). He demanded, therefore, that the lab teach "standard written English" (1) as one of its primary goals. The chair also underscored his desire to enforce standards in the lab through the ways in which he characterized the "right" kind of student. He argued that the lab ought to concern itself first and foremost with those students who "enter the university intent on learning to write within the conventions of standard written English" (1). But the lab should not concern itself, he argued, with those students who are purportedly "guided more by ethnic pride than a desire for immediate mobility," largely because these students typically "resist such instruction, hoping rather for a change in the dominant mores or for a separate Black economy and social structure" (1). In these ways, the chair insisted that the lab must work only with those students openly willing to accept the supposed superiority of white mainstream language and literacy practices at face value; it should not waste its time or effort working with militants who desired cultural or linguistic separatism.

This chair further translated his views into a new mission statement for the lab that he began circulating in the form of a February 1969 document titled "(Draft) Report and Tentative Plans: Writing Laboratory/Clinic." In this draft report, the chair insisted that the lab must be viewed as "remedial . . . with the goal of improving specific deficiencies" related to students' language backgrounds (1). He also argued that at stake in the lab "is sheer academic survival—at least for the student. Effective communication [should be] the prime . . . concern in the Writing Laboratory. For many underprivileged whites, certain rural students, and most ghetto blacks, college is at least another dialect to master. Sometimes it is the equivalent of a foreign language" (2). Finally, he insisted that this "remedial" philosophy of "survival" needed to be translated into standards-oriented teaching and assessment strategies within the lab. With regard to teaching, he recommended a series of drill activities to be conducted using audiotape, videotape, and computers, all of which might efficiently "substitute" for at least some tutor-student interactions (4). With regard to assessment, he requested a much

47

more rigorous quantitative evaluation plan for the lab, one designed to ensure that students were mastering white mainstream Standard English. This was needed, he said, because "measurement has been extremely meager in evaluations of the Writing Laboratory/Writing Clinic activities. . . . Evaluation has been hampered by two major factors. First there is the lack of explicit goals, stated in formal terms, at least some terms of which are translatable into correspondence rules that permit quantitative appraisal. Second, there is a lack of a resource person to detail what is measurable, create measures where they are not yet devised, supervise measurement, and carry out analytical studies. . . . Much valuable experimental evidence is presently being wasted in the Writing Laboratory/Clinic" (4–5).

The chair thus demonstrated his strong belief that the lab must maintain a primary focus on standard white mainstream language and literacy practices, a set of practices that he believed rendered black students (particularly "ghetto black" students) "remedial" in the eyes of the larger university and thus unlikely to "survive" without significant assistance.[22] Furthermore, he insisted that the lab must develop both a series of drill activities designed to instill this white mainstream Standard English into students as quickly and efficiently as possible and a new assessment program (one guided by a new "Director of Assessment") designed to determine students' mastery of this standard. Without such activity, he felt, lab function would be "hampered," and the opportunity to gauge students' acquisition of white mainstream language and literacy practices would be "lost." In this way, the chair advocated a lab-specific brand of bidialecticalism: while he conceded that race might matter to a small degree when considering the needs of EOP Rhetoric students in the writing lab, he remained adamant that these students ultimately required a good dose of Standard English for their institutional survival.

The Chair Takes Action

In addition to expressing his bidialectical views about the lab and its activities, this chair performed a number of actions to ensure that these views ultimately reshaped lab philosophy, practice, and structure in the short and the long term. Two examples of this lab reshaping are especially illustrative. In the first, the chair received a rather passionate complaint from one of the writing lab codirectors in fall 1968 regarding his earlier characterization of the lab as "remedial." In this complaint, the writing lab codirector wrote:

> I cannot help but take exception to your use of the word remedial. At least when it comes to working with the black students, our work is, and should be, teaching something *new* rather than with remediating something already learned. I would never want to try to make a student forget his dialect. My goal is to teach them to use their dialects in some situations and the so-called "standard English" dialect in others. Many of their writing "problems," including punctuation and grammar, are merely a reflection of a system different from the one we are most familiar with. These people need to have both systems if they are to adjust to college life and if they are not to lose [a sense of] how they have learned to relate to their own cultural community. It may seem strange to you that I am quibbling over the use of one term, but if I were to think of the Lab as remedial it would follow that I would feel that the majority of our students are pretty dumb. They know English and I think that we should show our respect for their knowledge by reflecting an understanding of what they are really learning. If I decided to use the term remedial, I would have to change the way I taught. (1)

Here, the lab codirector clearly rejected the idea that the lab was "remedial," insisting that to accept this characterization was to accept the idea that students are "pretty dumb" simply because they did not communicate in a way familiar to the white mainstream. In contrast, she felt that EOP students did in fact "know English." She also felt both that they deserved respect for this knowledge and that they should be encouraged to retain a sense of what it meant to communicate effectively within their home community in order to achieve university success.

In a short response memo dated just a few days later, however, the chair dismissed this codirector's critique somewhat bluntly: "We are not likely to view the term 'remedial' with the same connotations. . . . Should I go to France and have to converse with Breton sailors, I am sure my academic-economics-French would be deficient and I would have to remedy the deficiency. In this situation, I would feel neither pretty dumb, nor would I expect my tutor to regard me as such. I simply would not have a tool I needed for the task at hand. It is hard for me to see why the situation is any different in the Writing Laboratory" (letter to writing lab codirector, 28 March 1969, 1). The chair further remarked that "your letter is in no way quibbling, for there are enough meanings of remedy to accommodate a battlefield of semantics" (1). Yet he made no mention of striking the word *remedial* from his tentative mission statement for the lab, nor did he otherwise indicate that he would be changing his recommendations to the SCSE in light of the codirector's complaint.[23]

By responding to the codirector in this way, the chair clearly stressed his belief in the supposed superiority of white language and literacy standards. He insisted that just as he himself would need to adjust his own practices in recognition of the superiority of those used by the Breton sailors in the foreign context that he described, so too must EOP students adjust their own practices in recognition of the superiority of white mainstream Standard English within the predominantly white university context. These standards were nothing more, he felt, than the proper "tools . . . needed for the task at hand," and so it was quite "hard" for him to understand how anyone might rationally disagree with this view. The chair also underscored here his administrative power to define the lab as he saw fit: he refused, in effect, to make any changes to his draft report in response to these concerns or to otherwise modify his own recommendations to the SCSE, despite the codirector's request.

In the second of these examples, the chair had received written suggestions from the "Subcommittee on the Recruitment of a Director for the Writing Laboratory" in spring 1969 regarding the hiring of a full-time director for the writing lab in 1969–70.[24] With the NCTE liaison serving and writing as its chair, this subcommittee had made a number of race-conscious suggestions regarding the qualities they desired of a new lab director. It had also requested that these suggestions be circulated for full SCSE discussion in January 1969. In particular, the subcommittee had recommended that this new director possess

- A strong distaste for the idea that "the first step in teaching writing is to eliminate gross errors" (NCTE Liaison 2);
- A strong "interest in and some study of the interrelationships of various language activities" (3);
- A "respect for the power and the complexity of nonstandard dialects" (3);
- "Interest in and some study of the interrelationship of various language activities" (3);

- A "healthy suspicion of drill as a prime activity for a teacher or a tutor" (3); and
- A profound interest in "urg[ing] on his laboratory staff the greater responsibilities of attitudinal change and cognitive growth" (3), rather than in drill activities per se.[25]

The subcommittee was clearly convinced that any permanent lab director must be both race conscious and willing to implement a race-conscious agenda within the lab. It was also interested in persuading the larger SCSE to adopt this same perspective.

The chair received the subcommittee's recommendations and eventually passed them on to the SCSE. However, before he did so, he appended a short paragraph to them in which he argued, among other things, that

> the Writing Laboratory should prepare itself to offer the wisest, most eco-nomical instruction based upon available analysis of the contrast between the non-standard dialect and standard English. In such instances, drill can be appropriate and may be necessary. The transition from non-standard to standard writing or the addition of standard English to the repertoire of the student would be very slow otherwise. Not to provide this instruction would be a failure to capitalize on the essential motivation of these stu-dents. Although drill will not be the principal activity of tutors, continued exploration in the production and administration of drill materials will be an important activity in the laboratory. (letter to Subcommittee on the Recruitment of a Director, 21 January 1969, 1)

In this addendum, the chair clearly emphasized his standards argument yet again, highlighting in particular the need for any future lab director to focus explicitly upon drill activities aimed at promoting Standard English. Failure to do so, he insisted, would result in the "very slow" acquisition of white main-stream English on the part of EOP students, as well as a general failure on the part of the lab to "capitalize upon [students'] essential motivation." Further-more, by attaching this addendum to the subcommittee's original suggestions, the chair again asserted his power and authority to dictate the terms of SCSE discussion in ways that he saw fit: the SCSE may well have had to hear the subcommittee's race-conscious suggestions regarding a new director, but it would also have to hear the chair's bidialectical views alongside them.

In these examples including the writing lab codirector and the subcommittee, the chair of the SCSE attempted to shape the larger decision-making processes of the SCSE in light of the standards that he saw as so essential to the future of the lab. He was convinced that "mobility within the dominant economy and social structure is tied in some measure to command of standard written English." He was also convinced that he ought to influence discussion within the context of the SCSE to make sure that its other members were also persuaded of the correctness of this bidialectical point of view.

Institutional Outcomes and the Future of the Writing Lab

The larger body of the SCSE was ultimately persuaded by the chair's arguments and actions. In April 1969, it ratified the chair's original draft description of writing lab philosophy, practice, and structure, complete with its original wording, further advising that the chair's mission statement be adopted as the official statement of the writing lab "without delay" (Ad Hoc Committee on the Writing Lab, Report 1). In so doing, the SCSE effectively approved the chair's characterization of the lab as a "remedial" enterprise aimed at inculcating Standard English. It also agreed that its teaching practices must necessarily be rooted in both expanded drill and expanded quantitative assessment activities.

Furthermore, the SCSE opted to hire a new lab director for 1969–70 under the auspices of a position officially titled "director of assessment." When advertising for this position, the SCSE insisted that applicants must possess a "good background in research design, statistics and measurement, and the psychology of learning" (SCSE, "Job Description" 1). Ironically, however, it indicated that substantial training in writing instruction and administration was "desired, but not essential" (1).[26] Furthermore, when actually hiring an individual for this director of assessment position, the SCSE chose someone who emphasized both correctness and quantitative assessment much more strongly than had either of the previous writing lab codirectors. This new director of assessment decreed early in fall 1969, for instance, that the lab should divide its services into three tracks: section 103A for the student "whose needs are basically grammatical and [who] does not write standard English"; section 103B for the student who "already writes standard English but lacks discipline of language and a sense of logical pre-

sentation"; and finally, 103C for the student who "is well on his way to inde-
pendence in writing procedures but needs assistance in preparation of papers
for other courses" (SCSE, Minutes, 15 September 1969, 3). This director of
assessment's mention here of "grammatical" needs and Standard English as
the basis for instructional grouping suggested that the lab would begin
tracking students first and foremost on the basis of their nonstandard and
non-white language use, while relegating black English speakers to the lowest track. This new director also informed his lab staff later in fall 1969 that
students would be tested at least three times per semester for improvement
in terms of their usage, spelling, and punctuation skills ("To Rhetoric 103
Instructors" 1), ensuring in effect that assessment of students' facility with
Standard English was now central to lab activity in ways that it had not been
during the previous year. Both the larger SCSE and the new director of assessment thereby helped to translate some of the chair's emphasis upon the
superiority of white mainstream language and literacy practices into a
specific set of lab philosophies, practices, and structures. Their actions in
this regard made clear that, instead of the institution changing to meet the
needs of students, students would be changing to meet the needs and expectations of the institution.[27]

The Institutional Dynamics of Interest Convergence

The examples of administrative activity outlined throughout this chapter
demonstrate that significant institutional change occurred at UIUC during
the late 1960s and early 1970s to create an EOP Rhetoric writing lab where
one had not previously existed: new race-conscious administrators were
hired to direct the lab during its first year, the SCSE was transformed from
a long-standing campus literacy gatekeeper into a support mechanism for
the lab, and substantial funds were redirected in order to support this new
lab enterprise. Furthermore, this new lab ensured that the more than 550
African American students who had entered the UIUC campus for the first
time received race-conscious one-on-one writing instruction throughout
1968–69. It is also clear, however, that the chair of the SCSE, along with the
SCSE itself and the eventual director of assessment for the lab, imagined
and articulated clear standards-focused limits to such race consciousness

throughout 1968–69. This chair worked especially hard to articulate a bidialectical reenvisioning of the lab: he not only spoke regularly to the SCSE about the value of bidialecticalism but also performed administrative actions—that is, drafting new lab philosophies, shaping and reshaping SCSE discussions to his liking, advocating for the hiring of new positions, and so on—designed to promote his vision. As a result of his actions, the lab of 1969–70 was a decidedly less race-conscious place than it had been just one year earlier. In a crucial sense, the initial race-conscious promise of the lab was not fully realized even during its very earliest history.

These institutional events point to an important dynamic of institutional interest convergence taking place within the context of the lab in the midst of late-1960s and early-1970s concerns over racial crisis. The interests of those espousing race-conscious activist views of writing instruction and those espousing more mainstream approaches to this activity did converge around the initial development and implementation of the EOP Rhetoric program and its writing lab, and this convergence helped to create a lab that offered rather substantive change to institutional business-as-usual. Nevertheless, the changes wrought by institutional interest convergence were limited substantially by those espousing bidialecticalism in ways that had strongly reshaped the lab by 1969–70. Interest convergence helped to bring the lab into being, but limits placed on this convergence by powerful mainstream administrators quickly reined in some of the lab's more progressively race-conscious activities.

Racial Crisis and the Complexities of Interest Convergence

The context of the late-1960s and early-1970s racial crisis was clearly one of change brought on by various currents of interest convergence. Nationally, such convergence prompted the creation of hundreds of high-risk programs serving hundreds of thousands of students. At the level of the discipline, it helped to generate many important new race-conscious insights into language and literacy instruction within the field of composition and high-risk writing instruction. And institutionally, it resulted in the creation of the EOP Rhetoric writing lab at UIUC, which operated as the largest and most extensive program dedicated to serving the writing needs of minority students in the history of the institution. These changes were real and significant, and those of us interested in understanding the dynamics of high-risk program discussion should recognize (and perhaps even celebrate) them. But despite these changes, mainstream interests of the time still exerted a powerful influence to preserve fundamental aspects of the educational status quo. Nationally, high-risk programs proved reluctant to change standard views of students, of curricula, or of faculty responsibilities. At the level of the discipline, bidialectical views of standards were invoked as limits to the race consciousness being expressed within discussions of the time. And at the level of the institution, bidialectical views were invoked to promote the rapid reconfiguration of the EOP writing lab as a Standard English gate-keeping mechanism. In these ways, the real changes achieved during this era were not ultimately as extensive or as powerful as they could or should have been. Those of us with an interest in understanding the dynamics of high-risk program discussion need to come to terms with these important limits as well.

The dynamics of interest convergence outlined here, however, would soon shift as racial crisis concerns gave way to a new set of national, disciplinary, and institutional concerns with the "literacy crisis" during the mid-1970s. These mid-1970s concerns of a literacy crisis would shape discussion of high-risk activity through a dynamic of interest *divergence,* one in which race-conscious demands from activists were increasingly undermined and even reversed by appeals to standards and Standard English from those espousing mainstream interests and beliefs. Furthermore, these concerns would serve as the basis for actively reversing and dismantling even the limited changes achieved during the late 1960s and early 1970s.

The Mid-1970s

LITERACY CRISIS MEETS COLOR BLINDNESS

THE MID-1970s found many in the United States increasingly worried that societal troubles—the war in Vietnam, the pending energy crisis, the Watergate scandal, and other woes—were threatening the status of the country as the "hegemonic power of the West" (Genovese 61) and leaving it in a "weaker, less-independent position than at any time in the previous twenty-five years" (61). This era also found many mainstream whites increasingly convinced that these troubles were caused by an overemphasis on issues of race and racism within the Civil Rights Movement and other race-conscious reform efforts of the late 1960s and early 1970s. Omi and Winant have observed that many whites at the time felt that such efforts had produced a kind of "reverse racism" in which "*whites* were now the victims of racial discrimination in education and the job market. In attempting to eliminate racial discrimination, the state went too far. It legitimated group rights, established affirmative action mandates, and spent money on a range of social programs which, according to the right, debilitated rather than uplifted its target populations" (117).

Mainstream white fears regarding the disintegration of the country's social and racial order were further manifest within one of the most widely discussed higher-educational issues of this time period—the "literacy crisis" being championed throughout the mainstream media during the mid-1970s. A number of mainstream journalists, scholars, and politicians felt that U.S. students' language and literacy abilities had declined precipitously as a function of late-1960s and early-1970s educational experimentation in general and race-based educational experimentation in particular. They also felt that the only cure for this crisis was a swift and decisive abandonment of all such experimentation in favor of a return to the linguistic and literate "basics"— namely, training in Standard English and grammatical correctness—while eschewing any and all attention to unnecessary political issues such as race.

One especially well-known example of literacy crisis discourse was Merrill Sheils's 1975 *Newsweek* article "Why Johnny Can't Write," which opens with the bold claim that "if your children are attending college, the chances are that when they graduate they will be unable to write ordinary, expository English with any real degree of structure and lucidity. If they are in high school and planning to attend college, the chances are less than even that they will be able to write English at the minimal college level when they get there. . . . Willy-nilly, the U.S. educational system is spawning a generation of semiliterates" (58). Sheils located the roots of said crisis in the purportedly widespread late-1960s and early-1970s educational belief that "one form of language is as good as another" (Pei, qtd. in Sheils 58); in a general overemphasis on "'creativity' in the English classroom" at the expense of more traditional areas of study (60); and, especially significant given my purposes here, in the race-conscious writing instruction advocated by the CCCC within its final SRTOL document. Indeed, Sheils argued that the SRTOL was squarely rooted in "political activism of the past decade . . . . [an activism that] has led many teachers to take the view that standard English is just a 'prestige' dialect among many others, and that insistence on its predominance constitutes an act of repression by the white middle class" (61). She then condemned the SRTOL as "more a political tract than a set of educational precepts" (61), one that failed to recognize the real issue at stake within this crisis—namely, whether students could learn to speak and write correctly according to the tenets of Standard English. She argued that, "'prestige dialect' or not, standard English is in fact the language of American law, politics, and commerce, and the vast bulk of American literature—and the traditionalists [among which Sheils placed herself near the end of her piece] argue that to deny children access to it is in itself a pernicious form of op-pression" (61). After making these claims, Sheils concluded her piece with a resounding "back-to-basics" call, drawing an analogy between language use and a kind of servitude: "The point is that there have to be some fixed rules, however tedious, if the codes of human communication are to remain deci-pherable. If written language is placed at the mercy of every new colloquial-ism and if every fresh dialect demands and gets equal sway, then we will soon find ourselves back in Babel. In America today, as in the never-never world Alice discovered on her trip through the looking-glass, there are too many people intent on being masters of their language and too few willing to be its servants" (65). In these ways, Sheils clearly placed blame for stu-dent illiteracy at the feet of 1960s and 1970s "political" reform efforts rooted in issues of race. Furthermore, she insisted that these political reform efforts be abandoned and replaced with a return to the "fixed rules" of lan-guage use so that all students, regardless of background, could be properly taught their role as "servants" respecting the "masters" of the linguistic and literate mainstream.

By making these sorts of claims, Sheils (along with numerous others writ-ing during the mid-1970s) stressed what critical race theorist Kimberle Crenshaw has described as a discourse of "color-blindness" premised on three key ideas: first, that attention to issues of race and racial difference ought to be rejected as "irrational and backwards" (xiv), such that all "deci-sion-making based on the irrational and irrelevant attribute of race" (xv) was abandoned within social, political, economic, and educational realms; sec-ond, that mainstream white beliefs and values ought to be embraced as cultural universals necessitating "integration," "assimilation," and the vali-dation of "the basic myths of American meritocracy" on the part of non-white and nonmainstream individuals (xiv); and third, that any institutions or programs previously developed as mechanisms with which to offer "radi-cal or fundamental challenges to status quo institutional practices" or other-wise to implement "progressive thinking about race" ought to be dismantled and replaced with those deemed more "reasonable" in their approach to ra-cial issues (xiv).[1] Furthermore, by making such claims, Sheils underscored just how significantly the educational climate of the mid-1970s had changed. Gone was tentative late-1960s and early-1970s agreement between those es-pousing activism and those espousing mainstream discourses that some form of high-risk programmatic activity was necessary for the long-term health of U.S. higher education. Instead, mainstream thinkers of the mid-1970s insisted that high-risk programs were completely unnecessary: these programs were far more concerned with racial "politics" than with "educational precepts," and they clearly ignored the proper roles of "servant" and "master" within higher education.

This new educational emphasis on literacy crisis and standards during the mid-1970s was reflected within important changes to high-risk program sponsorship occurring at this time. The Open Admissions program at CUNY, for instance, was profoundly affected by what Lavin and Hyllegard described as "conservative voices . . . asserting the need for greater emphasis on educational excellence" (209), themselves bolstered by a "major fiscal crisis" in New York during the mid-1970s that prompted "severe reductions" to CUNY efforts and programs (209). In the wake of these conservative pressures, CUNY changed a number of its standards related to Open Admissions:[2] it raised minimum automatic admissions requirements for entry into the program from graduation in the top 50 percent of a New York City high school class to graduation in the top 35 percent (210); it required all students to obtain a minimum GPA of 2.0 by the time they had achieved twenty-five credits or risk being expelled (210–11);[3] and it decided to charge tuition of all students, Open Admissions or otherwise, for the first time in over a century (210).[4]

Views of national programs like SSS were changing at this time as well. For instance, the first federally sponsored study of SSS from 1975, titled *The Impact of Special Services Programs in Higher Education for "Disadvantaged" Students,* conceded, at least initially, that SSS programs promoted some positive attitudinal outcomes among high-risk students: for example, the "presence of Special Services Programs and/or disadvantaged students on the campuses seems to be associated with a change in campus attitude toward the disadvantaged, toward their more general acceptance and accommodation by faculty, administrators and other students" (Davis, Burkheimer, and Borders-Patterson viii). But this study ultimately drew several negative conclusions about SSS program effectiveness. It argued that SSS had no clearly measurable effects on either student experience or achievement with respect to standards: "There is no evidence that availability of or participation in support services activities systematically improves performance and satisfaction with college over that which may be expected from past performance" (viii). It also concluded that SSS programs should not receive additional federal money until they could demonstrate empirically that they improved student achievement with respect to standards: "After a reasonable time, program evaluation and renewal should be based on the success of students performing at a level that equals or exceeds that of their nondisadvantaged peers at that institution. Both internal and external evaluation should be built into contract requirements for renewal. Ongoing evaluation is a *sine qua non* for continuance, given the absence of proof of effectiveness of current efforts" (viii).[5] And notably, these new standards-focused federal attitudes toward SSS program effectiveness were accompanied by decidedly less supportive federal funding paradigms. In strong contrast to the period of significant early growth and support of the late 1960s and early 1970s, federal funding for SSS was frozen at $23 million from 1973 until 1977, thereby putting an end to all new program development during these four years (Chaney et al. 4-3). Furthermore, even as actual funding for need-based aid like Pell Grants increased significantly, from roughly $122 million in 1973 to $2.3 billion in 1979 (as measured in constant 2004 dollars) (Cook and King 28), the percentage of college costs covered by such aid actually declined steadily, from a high of 99 percent after 1975 (Cook and King 5). Consequently, high-risk minority students found it more difficult to gain access to SSS. In the midst of these changes, the number of underrepresented minority students enrolled in higher education began to decrease: whereas higher-education participation rates reached an apex of 27.6 percent for whites, 22.5 percent for blacks, and 20.0 percent for Hispanics in 1976, these rates dipped to 26.3 percent, 19.4 percent, and 16.1 percent, respectively, by 1979 (Snyder, Dillow, and Hoffman 296).

The Literacy Crisis and the Dynamics of Interest Divergence

Mid-1970s concerns about literacy crisis prompted a clear shift in thinking about the operation of high-risk programs. No longer was there agreement between activist and mainstream points of view, as there had been in the late 1960s and early 1970s, that high-risk programmatic activity was needed to ward off racial crisis. Instead, activists now found themselves supporting a kind of race-conscious high-risk programmatic activity that the mainstream openly rejected. This mainstream claimed that high-risk programs had focused far too much on contentious political issues like race and far too little on color-blind basics in ways that had actually caused the country's literacy crisis. As a result, the still-fledgling high-risk movement was exiting its late-1960s and early-1970s golden age and entering something of a mid-1970s dark age.

These mid-1970s trends therefore indicate an important dynamic of interest divergence emerging within U.S. higher education in the midst of literacy crisis concerns. Activists of this time period still possessed an interest in promoting race-conscious high-risk programmatic activity. However, their interests increasingly diverged from mainstream interests in preserving purportedly color-blind standards and the white linguistic status quo that these standards upheld. As these interests increasingly diverged, support for high-risk programs grew weaker and weaker, and the past race-conscious changes enabled by these programs were attacked, undercut, and even reversed. The white mainstream of the mid-1970s was actively reconfiguring previous race-based reform efforts in ways that demonstrated its profound power to dictate the overall course of racial justice, thereby reflecting Bell's assertions regarding the difficulty of race-based change once again.

From Lingering Race Consciousness
to Growing Color Blindness

The kinds of concerns over the literacy crisis routinely being articulated during the mid-1970s on a national level were also being articulated at the level of the discipline, a point illustrated by Richard Lloyd-Jones in his 1978 CCCC chair's address "A View from the Center." Lloyd-Jones remarked that composition scholars throughout the mid-1970s were routinely being asked to explain how and why those of us in composition "have now found our own place on the public stage as, suddenly, our fellow citizens have discovered writing. Or as the press usually puts it, 'the crisis in writing skills.' We are invited to make statements, and we have become the subjects of editorials. Though we might have doubted it, by the facts of public notice we now know that we exist" (24). Lloyd-Jones's statement concerning the ubiquity of literacy crisis concerns in composition was underscored by the appearance of a number of literacy crisis–inspired articles and books appearing at the time, including a 1977 special issue of *College English* dedicated to investigating literacy crisis, edited by W. B. Colley and Richard Ohmann, and the book *What's Wrong with American English,* written by Arn Tibbetts and Charlene Tibbetts. It was further underscored by the interest that scholars and teachers of high-risk writing instruction demonstrated in literacy crisis issues at this time. These scholars were compelled to grapple with the increasing conservatism of the mid-1970s era directly. Indeed, in response to literacy crisis concerns, some high-risk scholars and teachers of the mid-1970s certainly continued to argue for race-conscious instruction, often explicitly rejecting literacy crisis concerns as racist attempts to affirm white mainstream power and privilege. However, two other types of disciplinary response became common at this time as well. The first of these openly dismissed all race-conscious high-risk efforts as both racist and unnecessary while simultaneously advocating a prompt return to the color-blind basics, thereby directly echoing the logic of Sheils's "Why Johnny Can't Write" argument. The second, often appearing under the moniker of the new "basic writing" (BW) movement, appeared initially to defend the race-conscious goals of many high-risk programs in the face of literacy crisis critique. However, this work also ultimately demanded a shift away from race consciousness and toward color-blind cognitive approaches to meeting students' perceived needs.

Shifting Disciplinary Points of View

At least some of the mid-1970s scholarship generated by high-risk/BW scholars and teachers was openly race conscious in substance and tone. Harvey Daniels's 1974 *English Journal* opinion piece, titled "What's New with the SAT?," for example, offered a scathing critique of the Educational Testing Service's (ETS's) recently introduced Test of Standard Written English (TSWE), a multiple-choice test of students' ability to detect written deviations from Standard English. In this piece, Daniels argued that the TSWE had emerged directly from literacy crisis concerns articulated by "those who seek a return to the basics" (12) and who demanded "the production of white, middle-class speech styles" (11) from all students regardless of background. He also expressed concern that widespread adoption of the TSWE may have marked "the symbolic end to the period of minority recruitment in higher education. While we have recently seen some fairly dramatic and important attempts by colleges to diversify their student bodies, and have even come to expect them, [the TSWE suggests that] the official retreat has already begun" (12). In light of his assertions, Daniels rejected the TSWE outright: "A more regressive, backward-looking, and muddle-headed innovation would be hard to imagine. Professional testers and college admissions officials, it seems, are eager to endorse linguistic prejudice; willing to downgrade the natural speech styles of linguistically normal adolescents; and cheerfully ready to penalize those who come from non-mainstream backgrounds" (11). He also urged NCTE members to reject openly both the TSWE and the logic of literacy crisis driving its adoption: "If we can shake them up some more, the test just might be dropped. Let's get at it" (12).[6]

Throughout each of these passages, we see Daniels engaging in race consciousness similar to that of Smitherman and the SRTOL (see chapter 2). He asserted directly that race mattered to language and literacy instruction in ways that required the interrogation of white mainstream standards. He further used this critique as a means to attack tests like the TSWE that he felt accepted these standards uncritically, insisting that they both threatened "minority recruitment in higher education" and "penalize[d] those who come from non-mainstream backgrounds." And finally, he urged scholars to act on their race-conscious knowledge and reject the TSWE unequivocally.

Standing in important contrast to this color-blind work, however, was the work of scholars espousing a Sheils-inspired rejection of high-risk programmatic activity. Notable in this regard was Geoffrey Wagner's 1976 *College English* article "On Remediation," which discussed Open Admissions at CUNY in ways that prefigured some of the scathing arguments upon which he would expand in his 1976 book *The End of Education*.[7] Wagner decried the mid-1970s rash of "adult illiteracy" (153) being caused by the race-conscious ideologies that undergirded open admissions programs and their activities. He then declared that CUNY's Open Admissions program had always been run by "academic politicians" (153) who both "ordained that remediation shall be known as *compensation,* presumably for past injustices" (153), and who concerned themselves much more with "teaching . . . about the injustices of society outside the classroom than the use of punctuation within it" (153). These academic politicians encouraged "Johnny to read his racist writers, [and] publicly-honored Malcolm X and Eldridge Cleaver" (155), such that there was "little wonder when Johnny gives [them], at college level, the thick jeer—Why should I take Whitey Math and Whitey English, to enter a Whitey World?" (155). The result, Wagner concluded, was "a huge accretion of minority students" (157) who refused to "lift [themselves] up by their own bootstraps" because they "insist on cutting them off all the time" (158). Wagner demanded, therefore, that race-conscious high-risk programs be abandoned and replaced with programs that doggedly refused to "shirk the duty of hardcore remediation" (158) any longer.

Here we can see Wagner decrying virtually all aspects of race-conscious high-risk writing instruction in the midst of literacy crisis concerns. He dismissed the idea of "compensation" for "past discrimination" as a kind of reverse racism, one unnecessarily benefiting minorities at the expense of mainstream white students. He insisted, too, that such race-conscious education foolishly rewarded minority students for dismissing a "Whitey" world and ignoring "bootstraps" ideologies of hard work, individual effort, and adherence to standards within the higher-educational enterprise. Wagner concluded, therefore, that all race-conscious high-risk efforts should be immediately abandoned and replaced with programs that emphasized "hardcore remediation."

In a mode similar to Wagner, Elissa Guralnick published a 1978 *College English* article titled "The New Segregation: A Recent History of EOP at the University of Colorado, Boulder," noteworthy for making one of the more explicit links within English studies journals of the time between educational opportunity programs and "reverse discrimination."[8] Guralnick argued that EOP programs like the one at Colorado embodied a "potentially dangerous, if ostensibly benevolent, form of separatism" (970) that both posed a direct threat to "academic standards" (970) and resulted in "daily complaints from faculty and students alike" regarding students' poor literacy skills (965). Guralnick continued to declare that such EOP programs had for too long sidestepped these standards and served as "separate-but-equal [facilities] for the teaching of composition to minority students . . . tacitly defying the Supreme Court's decision (*Brown v. Board of Education,* 1954) that separate facilities cannot be equal—a decision intended to protect minority students from the kind of discrimination that EOP controlled-enrollment courses necessarily represent" (969). Finally, after warning that the entire university system currently sat perched on "the edge of an abyss" (974) as a function of such obvious reverse discrimination, Guralnick argued that EOP programs should be dismantled and replaced with color-blind remedial mechanisms designed to enforce language and literacy standards: "Common sense dictates that if an Educational Opportunity Program is to promote the integration of groups into American society, it must do so by eschewing separatism. It must discover ways of offering special opportunities to educationally disadvantaged minority students—and to educationally disadvantaged non-minority students as well—without conferring upon them the special privileges inherent in exemptions from normal admissions standards and course requirements. It must help these students adjust to a university life without offering them a dubious protection from social and academic stress by segregating them into controlled enrollment classes" (972).

Here we see Guralnick similarly rejecting race consciousness in favor of programmatic color blindness. She claimed that "academic standards" were under attack within EOP programs because such programs exempted students from "normal admissions standards and course requirements." She further insisted that such exemption promoted racial "segregation," along with a kind of "separate-but-equal" mentality that flew in the face of the proper goals of high-risk instruction. And she concluded that in order to avoid having this entire institutional arrangement fall into an "abyss," EOP-type programs must be dismantled and replaced with color-blind remedial efforts focusing on the basic skills that all students ostensibly needed in order to get ahead.[9]

Somewhat different from these overtly color-blind responses of the mid-1970s were more subtly color-blind arguments from those who would become identified with the burgeoning BW movement.[10] These BW scholars would seem rather race conscious in the ways that they explicitly rejected literacy crisis discourse while defending the race-conscious motivations undergirding many high-risk programs. But their work nonetheless drew color-blind conclusions regarding students and their language and literacy needs, especially as it advocated for standards-based and error-focused instruction.

One important example of this second type of work was Mina Shaughnessy's 1976 speech to writing instructors at CUNY titled "The Miserable

Truth," one of Shaughnessy's more pessimistic commentaries of the time concerning the threat posed to high-risk writing instruction by literacy crisis concerns. Shaughnessy opened her speech by lamenting how "the national press spreads alarm about the state of literacy in the country" (110) in ways that have "allowed the society to settle back into its comfortable notions about merit . . . [and to perpetuate] the various brands of race and class prejudice that have pervaded this society since its creation" (110). She sharply criticized those who espoused such literacy crisis discourse and its back-to-basics mentality for tolerating the "unconscionable failure to meet the educational needs of the poor and the dark-skinned" (111). She also worried that any attempt to encourage the continuation of high-risk writing instruction in light of the clear anti–open admissions and anti–minority student tenor of the time seemed rather hopeless, akin to "trying to give a pep talk on the *Titanic*" (109).

Throughout these remarks, Shaughnessy seemed to be offering an openly race-conscious critique of literacy crisis. She suggested that literacy crisis discourse did in fact have a racialized component, rooted in both "comfortable notions about merit" and "race and class prejudice," and asserted as well that such discourse operated against the best interests of the "poor and dark-skinned." She also worried that it would be difficult to convince even advocates of high-risk instruction that such instruction was not the equivalent of a sinking ship in a sea of literacy crisis concern.

Shaughnessy ultimately argued, however, that it was possible to imagine preserving high-risk writing instruction in the face of literacy crisis concerns—at least if programs were to abandon an overt focus on issues of race and racism in favor of a decidedly scientific and decidedly color-blind research and teaching agenda. This agenda would properly focus on the cognitive dimensions of successful writing by analyzing "the writing process itself: how accomplished writers behave when they write; what sorts of stages they go through; what coordinations and perceptions are required of them; and how the behavior of our students as writers differs from that of accomplished writers—are they, for example, in the habit of rescanning their sentences, can they objectify their own pages, looking at them at one moment for semantic sense and at another for formal correctness?" (112). It would further require that teachers "keep learning how to teach writing" (114) by focusing on student cognition rather than by interrogating issues of race and racism directly.

Within these assertions, we see a subtle but important stress on cognitivist color blindness as the solution to literacy crisis concerns. Shaughnessy argued, in effect, that continued talk of student backgrounds and the unhappy political situation of the mid-1970s was ultimately less useful than the study of scientifically based and color-blind cognitive inquiry regarding students' writing processes, study that would reveal what it is that "accomplished writers" do as a function of their writing "behaviors" and "habits." She also made mention of "formal correctness" in ways that began to suggest the role of standards and Standard English within BW instruction: in her view, adherence to or deviation from these standards would indicate whether or not a writer was actually "accomplished." Shaughnessy thereby argued that color-blind cognitivism gave teachers and scholars the best chance of making sure that, to return to her nautical metaphor for a moment, students' educational future would lie not in a watery grave, but rather securely on the shores of mainstream integration, happiness, and prosperity.

Related arguments can be found in Shaughnessy's famous *Errors and Expectations,* a text widely regarded as a centerpiece of the new BW movement. In both the introductory and the concluding sections of this book, Shaughnessy once again seemed explicitly critical of literacy crisis discourse and its racist implications. She argued, for example, that this discourse ignored the fact that many high-risk students came from "racial or ethnic enclaves" and spoke "other languages or dialects at home," such that they might find it challenging to "reconcile the worlds of home and school" (3). She also argued that this discourse ignored the "generally humiliating encounter with school language, which produces ambivalent feelings about mastery, persuading the child on one hand that he cannot learn to read and write and on the other that he has to" (10), that was routinely experienced by many high-risk students.

Ultimately, though, Shaughnessy insisted throughout most of *Errors and Expectations* that attending to students' racial backgrounds within the context of instruction was unnecessary. Instead, she thought it necessary to attend to what students were cognitively capable or incapable of doing as writers as measured by their deviation from mainstream Standard English. She argued, for instance, that regardless of their racial or ethnic background, all high-risk writers were best viewed as the same kind of "beginners, [who] like all beginners, learn by making mistakes" (5). She also argued that writers' mistakes ought to be defined as "errors," as "unintentional and unprofitable intrusions upon the consciousness of the reader" (12) to be understood via analysis of "the underlying patterns that govern the language that [students] are learning" (10) and "the degree of predictability and efficiency in [students'] use of language" (10). Such a view of error was particularly necessary, she said, given "the reality of academia," which was rooted in the "fact that most college teachers have little tolerance for the kinds of errors that BW students make, that they perceive such errors as indicators of ineducability, and that they have the power of the F" (8).

For the balance of her book, Shaughnessy cataloged and analyzed the sorts of errors that the students whom she was describing tended to make with respect to Standard English. While offering a detailed analysis of difficulties with "handwriting and punctuation" in chapter 2, she argued, "The teacher must try to decipher the individual student's code, examining samples of his writing as a scientist might, searching for pattern or explanations, listening to what the student says about punctuation, and creating solutions in the classroom that encourage students to talk openly about what they don't understand" (40). While attempting to theorize students' problems with "syntax" in chapter 3, Shaughnessy claimed that three issues were at stake: "what the student has not internalized in the way of *language patterns* characteristic of written English . . . his [or her] unfamiliarity with the *composing process* . . . and his attitude toward himself within an academic setting" (73). Finally, Shaughnessy concluded that BW programs ought to adopt a three-semester writing sequence in order to formalize and institutionalize cognitivist error analysis and correction. The first semester within this sequence ought to focus on "the conventions of written English that are unfamiliar and troublesome to [the BW student]" (290); the second ought to feature assignments designed to help this student "sustain commentary over longer and longer units of discourse without losing his or her readers' bearings" (290); and finally, the third ought to deal with the composition of a "research paper," in which "rigorous procedures for directing and sustaining a line of inquiry that will meet academic criteria for thoroughness and correct form" were followed (290).

Across these detailed discussions, Shaughnessy asserted repeatedly that it was not race but rather cognition that mattered most when dealing with high-risk students. These students ought not to be viewed as linguistically or culturally different; rather, they should be viewed as cognitive "beginners" who committed "errors"—that is, deviations from Standard English. Indeed, these beginners had not yet mastered the sorts of language and literacy skills expected of them within the "reality" of the college environment as it is shaped by the "power of the 'F'." Shaughnessy also assumed that this particular version of reality did not reflect any sort of racialized power or privilege; instead, it reflected a set of deracialized and apolitical cognitive challenges that each successful student must learn to negotiate in the same basic way. Race thereby dropped out of Shaughnessy's prescriptions for successful writing instruction, and it dropped out quite entirely.

Regardless of the type of crisis-inspired work from which it emanated, it is clear that much disciplinary discussion of high-risk writing instruction of the mid-1970s focused on very different kinds of concerns than those common during the late 1960s and early 1970s:

- How to identify the linguistic and literate deficiencies that writers possessed, especially by studying the types of "errors" that they committed with respect to the expectations of Standard English;
- How to begin identifying and correcting these deficiencies both quickly and efficiently;
- How to transform existing race-conscious high-risk programs into programs dedicated to the color-blind remediation of student deficiencies with respect to Standard English.

These concerns were clearly premised on the notions that race ultimately did not matter when dealing with students' linguistic and literate deficiencies, that mainstream notions of standards and correctness must be embraced and enforced in order to facilitate remediation, and that any race-conscious institutional structures of writing instruction needed to be fundamentally reconfigured in order to return to the color-blind basics.

Color Blindness and the Disciplinary Dynamics of Interest Divergence

Mid-1970s high-risk/BW disciplinary discussions of literacy crisis indicate a clear shift away from race consciousness and toward color blindness. Even though activist scholars continued to advocate for race-conscious approaches to high-risk instruction, their race-conscious scholarship seemed less influential than either scholarship unabashed in its Sheils-like criticism of high-risk instruction or scholarship asserting that high-risk writing instruction ought to be transformed into BW instruction through a focus on color-blind cognitivism. In a key sense, then, the discipline of the mid-1970s was increasingly convinced that white mainstream standards in general and white mainstream Standard English in particular were not "white" but simply "right." The discipline also increasingly accepted the notion that race-conscious programs critiquing this "rightness" needed to be rejected and replaced with others possessing a clearer understanding of what these standards meant and how best to inculcate them.

Literacy crisis–era disciplinary discussions thereby reveal an important dynamic of disciplinary interest divergence emerging during the mid-1970s. While some scholars retained interest in preserving race-conscious high-risk writing instruction, their interests clearly diverged from those demanding a color-blind disciplinary return to standards. This divergence generated a very different disciplinary climate in comparison to that which had operated in the late 1960s and early 1970s: gone were numerous race-conscious disciplinary pronouncements such as the SRTOL, demanding respect for students' home languages and literacies; replacing them were numerous disciplinary pronouncements demanding response to literacy crisis through color blindness of one kind or another. Such divergence made it seem as though, in the words of BW critic Jeoffrey Youdleman, "the spirit of the people's 60's was over. . . . It was time again for the official policy of benignly neglecting critical questions" (564) related to race and racism within high-risk/BW language and literacy instruction.

Literacy Crisis Comes to Campus

The same sorts of general mid-1970s conservatism and literacy crisis concerns circulating nationally and at the level of the discipline were also circulating at UIUC with respect to EOP Rhetoric. Both EOP Rhetoric and its parent EOP program had already been experiencing a drop in enrollment and potential budget cuts, trends noted repeatedly at the time by the dean of EOP ("Dean B"). Dean B noted in a 1975 report that overall EOP enrollment had shrunk from 550 new students in 1968 to just over 150 new students in 1973 (Dean B, "Educational" II-7). He also expressed concern in another related report that, even though efforts to increase this enrollment were under way, EOP faced the threat of significant "budget constraints" that might undermine "many of the activities undertaken to increase [minority] enrollment (i.e., bringing accepted students to the campus, home site visits, mass mailing of various financial information, etc.)" ("Annual Report: Addendum" 1). He continued: "The tendency to cut 'frills' or other activities which are perceived as being expendable during periods of financial stringency, presents a problem, too. Certainly, the danger exists that those who question the wisdom of the University's involvement in an EOP-type endeavor may attempt to divert the Program's resources to other activities" (2). In the eyes of Dean B, both EOP Rhetoric and its parent EOP program were clearly facing significant mid-1970s questions about their institutional futures.

The EOP Rhetoric program was also facing a larger mid-1970s UIUC climate profoundly concerned with literacy crisis and its effects on students. One UIUC professor of business and technical writing complained to the College of Liberal Arts and Sciences (LAS) in 1976, for instance, that UIUC students were routinely displaying "fuzzy thinking, ill-developed ideas, and illogical expression," as well as manifesting "defective natural equipment" for thinking in sustained terms (letter to dean of LAS, 23 February 1976, 1). To correct this problem, the professor advised that LAS "develop and adhere to sensible standards of performance, to make every effort to counter the widespread tendency of indiscriminately assigning A's and B's to what is often hopelessly inadequate work" (2). Meanwhile, the director of undergraduate studies for the Department of English at UIUC insisted even more publicly—in fact, insisted openly in the pages of Sheils's "Why Johnny Can't Write" piece—that UIUC was experiencing literacy crisis in large part because K–12 teachers in Illinois were not doing their jobs. This director was quoted by Sheils while complaining that K–12 teachers across the country had regularly "shortchanged instruction in the English language" and that "things have never been good, but the situation is getting a lot worse. . . . What really disturbs us is the students' inability to organize their thoughts clearly" (qtd. in Sheils 60).

Perhaps most significant for the mid-1970s EOP Rhetoric program, however, was the literacy crisis–inspired creation of a new LAS committee called the Committee on the Use of English (CUE) in 1975. The CUE was convened by the dean of LAS at the time to investigate what he described as "the continuing drop in verbal SAT scores as reported by the College Entrance Examination Board," along with what he termed a sharp decline in "the quality of student writing . . . in recent years" (CUE, minutes, 29 October 1975, 1). Across numerous meetings during 1975–76, the CUE discussed past efforts at UIUC to address problems with student writing, including the former operation of the SCSE and its EQE exam (minutes, 2 December 1975, 1); it debated the relevance of standardized testing, especially in "Standard English," to this problem (minutes, 11 February 1976, 1); and it weighed possible steps to be taken by the campus in light of this crisis (minutes, 15 January 1976, 1). The CUE also recommended in its final report that the EOP Rhetoric program be reconfigured as a color-blind and remedial writing program designed to address literacy crisis problems at UIUC. Even though the CUE noted that the current EOP Rhetoric program offered "intensive tutoring in basic writing skills for students identified as having special problems" ("Report" 35), it concluded that the type of remedial instruction that EOP Rhetoric offered ought to be made available to all students regardless of background—that is, all "who need special help, regardless of their fields of concentration and in spite of the reasons for their deficiencies" (49). The CUE advocated, in essence, that EOP Rhetoric be discontinued as a race-conscious high-risk program and reconstituted as a wholly color-blind remedial program. In so doing, it asserted that race-conscious writing instruction had no clear institutional place at UIUC during this era of literacy crisis.

Shifting Administrative Points of View

The pressures being placed on EOP Rhetoric within this mid-1970s context of literacy crisis were also being felt acutely by two new administrators directly responsible for the larger EOP program and partially responsible for the EOP Rhetoric writing lab during the mid-1970s: "Director B," who served from 1972 to 1975, and "Director C," who served from 1975 to 1977. Both directors B and C made clear on numerous occasions that they were deeply concerned about this mid-1970s context of crisis and its potential effects on EOP Rhetoric and its writing lab. However, both also made clear that they wanted to reconfigure these programs in a decidedly color-blind and standards-oriented fashion in response to these pressures.

Director B had assumed her position as director of the lab in 1972 after serving as the assistant to the writing lab's director of assessment (see chapter 2) from 1969 through 1972. Beginning in about 1974, she became profoundly concerned with literacy crisis and its implications for writing instruction on the UIUC campus—concerned enough that she decided to circulate a document titled "Proposal for Change in the Rhetoric Placement Policy at the Lower Level" to both the English Department and the College of Liberal Arts and Sciences in January 1974. In her document, she insisted that literacy crisis was a pressing issue at UIUC, as "some recent surveys indicate that, unfortunately, students' writing ability is not necessarily getting better and better" (1). She also presented a litany of crisis-inspired evidence, including a National Commission on the Reform of Secondary Education report observing that "students possess a 'low level of competency in the mechanics of writing at every age level'" (1), SAT data showing that average verbal scores had dropped over thirty points in the previous decade (1), and a *New York Times* article contending that "elementary schools and secondary schools are not preparing students as well in verbal . . . skills as they did in former years" (1).

After presenting her evidence, Director B asserted that the best way to address literacy crisis at UIUC was to ensure that the campus develop a more widely available remedial program for all of its students, one that could help to turn the tide of poor scores and declining proficiency sweeping both the country and the campus. But she quickly insisted that precedent for such a program was lacking in recent years because UIUC had decided to "abolish remediation" in 1960 and had since only provided for "partial remediation" with the development of the EOP Rhetoric program in 1968.[11] The reason that EOP Rhetoric constituted only "partial remediation," she felt, was that it was open only to those minority students admitted through EOP. This had caused two related problems: it prevented regularly admitted students from enrolling in "remedial" rhetoric, such that "the educational value of the course is lost to most [of them]" (4); furthermore, it created a context of "racist bias" in which minority students were funneled into the "remedial" track, thus creating a situation in which "only EOP students can qualify for remediation, regardless of widely varying placement scores" (5).

Given this growing sense of literacy crisis on one hand and the purported problems with race-based placement on the other, Director B concluded that only one course of action was advisable: the reconstitution of EOP Rhetoric as an expanded color-blind remedial program open to all students and focused directly on standards. She argued that this new program should "remove the stigma of 'remedial' or 'EOP' with a placement designation for all freshmen of 1) Rhetoric 104 plus Rhetoric 103 followed by Rhetoric 105, 2) Rhetoric 105 only, 3) Rhetoric 108 [i.e., 'honors' composition], or 4) proficiency out of the course. This would be the fairest, least racist, most educationally sound policy" (6). Such programmatic reconstitution, she concluded, should both provide access to "remediation" for all students and ensure that the "racism" inherent in the present system was eliminated. It would also help to assure that money currently being spent on EOP students was more fairly distributed among all those who were truly deficient in terms of their writing skills.[12]

Upon assuming the EOP Rhetoric directorship in 1975, Director C made similar arguments as part of her own efforts to address the problem of literacy crisis. In one program-description document titled "The Directive: Rhetoric 104," for instance, Director C initially granted that EOP student background might play a role in shaping both the kind of language and literacy skills that students possessed and the kind of instruction that they required within this literacy crisis context. She argued that "most of the errors in EOP students' writing result from the difference between their spoken dialect and the structure of Standard English" (1). She also suggested that students should be "taught to recognize this difference. By explaining the structure and function of written Standard English, we teach students to respect both Standard English and their own dialects" (1).

Yet Director C quickly clarified that cultivating such "respect" had little (if anything) to do with recognizing students' race, but instead much to do with improving students' ability to eliminate errors and produce mainstream Standard English. She wrote in a separate memo from this time that, across the EOP Rhetoric program, "our first task is to eliminate a large number of mechanical and idiomatic errors" present in student writing ("To the Rhetoric" 3). She further asserted in another program-description document that the main goal of the EOP Rhetoric writing lab in particular ought to be "to teach students how to improve their writing by teaching them why they have made mistakes in papers and how to correct them" ("Directive: Rhetoric 103" 1) using the following protocol: "As often as possible have students write sentences and paragraphs in tutorial. Focus first upon the smaller elements of the students' writing: spelling, word choice, 'ed' and 's' verb endings, verb tense, pronoun reference, structure of individual sentences, etc. When simpler problems are eliminated, move to more sophisticated problems such as diction, conciseness, coherence, transition, methods of support, complexity of thought, etc." (2). In the course of articulating these arguments, Director C argued that both the EOP Rhetoric program and its writing lab should be further transformed under her leadership into fully color-blind and decidedly remedial enterprises along the lines of what scholars like Shaughnessy and others were advocating at the time.

Within these arguments, both Director B and Director C revealed a number of profound differences between their views and those of their race-conscious administrative predecessors of the late 1960s and early 1970s. To begin, both directors insisted that race did *not* ultimately matter in terms of understanding EOP students' linguistic and literate deficiencies: Director B argued that the "fairest, least racist" way to understand the writing problems that EOP students faced was not to examine their existing racialized language and literacy skills, but rather to measure "objectively" their existing deficiencies through administration of a color-blind placement test; Director C similarly implied that the best way to afford "respect" to EOP students was not to identify their existing racialized language and literacy skills, but rather to assess the cognitive nature of their deviations from Standard English in decidedly Shaughnessian terms. Second, both directors insisted that the primary cure for students' deficiencies was to embrace mainstream standards within EOP Rhetoric rather than to critique them: Director B demanded that the EOP Rhetoric program offer "remediation" aimed at helping students achieve (among other things) "competency in the mechanics of writing" as defined by a mainstream audience; similarly, Director C called quite openly for adopting color-blind remedial instruction with the "first task" of "eliminating" student errors with respect to standard grammar, style, and usage. And finally, both directors demanded that past race-conscious EOP Rhetoric and writing lab structures be dismantled and reconstituted as error focused and remedial: Director B called for the fundamental reconstitution of EOP Rhetoric as a color-blind enterprise open to all students with writing problems, thus eliminating alleged racist bias; relatedly, Director C insisted that EOP Rhetoric and its writing lab operate first and foremost as color-blind and error-focused entities. Clearly, then, both directors felt that the very same status quo for language and literacy use that had been racialized and criticized as unfairly "white" by previous program administrators like Director A should, in the context of the mid-1970s literacy crisis, now be embraced as "right." Only in this way, they insisted, could EOP Rhetoric and the writing lab help students escape the clutches of literacy crisis.

These statements from directors B and C clearly illustrate a shift in administrative thinking, away from race consciousness and toward a kind of color-blind error correction in EOP Rhetoric, one akin to that occurring both nationally and on the level of the discipline during the mid-1970s. Indeed, the race-conscious interests of previous administrators were perceived by these new directors as antithetical to the true needs of a program faced with crisis: EOP Rhetoric did not need to recognize or cultivate students' existing racialized language and literacy skills; instead, it needed to identify and eliminate students errors with respect to Standard English as quickly and efficiently as possible. But much like the chair of the SCSE before them (see chapter 2), these two administrators did much more than simply state their color-blind views in the context of mission statements and program documents: both worked quite actively, in tandem with a number of their administrative superiors, to ensure that their views reshaped the institutional structure and function of the EOP Rhetoric writing lab.

The EOP Rhetoric Writing Lab in the Early 1970s

As noted in chapter 2, the EOP Rhetoric writing lab had possessed a dual administrative structure from its inception: administrators from the English Department/EOP Rhetoric program oversaw the staffing of lab tutors, along with day-to-day lab operation, while a campus administrative entity known as the Senate Committee on Student English (SCSE) oversaw the larger mission and administration of the lab. Beginning in mid-1971, however, a sense grew across the campus that this dually administered writing lab was not fully meeting the needs of EOP students. A May 1971 letter from the dean of liberal arts and sciences (LAS) to the head of the English Department stated, "The belief that the Writing Laboratory is not doing the job for the EOP students appears to be widespread on the campus. In view of our heavy investment in the program, it seems necessary to ask whether or not the effectiveness of the program does, in fact, justify the cost" (1).

Around this same time, word had also begun circulating that a new student service entity known as the Expanded Encounter with Learning (EEL) program had been formed under the umbrella of the EOP program with the help of a federal grant. The sole purpose of this new EEL program was to assist those students who were seen as "lacking the language and skills developments necessary to effectively negotiate the academic demands of the University" ("Expanded" 6), and it aimed at cultivating race consciousness quite explicitly. For instance, in a 1971 program description titled the "The Expanded Encounter with Learning Program," the EEL argued that it tried to "provide [students] with a comprehensive, totalistic and interdisciplinary approach to learning. [The program] will recognize that the students come with skills and past experiences that are invaluable to the students' further academic development. . . [and will foster] student discussion of past experience in school, family, and community" (6). This program description further stressed that both EEL administrators and instructors should share, whenever possible, students' "ethnic and cultural background since we intend to utilize students' prior experience and learning as part of a holistic approach to academic learning" (10). Similarly, within a memo written to administrators, faculty, and students designed to characterize EEL in light of commonplace questions about its mission and activities, the director of the EEL offered a number of openly race-conscious characterizations of the program. For instance, in response to the hypothetical student question "Don't these special courses discriminate against us and hold us back?" the director of the EEL was insistent:

No, the "discrimination," if it must be called that, was done before the University ever met you. Perhaps your parents and teachers and you yourself did all you could to prepare you for college and yet your preparation is still somewhat deficient compared to other students. So the University distinguishes among its students' preparation in order to give each individual the learning that he personally needs. If we followed any other policy (such as putting every entering freshman into calculus, seminars in poetry and international relations, etc.), then the University would be unrealistic.

Treating every student equally means giving every student the program he individually needs—NOT giving every student the same program. (Memo to "Administrators, Faculty and Students," n.d., 3)

Throughout this passage, the EEL consistently characterized its actions in race-conscious terms: it described students' racialized backgrounds and experiences as "invaluable to [their] further academic development," as well as central to increasing the "the number of tools" that they could use in order to negotiate the academic environment; it stressed the ways in which administrator and teacher background ought to match student background whenever possible as a means to foster a "holistic approach to learning"; and it even argued that while parents, teachers, and students may have done "all [they] could" to capitalize on available educational opportunities, the larger social and racial forces of "discrimination" may have nonetheless limited students' chances for success.

In response to these widespread complaints about lab effectiveness, the campus chose to cede the SCSE's portion of lab administration to the EEL beginning in 1972. This decision created a new dual administrative structure in the lab: the English Department and EOP Rhetoric program would continue to exercise the same staffing and oversight responsibilities that they had previously, but now the EEL would oversee lab operation and begin hiring additional tutors with its own funds. This decision also meant that these two branches of the lab's new dual administrative structure operated at odds with each other: the directors of EOP Rhetoric, first Director B and later Director C, were now openly color-blind and convinced that such color blindness was necessary to long-term lab functioning; in contrast, the EEL was openly race conscious and adamant that race consciousness be reflected in its approach to the lab.

The Mid-1970s Struggle for Lab Control

The difficult administrative situation in the lab eventually led to an administrative battle over lab control in fall 1974, manifesting itself in a number of complaints against the EEL from members of the English Department/ EOP Rhetoric. The first of these complaints was issued by the head of the English Department ("Head A") in a September 1974 letter to the dean of LAS. In his letter, Head A argued that the EEL was unnecessarily duplicating the services of the larger EOP Rhetoric program within the context of the lab. He described such duplication as "almost extravagantly expensive" (24 September 1974, 1). He also characterized EEL activity as a primary cause of "frequent dissention when the two tutors [i.e., one hired by the EOP Rhetoric program and one by the EEL] and the instructor give conflicting advice" (2). Head A insisted that such duplication was creating an openly racist lab environment by reinforcing the purported belief among "many of those involved in the program—both EOP staff and students"—that "EOP Rhetoric is racially discriminatory. They report that the course sequence is almost universally regarded as a 'put down.' Resentful students view the predominantly black classes as evidence of segregation and complain that white students with the same low [program placement] scores are not subjected to the same humiliation of being required to take 'bonehead English' or to report for long tutoring sessions, which take large blocks of time from their day" (2). Given his displeasure with the EEL, Head A requested formal administrative "reconsideration of the Equal Opportunities Program and its funding, especially the allocation of federal funds which provide an overlap of services" (2), so as to "subsidize to a greater extent the important services [the English Department] renders in this most fundamental of course sequences" (2).[13] Head A wanted, that is to say, both the rededication of the EOP Rhetoric program to "remediation" and the rededication of EEL funds to the English Department itself so that both could be (purportedly) better managed.

In the wake of this complaint, Director B filed two complaints of her own. In an initial October 1974 memo addressed to the head of the English Department, Director B argued that the EEL program and its director were causing "interference" with day-to-day lab activities, along with significant "suffering" for many lab tutors hired by the EOP Rhetoric program (17 October 1974, 1). Then, in a follow-up meeting with the dean of LAS and the department head, Director B further charged that "the EEL is encroaching upon services which rightfully belong in the Writing Laboratory" and that students were "receiving conflicting advice from . . . two sets of tutors" within the context of their Lab work ("Notes on Meeting" 1). As proof of such purported interference, Director B referenced a short memo written to her by the director of the EEL, one in which he wondered whether one particular male tutor originally hired by Director B "might not be too severe in giving grades" (15 October 1974, 1). More specifically, the director of the EEL had written that this tutor "originally praised certain papers and gave little indication of how serious [one female lab student's] mechanical errors were. [However, when] she wanted to take the papers to show her mother, he wrote D's and E's on them, along with brief comments that were basically negative. [This student's] questioning of him brought little satisfaction, since he apparently wanted the low grades to motivate her to improve" (1). For her part, Director B described this memo as an example of what she and her staff had been forced to "put up with" when dealing with the director of the EEL (memo, 17 October 1974, 1). She also expressed her wish that, in light of this memo, the administrative arrangement in the lab might be changed such that the EEL would no longer have to be "consulted" regarding administrative, budgetary, or hiring matters ("Notes on Meeting" 1).

Within these initial complaints, we can clearly see a shift away from administrative race consciousness toward a kind of administrative color blindness relative to the lab. Indeed, Head A accused the race-conscious EEL of creating general "dissention" in the lab by giving students direction and advice that differed from that offered by EOP Rhetoric writing lab tutors. He also explicitly accused the EEL of contributing to racism within the lab by "segregating" students into "predominantly black" tutoring arrangements, making students feel "put down" and otherwise less capable than their white peers, and forcing students to spend "large blocks of time [in] their day" working with language and literacy skills under these purportedly racist conditions. And in light of these problems, he made a direct request that the money and power being funneled through the race-conscious EEL be redirected to a color-blind English Department/EOP Rhetoric administration that he believed was much better prepared to uphold the goals and values of color-blind remediation.

Director B also accused the EEL of malfeasance: in particular, she was upset that the openly race-conscious director of the EEL would dare to raise questions about "mechanical errors" and their relationship to the assessment of minority students within the lab context. After all, Director B had already expressed her views about the need for color-blind and standards-focused instruction and assessment within all EOP Rhetoric activities in her January 1974 proposal; she had also apparently been arguing to many of her staff members during this time period that the "writing problems of different ethnic groups are not substantially different and that anyone can handle them," such that "Latinos [need not] tutor other Latinos" within the lab (writing lab staff member, memo, 1 October 1974, 1).[14] Thus, Director B's request for reconfiguration of the lab served as another direct administrative request for color blindness—a request that Director B and the rest of her EOP Rhetoric staff be allowed to conduct lab business and focus on standards without having to work with (or, perhaps more accurately, work around) a race-conscious EEL administration.

Institutional Responses and Outcomes

These two official complaints against the EEL rose up the chain of administrative command at UIUC fairly quickly, arriving first on the desk of the dean of LAS and shortly thereafter on the desk of the vice-chancellor for academic affairs (VCAA). For his part, the dean of LAS characterized these complaints as follows in an October 1974 letter to the VCAA: "The Department of English, which is responsible for the administration of the rhetoric requirement, thinks that there is not the degree of cooperation that might be expected [between English and the EEL]; different approaches and different evaluations and strategies are employed, and the situation appears to be somewhat unsanitary. . . . The Department of English is not satisfied with the present arrangement for its writing laboratory and would like, if it is to retain responsibility, to make a strenuous effort to strengthen the Writing Lab. It cannot do so unless questions of control and authority are straightened out" (21 October 1974, 1). In response, the VCAA noted in a January 1975 letter to the LAS dean that the EOP Rhetoric program/English Department would be granted full administrative control over the lab. He wrote, "There should be no question that the English Department [as administrative home of the EOP Rhetoric program] is in charge of this supportive service and that the EEL willingly offers its considerable experience to planning a stronger writing laboratory. Questions on this level ought to be resolved immediately" (22 January 1975, 1). He also noted that "what is therefore needed is a clearly stated policy affirming this understanding and the construction of guidelines by which the two units can work cooperatively for the students' benefit" (1), a policy that would begin to address the ways in which the campus might begin to develop a "future writing laboratory help for non-EOP students who also need it" (1). The VCAA did not mandate here that the lab stop serving EOP Rhetoric students exclusively at this time, but he did imply that it might stop serving these students exclusively in the future.

Finally, this decision on the part of the VCAA was translated into official institutional operation in fall 1975 by Director C. In an October 1975 letter to the director of the EEL, Director C wrote that "the Vice Chancellor determined . . . that the English Department is in charge of the supportive services of EEL and that any referrals made are to be made by the [Director of EOP Rhetoric]" (6 October 1975, 1). She also offered a detailed interpretation of what this decision ought to mean for the EEL's role in lab philosophy and practice: whereas the EOP Rhetoric program would now be solely responsible for "basic writing skills and usage" (2), the EEL program would retain responsibility only for teaching students about "use of the library," "examination skills," "study habits," how to improve "class participation," how to maximize use of "conferences" in the writing lab, and "word skills" like dictionary use and spelling (2). Director C concluded her letter by admonishing, "I hope that you will willingly, and of your own initiative, assist the EEL student in these areas" (1).

Across their first set of responses, both the dean of LAS and the VCAA were convinced that the race-conscious EEL was unnecessarily impeding lab function. The dean of LAS had determined that the race-conscious EEL was not "cooperating" with various color-blind efforts to "strengthen" the lab in the face of crisis: he declared, too, that the situation was "unsanitary" and demanded that these issues of "control" and "authority" be resolved to the "satisfaction" of the EOP Rhetoric program and its parent English Department. The VCAA decided that the EOP Rhetoric program would assume immediate primary control over all instruction taking place within the context of the lab; he also demanded that it begin theorizing how best to offer such remediation to all students regardless of their racial or ethnic background. So although neither the dean of LAS nor the VCAA went so far as to mandate the full exclusion of the EEL from the lab, both determined that EOP Rhetoric should possess full authority over the EEL in all lab matters, especially those related to standards, thereby ensuring that color blindness would become the official guiding principle of the lab for the immediate future.

Finally, Director C saw to it that these sorts of color-blind complaints were transformed into color-blind and standards-focused institutional activity. By spelling out in detail a new institutional power relationship within the lab, Director C ensured that the EOP Rhetoric program would assume sole control over the central features of writing instruction—that is, basic writing "skills and usage"—along the color-blind lines of what she had described in documents of the time. She also ensured that the EEL program would retain control only over ancillary aspects of writing activity—that is, "use of the library," "examination skills," "study habits," "class participation," "conferences," "word skills," and so forth. In effect, then, Director C officially established a new administrative division of labor in the lab, one ensuring that no further interference with the EOP Rhetoric program's goal of color-blind remediation was possible.

Color Blindness and the Institutional Dynamics of Interest Divergence

This volley of administrative correspondence and decision making within the UIUC writing lab illustrates the degree to which key administrators during the mid-1970s era of literacy crisis concerns both promoted institutional color blindness and ultimately reshaped lab administration in light of it. The head of the English Department and Director B both clearly rejected the EEL's contention that race ought to shape the ways that the lab should "utilize students' prior experience and learning as part of a holistic approach." Accordingly, these two administrators issued complaints designed to elicit support from other more powerful administrators, demanding a color-blind administrative reconfiguration within the lab that was oriented to the teaching and learning of standards in general and Standard English in particular. In turn, both the dean and the VCAA recognized these complaints and decided that they should form the basis of a new administrative structure within the lab. And finally, at their urging, Director C reconfigured the previous dual administrative structure of the lab such that the English Department/ EOP Rhetoric program assumed sole control over the substantive components of lab activity—namely, error identification and correction with respect to Standard English—while the EEL controlled only ancillary components of lab instruction. The lab of the mid-1970s was, therefore, a very different place than it had been under the EEL: it now had two new directors who saw BW-style error analysis and correction as fundamental priorities; it now had a very different administrative structure that was fundamentally dedicated to color-blind remediation; and it now had the backing of the highest levels of the UIUC administration for these changes.

In addition, the various decisions at UIUC demonstrate that institutional interests had clearly diverged within the context of the campus and the lab by the mid-1970s. Some activists of the time (e.g., administrators and teachers involved in the EEL) did retain an interest in race consciousness. However, this interest diverged considerably from the more color-blind interest espoused by EOP Rhetoric administrators themselves during this time. In turn, this divergence resulted in a number of substantial institutional changes to EOP Rhetoric, ensuring that the color-blind interests of the mainstream reshaped lab structure and function in ways that largely reversed the race consciousness that had been originally achieved within the lab during 1968–69 by Director A, the NCTE liaison, and the writing lab codirectors, which had later been briefly revived from 1972 through 1974 by the EEL. In this crucial sense, the lab of the mid-1970s was a decidedly more color-blind and standards-oriented place than it had been previously—a place in which white mainstream standards and Standard English were now explicit guiding principles.

Literacy Crisis and High-Risk/BW Activity

I concluded chapter 2 by arguing that a level of interest convergence occurring during the late-1960s and early-1970s context of racial crisis, while certainly limited in key respects, nonetheless fostered the development of many high-risk writing programs, along with some degree of race-conscious change to national, disciplinary, and institutional thinking about them. Here I must conclude by asserting that things had changed by the mid-1970s, largely for the worse. Nationally, this time period witnessed diminished support for program activity and funding. At the level of the discipline, this period witnessed widespread rejection of race-conscious high-risk programs, along with embrace of standards-oriented BW programs. And institutionally, this period witnessed UIUC's administrative rejection of past race consciousness in EOP Rhetoric and the writing lab in favor of new forms of color blindness. So while race-conscious high-risk writing instruction may not have been completely gone by the mid-1970s, its power had been considerably weakened: high-risk instruction and its high-risk/BW counterpart had clearly transitioned from a late-1960s and early-1970s golden age to much more of mid-1970s dark age.

Importantly, however, this dynamic of interest divergence was about to change once again in light of a new set of cultural concerns about student "competence." In the wake of the famous 1978 *Bakke* decision, a number of mainstream legal and governmental institutions would begin advocating a return to at least some level of race consciousness within higher education in general as a means through which to determine and assess student competence. This advocacy, in turn, hastened something of a reconvergence between the interests of race-conscious activists and the mainstream regarding high-risk instruction—although again with some important mainstream limits attached.

The Late 1970s and Early 1980s

COMPETENCE CONCERNS IN THE AGE OF <u>BAKKE</u>

ONE OF THE most pressing issues facing U.S. higher education during the late 1970s and early 1980s was that of student "competence"—that is, how best to define and measure what it meant for a student to have achieved (or failed to achieve) a certain level of educational attainment or proficiency. Of the many contexts in which issues of competence were being debated at this time, the most famous was the 1978 Supreme Court case *University of California Regents v. Bakke. Bakke* centered on the claim of a white medical school applicant, Allan Bakke, who argued that he had been denied admission to medical school at the University of California–Davis (UC-Davis) because a number of spaces within the Davis program each year were reserved for racial and ethnic minorities who were not competent according to usual measures such as test scores or undergraduate class rank. When the case came before the Supreme Court, UC-Davis stood as the plaintiff, arguing that it had fairly and justly considered issues of race as part of its overall assessment of student competence to enter graduate school. Davis stressed its desire to use its existing policies for determining competence as a means to admit, support, and graduate minority physicians who "are likely to return to those disadvantaged areas from which they came" (qtd. in Schwartz 16). Meanwhile, Bakke stood as the defendant, arguing that Davis's policy was unconstitutional because competence with respect to medical school admissions ought to be determined in entirely color-blind fashion.

The court offered two separate decisions in the case, each decided by a 5–4 vote. In the first of these decisions, the court ruled the specific Davis admissions program to be unconstitutional, finding that it had utilized a race-based quota to discriminate between non-white and white applicants in terms of their overall admissibility.[1] In the second of these decisions, however, the court ruled that some level of race consciousness could be constitutional, asserting that mainstream colleges and universities must have the freedom to pursue "the attainment of a diverse student body" (*Regents . . . v. Bakke* 311) in ways that could include "the competitive consideration of race and ethnic origin" (320). This principle was important in the case of medical school admissions because "physicians serve a heterogeneous population. An otherwise qualified medical student with a particular background— whether it be ethnic, geographic, culturally advantaged or disadvantaged— may bring to a professional school of medicine experiences, outlooks, and ideas that enrich the training of its student body and better equip its graduates to render with understanding their vital service to humanity" (314). But this principle was perhaps even "greater . . . at the undergraduate level" (313) because undergraduate students needed exposure to "the ideas and mores of students as diverse as this Nation of many peoples" (313). In these important ways, the Supreme Court did seem to be promoting at least some level of race consciousness within one of the most important discussions of student competence of the time period: race could matter to admissions at the undergraduate level under certain circumstances.

Importantly, however, as the court continued to outline what exactly it meant by "competitive consideration of race and ethnic origin," it articulated some key limits to its apparent race consciousness. It asserted that "race or ethnic background may be deemed a 'plus' in a particular applicant's file, yet it does not insulate the individual from comparison with all other candidates for the available seats" (317). This notion of race as a "plus" imagined "each applicant as an individual in the admissions process. The applicant who loses out on the last available seat to another candidate receiving a 'plus' on the basis of ethnic background will not have been foreclosed from all consideration for that seat simply because he was not the right color or had the wrong surname. It would mean only that his combined qualifications, which may have included similar nonobjective factors, did not outweigh those of the other applicant. His qualifications would have been weighed fairly and competitively, and he would have no basis to complain of unequal treatment under the Fourteenth Amendment" (318). Furthermore, the court asserted that this logic of race as a plus was validated by Harvard's admissions policies—even going so far as to quote the assertion of Harvard's admissions committee that, when assessing the competence of "the large middle group of applicants who are admissible and deemed capable of doing good work in their courses, the race of an applicant may tip the balance in his favor just as geographic origin or life spent on a farm may tip the balance in other applicants' cases" (qtd. on 316). This approach did not constitute a "quota" system or otherwise trump an emphasis on traditional standards of admissibility, argued this committee; instead, it meant "only that in choosing among thousands of applicants who are not only admissible academically but have other strong qualities, the Committee, with a number of criteria in mind, pays some attention to distribution among many types and categories of students" (qtd. on 316–17).

Within these crucial passages of its ruling, the court argued that race could only be considered within overall determinations of competence as an addition to otherwise traditional assessment of student ability. Such considerations of race most definitely could not challenge traditional institutional standards themselves. If anything, the court felt that traditional standards must be maintained such that institutions could "fairly and competitively" make "comparison[s]" between and among "candidates for the available seats." Furthermore, the court determined that Harvard stood as a model for how best to account for race in this way: it praised Harvard explicitly for its treatment of race, including the way it managed to place racial diversity on par with the diversity created by "geographic origin" or "life spent on a farm." *Bakke,* therefore, fell prey to two critiques recently leveled by Derrick Bell. First, the decision failed to interrogate mainstream standards in any meaningful way within the admissions process: "[By] simply recognizing minority exceptions to traditional admissions standards based on grades and test scores," *Bakke* "served to validate and reinforce traditional policies," rather than to critique them in any fundamental sense (*Race* 255). Second, *Bakke* defined racial justice not according to the needs or desires of minority persons, but rather according to the needs of mainstream white institutions themselves —that is, as part of a "broad range of discretion that universities have long exercised in the admissions process," rather than as a racial justice benefit owed directly to students of color "because of past discrimination" (256).[2] In these important ways, the *Bakke* decision might have seemed race conscious in certain aspects, but it was ultimately defined according to mainstream standards and in light of overarching mainstream institutional interests.

While the actual *Bakke* decision was not explicitly concerned with high-risk programs, its logic nonetheless had important implications for high-risk programs and other related minority recruitment efforts of this time period. For instance, educational historians Elizabeth A. Duffy and Idana Goldberg have noted that, in the wake of *Bakke,* many "educators and policy makers became increasingly concerned about the growing disparity in educational achievement among the country's various ethnic groups" (154–55). In particular, many of the elite four-year institutions that Duffy and Goldberg analyzed began to reinvigorate their high-risk and other minority recruitment efforts beginning in the late 1970s and early 1980s, renewing efforts in which they "visited predominantly minority high schools, extended [institutional] minority alumni networks, dedicated additional admissions counselors to minority recruitment, and produced more targeted mailings and publications. . . . [Some also] expanded or introduced summer enrichment programs for minority high school students" (157). In the wake of *Bakke,* it had apparently become acceptable for mainstream four-year institutions to resume race-based recruitment and admission efforts, presumably in the interest of creating a "diverse" class.

A return to some level of race consciousness at this time was also evident within institutional contexts such as the Open Admissions program at CUNY, which began publicly reaffirming the value of the "Search for Education, Elevation, and Knowledge" (SEEK) program at the close of the 1970s. SEEK was originally developed in 1966 to "recruit economically and educationally disadvantaged students, admit them to the student body, and provide them with counseling and compensatory education" (Renfro and Armour-Garb 22), but it was also widely acknowledged as a mechanism by which to "provide adequate racial integration of the senior colleges" at CUNY (22). In 1978, the CUNY administration publicly praised SEEK as "an intrinsic part of the mission of the senior colleges" (qtd. in Renfro and Armour-Garb 35). It also argued that CUNY should issue "comprehensive guidelines for the program" within all senior colleges (35) and that "each senior college campus should have a SEEK department with a permanent status" (35). In stark contrast to the mid-1970s, then, the CUNY administration of the late 1970s and early 1980s seemed willing to recognize, even celebrate, some manifestations of race consciousness within its four-year schools.

Something of a return to race consciousness was also evident within the dynamics of SSS during this time. For instance, in contrast to the generally negative findings of the 1975 federally sponsored study of SSS (see chapter 3), 1983's *Evaluation of the Special Services for Disadvantaged Students (SDSS) Program: Final Report* drew largely positive conclusions concerning the overall impact of SSS on high-risk students.[3] This 1983 report stressed that SSS academic services such as tutoring were associated with gains in terms of students' time of enrollment, number of course hours attempted, and course hours completed (Coulson and Bradford 7); it further asserted that SSS nonacademic services such as personal counseling and career counseling promoted similar benefits along with improvement in students' GPA (7). The report even framed its more negative findings in generally positive terms. For instance, when it reported that students receiving a considerable amount of SSS services tended to achieve "poorer long-term academic outcomes" than those students receiving fewer services (8), it proposed that these outcomes were less likely a "negative effect of the [SSS] services" themselves (2) than a result of the fact that students receiving the most services tended to possess "poor entry skills" (2). This newly positive federal attitude toward high-risk instruction was also accompanied by more financial support than had been available at any point since the early 1970s: over 120 new SSS programs were developed in 1978 alone, aided by the help a $45.2 million total budget in federal spending (Chaney et al. 4-2), while 150 additional programs were developed and supported by 1985, with a yearly total budget of $70.3 million (Chaney et al. 4-2).

In these important ways, the late 1970s and early 1980s witnessed a clear renewal of race-conscious high-risk activity. However, just as the Supreme Court ultimately framed its apparent return to race consciousness in *Bakke* within a larger context of mainstream standards, so too did many of these renewed race-conscious high-risk efforts. For example, the revitalized support for minority recruitment among elite institutions mentioned by Duffy and Goldberg previously was accompanied by a clear sense that such recruitment should not target high-risk minority students, but instead "high-achieving" minority students—that is, students who already possessed clear facility with white mainstream standards as evidenced by test scores, class rank, and other traditional measures of student success. Indeed, Duffy and Goldberg noted that, in contrast to the late 1960s and early 1970s, when "commitments to equal opportunity and redressing the past wrongs of society led many colleges to pursue 'ghetto youth' or severely underprepared students" (154), by the "late 1970s, possibly as a result of the tensions experienced in the earlier decade, and possibly due to what was perceived by some as unfair advantages given to less qualified students, colleges began to look for minority students who more closely fit the profile of their class" (154). Race may have begun to matter to these campuses, in other words, but not in ways requiring that they continue to pursue students whom they perceived to be "risky" in terms of their familiarity with white mainstream standards.

CUNY's affirmation of programs like SEEK was similarly accompanied by a renewed push to enforce new mainstream standards within other parts of its system. In particular, CUNY decided in 1978 to implement a system-wide testing mechanism requiring that all incoming freshman, as many as forty-five thousand per academic year, be required to take mandatory standards-oriented placement exams in reading, writing, and math, tests collectively known as the Freshman Skills Assessment Tests (FSAT) (Renfro and Armour-Garb 34).[4] Furthermore, in 1980, CUNY mandated that all students placed in remedial courses as a result of poor scores be required to retake and pass these FSATs before completing sixty credits (34). So even as CUNY championed SEEK, it simultaneously mandated an extensive testing mechanism designed to screen out those students who did not already possess a certain level of facility with white mainstream standards.

Finally, the student aid practices directly affecting high-risk programs such as SSS were strongly influenced by a standards-oriented shift in student aid patterns during the late 1970s and early 1980s. Students entering SSS programs were confronted with the fact that federal, state, and institutional need-based aid was increasingly being replaced by "merit-based" aid provided to students on the basis of GPA, test scores, and traditional measures of academic performance—a shift designed to help mainstream institutions "recruit the best and the brightest" (Porter and McColloch, qtd. in Duffy and Goldberg 207) according to traditional measures of competence. One survey of the time demonstrated that by 1983, over 80 percent of the institutions surveyed relied on merit-based aid either to "a great extent" or "some extent" as a way to support students (Porter and McColloch, qtd. in Duffy and Goldberg 207); in contrast, the overall proportion of need-based aid offered by federal, state, and institutional sources to the average student declined from 80 percent in 1977 to 48 percent in 1987 (Eaton 17). This shift in aid support away from need and toward purported merit ensured that high-risk minority students were less likely to receive financial support than their white mainstream counterparts, a shift that educational historian and funding expert Judith Eaton described in 1991 as "sustain[ing] the availability of education for the predominantly white, middle-income population," rather than forcefully addressing "the urgent problem of financing access to higher education for the low-income and minority populations" (122). And importantly, this shift in aid practices was also accompanied by a decline in the percentages of black and Hispanic enrollment in higher education: black participation decreased to 19.4 percent, while Hispanic participation decreased to 16.1 percent by 1980, a drop of 3.1 percent and 3.9 percent respectively from 1976 levels (Snyder, Dillow, and Hoffman 296).

Competence Concerns and the Dynamics of Interest Reconvergence

The complex dynamics of high-risk instruction during the late 1970s and early 1980s point to a partial resurgence of race consciousness with respect to high-risk programmatic activity in the midst of competence concerns. Through *Bakke,* the Supreme Court determined that some level of race consciousness could be used in assessing students' overall competence. And in light of this decision, mainstream predominantly white colleges and universities across the country reaffirmed at least some of the original race-conscious goals of the high-risk movement: new minority student recruitment efforts were again being developed and implemented, high-risk programs at places such as CUNY were being publically praised for their race consciousness, and national efforts such as SSS were once again being supported. The high-risk movement of the time had begun, at least in some sense, emerging from the dark age of the mid-1970s and experiencing something of late-1970s and early-1980s race-conscious renaissance. But this renaissance was nonetheless limited by traditional standards. *Bakke* itself mandated that race consciousness should apply only after routine standards of test scores, class rank, and so on were met, and it further insisted that these standards were not to be subject to any kind of substantive scrutiny. Mainstream predominantly white schools across the country followed suit: elite institutions developed minority recruitment mechanisms that were aimed not at high-risk but at high-achieving minority students, institutions such as CUNY implemented standards-based testing and screening mechanisms designed to enforce standards yet again, and entrance into programs such as SSS was affected adversely by the replacement of need-based funding with merit-based funding that was predicated on students' existing facility with white mainstream standards.

This limited return to race consciousness demonstrates that an important dynamic of interest reconvergence was emerging during the late 1970s and early 1980s. Race-conscious activists were certainly advocating for their interests in promoting race-based institutional change. In turn, their interests seemed to reconverge with mainstream interests in promoting diversity within the student bodies of predominantly white mainstream institutions. But not surprisingly, this reconvergence occurred only to the degree that it did not threaten traditional white mainstream standards or the role of these standards in determining student competence. This convergence did not, in other words, prompt an institution such as Harvard to transform its existing standards in order to promote greater racial and ethnic diversity. Instead, it prompted other mainstream institutions around the country to emulate Harvard's existing policies by defining diversity according to their perceived institutional needs. This dynamic of reconvergence thereby revealed, once again, the extent of white mainstream control over racial justice efforts: although racial justice was perhaps being pursued more actively during the late 1970s and early 1980s than it had been during the mid-1970s, this pursuit was again clearly defined by the desire of white mainstream institutions to achieve their goals without compromising their sense of standards.

Interest Reconvergence and Its Limits

The national concern being directed toward issues of competence in *Bakke* throughout the late 1970s and early 1980s was also being directed toward writing programs in general and high-risk/BW programs in particular. Writing in 1986, for example, high-risk/BW assessment scholars Karen Greenberg, Harvey Wiener, and Richard A. Donovan noted that, since the late-1970s, "state legislatures and boards of education across the country have mandated large-scale writing assessment programs, inspired in part by public outcry for a return to basics, and in part by a general lack of interest from teaching faculty in taking early initiatives to develop tests measuring basic skills. These legislatures, wary of committing tax dollars to educational programs whose successes and failures do not submit to measurement, have pressed chief academic officers to produce data on how students write before and after the completion of writing courses" (xi). Widespread concern with writing competence was perhaps to be expected, given that literacy crisis concerns had been so widely and loudly proclaimed just a few years earlier: the mainstream had long been wondering why "Johnny couldn't write," so it seems only logical that this mainstream now wanted measurable proof that now Johnny could.

During the late 1970s and early 1980s, numerous scholars within composition and high-risk/BW began to explore issues of competence and assessment, a point underscored by numerous publications: for example, the 1978 issue of *JBW* dedicated to assessment; the 1982 special issue of *CCC* dedicated to assessment; edited collections including the 1981 Cooper volume *The Nature and Measurement of Competency in English,* the 1981 Farr Whiteman volume *Variation in Writing: Functional and Linguistic-Cultural Differences,* and the 1986 Greenberg, Wiener, and Donovan collection *Writing Assessment: Issues and Strategies;* and books such as White's 1985 *Teaching and Assessing Writing.*[5] The time period also witnessed the development of national groups such as the National Testing Network in Writing (NTNW), operating out of CUNY, for "the people who develop, implement, and grade [writing] tests to exchange ideas and learn from each other" (Greenberg, Wiener, and Donovan xiv), along with the widespread development of writing assessment programs designed to help institutions measure students' competence.

Two of the most well-known of the writing assessment programs at this time were the Writing Assessment Test (WAT) at CUNY and the English Placement Test (EPT) in the California State University system. CUNY began offering its test as part of its new suite of FSAT exams in 1978. This WAT was "based largely on Mina Shaughnessy's conception of the skills which basic writing students must master, defin[ing] these competencies as the abilities to introduce and develop an idea, to present adequate supporting detail, to organize these details logically, and to demonstrate sufficient command of vocabulary, syntax, and grammar" (Greenberg 369). The WAT required students to write fifty-minute essays about open-ended questions (e.g., by asking students to "agree or disagree" with a particular assertion while "explain[ing] and illustrat[ing] your answer from your own experience, your observations of others, or your reading" [Troyka 35]). Initially, it was used as a placement test for as many as forty-five thousand CUNY students per year (27); however, because as many as half of the students taking the WAT typically failed it on the first try (Greenberg, "Competency" 370), it also became a kind of gatekeeper to upper-level study, with CUNY mandating in 1980 that all students pass the WAT before earning their sixtieth credit hour (Troyka 31).

Meanwhile, the California State University system developed and debuted its English Placement Test (EPT) in 1977 as part of an effort to "provide placement information for entering freshmen in the appropriate composition course" (Brekke 25), as well as to provide "reliable new information and potential new power to writing program administrators in the California State University system" (White, "California" 22). As its name implied, the EPT was used first and foremost as a placement mechanism, not as a gatekeeper per se: its primary purpose was to provide the campuses with "an indication of [students'] general skill in reading and in written communication," along with "a brief description of [students'] strengths and weaknesses" as readers and writers (qtd. in White and Thomas 277). It featured timed essay writing in response to open-ended prompts, along with sets of multiple choice questions designed to elicit students' understanding of "reading" (e.g., "For each of the sentences, decide the best word to substitute for the nonsense word *gliff*" [qtd. on 282]), "sentence construction" (e.g., "Select the best version of the underlined part of the sentence" [qtd. on 282]), and "logic and organization" (e.g., "Choose the object that is a specific example of the category underlined" [qtd. on 283]). Like the WAT, the EPT was a massive endeavor: its first administration reached about eleven thousand students (278), and it had been administered to over fifty thousand students in the Cal State system by 1980 (White, "California" 20).

The proliferation of late-1970s and early-1980s scholarship, testing organizations, and testing programs demonstrates that issues of competence assessment were the focus of significant discussion in the wake of *Bakke*. Many in composition and high-risk/BW at this time were profoundly concerned both with understanding how to define students' writing competence and with developing and implementing testing programs that could be used to determine this competence. Notably, these disciplinary discussions and the testing programs enabled by them would demonstrate similar Bakkean dynamics of interest reconvergence: they, too, would promote some measure of race consciousness even as they ultimately limited this consciousness through a traditional stress on mainstream standards and especially Standard English.

Disciplinary Race Consciousness versus the Affirmation of Mainstream Standards

In the midst of the larger context of competence concerns during the late 1970s and early 1980s, a number of scholars in high-risk/BW maintained an overtly race-conscious approach to their work. One example was Richard Hendrix's "The Status and Politics of Writing Instruction," a chapter included in the volume *Variation in Writing: Functional and Linguistic-Cultural Differences,* edited by Marcia Farr Whiteman.[6] In his chapter, Hendrix warned that "the increased use of testing [in this competence era] is ambiguous in its effects, and may inhibit efforts to improve writing for those with the greatest need" (60). He also cautioned that both uncritical holistic assessments of competence (i.e., testing "based on overall impressions [of student writing] which involve common values and norms" [61]) and uncritical objective assessments of competence (i.e., those geared toward measuring "the features of standard English" [60]) could promote racism. Both types of assessment, Hendrix asserted, threatened to adopt "the norms of one fairly homogenous group as a standard. Of course all norms belong to individuals, though some may be more universal than others. In the case of writing assessment, the norms of standard written English are very nearly the norms of white, middle class faculty. This at least is a fair description of those who make the judgments, and when the content of an essay is part of what is judged, the experience of writer and reader are at issue" (61). Both types of assessment also ran a serious risk of ignoring the "likelihood that the typical judgments of writing teachers will penalize working class and minority students. Almost everyone expects (though few point it out) that these students will do worse with increased testing. Cultural unfairness may arise even apart from questions of content. . . . Speakers of nonstandard English (blacks and others) may be on their way to developing quite effective writing abilities, even while some of the surface features of their writing (e.g., noun/verb agreement) are persistently incorrect" (61–62). Accordingly, Hendrix concluded that all assessments of student competence, whether holistic or objective, must recognize and explicitly address the possibility of racism and its relationship to traditional standards: "Writing is hard enough to master in its own right, without becoming the arena for unacknowledged social differences. . . . Writing instruction should be an opportunity for learning, expression and empowerment. But writing will simply become an obstacle and an object of mistrust for those outside the dominant culture, if we let it" (62).

Hendrix stressed here the same type of overt race consciousness that predecessors like Smitherman, the authors of the SRTOL, and many others did before him. He insisted explicitly that assessors must develop both holistic and objective measures of student competence that strove actively to recognize and accommodate what it was that students bring with them to the context of learning. He also criticized the role that standards typically played within both forms of assessment: these standards were very much of the "white middle class" and were therefore likely to be wielded in ways that "penalize working class and minority students" if not carefully scrutinized.

Very different from Hendrix's approach were other common discussions of competence that seemed to be race conscious on a number of levels but that ultimately asserted the unassailable centrality of mainstream standards within competence assessment mechanisms. One example of such a discussion was Roscoe C. Brown Jr.'s text "Testing Black Student Writers," a chapter focusing directly on the WAT and its effects, included in the 1986 Greenberg, Wiener, and Donovan volume *Writing Assessment: Issues and Strategies.* Brown began his arguments in seemingly race-conscious fashion: after noting that "minimum competency testing programs [are] now offered in at least 40 states" (101), he argued that "the issue of [competence] testing must, of course, be viewed in the larger context of equal educational opportunity, a multifront war wherein the battles over affirmative action, desegregation, and federal support of public education have been fought. In that context, our criticism should represent steps toward compensation for past injustices and prevention of future injustices" (98). Brown further advocated what appeared to be a race-conscious approach toward holistic assessment of competence, highlighting its relationship to what testing theorist Paul Ramsey describes as "scribal fluency": "While we must trust essay tests, we must be concerned about how they are scored. Most essay tests are read holistically, to get a general impression. Some critics of holistic scoring say it merely assesses 'scribal fluency,' and if that is so, dialect features will influence the general impression left with the reader. An interesting area for research is whether primary trait analysis of holistically scored tests would change the scores of minority students" (104). Brown even went so far as to reference the *Bakke* decision directly as a catalyst for widespread race-conscious discussion of competence: "In 1978 the controversial case pitting the Regents of the University of California against Allan Bakke exacerbated this sense of crisis [concerning student competence], focusing national attention on the selection process for admissions to professional schools. In a split decision, the Supreme Court at once reinforced the legitimacy of testing as a predictor of future performance and supported the use of race as one criterion meriting consideration in the selection process" (99).

Across each of these assertions, Brown clearly advocated at least some attention to issues of race and racism. He argued that judgments concerning competence could not be separated from the social context of "equal educational opportunity"; from a larger "multifront war wherein the battles over affirmative action, desegregation, and federal support of public education have been fought"; or from the *Bakke* decision itself. Brown further argued that holistic assessments of such competence risked assessing little more than "scribal fluency" in racist ways if they were not carefully conducted.

In spite of his apparent race consciousness, however, Brown ultimately concluded that the competence of high-risk students must be measured in light of white mainstream standards for language and literacy, standards that he frequently referred to as "basic skills." To this end, Brown reasoned that "despite the consequences of testing programs that may be flawed or biased, the concept of minimum competency is nonetheless sound. The principle behind minimum competency tests is that students should be assessed periodically to determine the extent to which they demonstrate mastery of basic skills in reading, computation, and writing. . . . Any serious examination of today's job market will show that reading and mathematics skills are necessary for advancement in a society that is becoming increasingly verbal and computational" (102). He also argued that "as educators continue to examine the principle of assessment, we should ensure that conflicts over specific techniques of testing do not obscure the need to place increased emphasis upon basic skills. The acquisition of these basic skills is not merely desirable; it is essential" (99–100).

Finally, Brown highlighted CUNY's WAT test as an important model for what he thought responsible competence assessment should look like, describing it as a "pioneering . . . use of minimum competency tests" (105). He argued that the WAT had clearly "taken steps in the right direction" (105) by providing "a clear standard . . . requiring that, upon entering the university, 'students should already understand the basic form of academic, professional, and business discourse' and 'be able to formulate and state a position in reasonably correct standard written English'" (105). He asserted that the WAT therefore stood as proof that "we should use every tool at our disposal, including tests, and use our professional judgment and positions to ensure that all students receive a quality education, for it is through quality education that we will move toward closing the educational and socioeconomic gap between the majority and minority group populations" (106).

Brown insisted throughout these passages that student competence could not be assessed without recognizing and accepting the power of extant standards. He was adamant that such acceptance was "sound"—even "essential" —given "any serious examination of today's job market." He also posited that the CUNY WAT test served as a model for competence assessment that was quite clearly taking "steps in the right direction" because it focused on these standards directly. In these ways, Brown concluded, scholars and teachers should pay some attention to issues of race and racism within assessment, but they should not do so in ways that questioned standards themselves.

A similar argument regarding race and competence was articulated in Edward White and Leon Thomas's 1981 "Racial Minorities and Writing Skills Assessment," appearing in *CCC,* one of several articles of the time to discuss the genesis and evolution of Cal State's EPT.[7] White and Thomas began their discussion by stressing that the EPT used holistic assessment techniques constituting the most effective means by which to assess and place minority students within predominantly white college and university environments— much more effective, they insisted, than traditional tests of correctness like those featured in the College Board's Test of Standard Written English (TSWE).[8] Specifically, White and Thomas argued that the EPT was designed to eschew "isolated questions of usage except as they relate specifically to sentence structure or to logic and organization" (277), in favor of "scoring criteria that direct [assessors'] attention to many matters in addition to correctness" (277). In contrast, they claimed, the TSWE served merely to "examine 'correctness' first and foremost in terms of standard English through questions about isolated items [while relying] on data that shows a high correlation between writing ability and ability to answer usage questions correctly" (277). White and Thomas tried, in this way, to draw a strong distinction between what they perceived to be the more race-conscious holistic view of writing ability operating within their EPT and the exclusive color-blind emphasis on Standard English featured in the TSWE.

White and Thomas continued that their EPT yielded "very different score distributions" (278) for high-risk minority students (including those from Cal State's own EOP program [278]) than those achieved by the TSWE: "While [minority] students have a lower EPT total mean score than the majority, they are distributed along the whole range of scores . . . [in ways that are] desirable for placement testing" (280); conversely, the TSWE tended to bunch minority students' scores at the low end of the score spectrum— even going so far as to place "eleven percent of the black students at the lowest possible score" (280)—in ways presuming that minority students had generally low language and literacy skills. From these results, White and Thomas concluded that their EPT test was more racially sensitive than objective tests like the TSWE: the EPT was more "likely to produce more accurate distributions of scores [for placement purposes], at least in relation to faculty judgments of writing ability," than a test such as the TSWE was (282).

Throughout these assertions, White and Thomas seemed openly attentive to issues of race and racism. They argued that their EPT exam did a significantly better job of race consciously recognizing the holistic dimensions of students' competencies than did more traditional objective and Standard English–oriented tests like the TSWE. They also insisted that the EPT did a better job of correctly placing minority students into courses than did the TSWE.

Although their claims in these passages certainly seemed race conscious, White and Thomas ultimately stressed the centrality of white mainstream standards within the EPT and the picture of competence that it painted. One example can be found in their aforementioned assertion that the EPT was designed to "direct [assessors'] attention to many matters *in addition to* correctness" (my italics), a statement implying that linguistic correctness of the sort condoned by the white mainstream was actually foundational to the EPT. Another example appeared in their assertion that "it is important to note that this issue [of holistic placement] has nothing to do with 'standards' or with the value of teaching students appropriate usage for formal writing situations. Both of the tests under discussion, and all factions in the dispute, agree on the need for high standards and appropriate usage. The EPT cautions students that 'of course, the rating your essay receives from the faculty members who score it will, to some extent, also be dependent on how well you spell or punctuate and how carefully you follow such conventions of standard written English as subject-verb agreement'" (278). White and Thomas felt strongly, then, that even the EPT's holistic version of competence assessment needed to recognize and assess students' facility with white mainstream "standard written English"—a point about which "all factions in the dispute" supposedly "agreed."

Finally, against this backdrop of standards, White and Thomas concluded that the racialized disparities yielded by the EPT, while perhaps unfortunate, were nevertheless accurate. As they attempted to explain the reasons that minority students still "have a lower EPT total mean score than the majority" (280), they acknowledged that some readers might suspect overt racism—that is, that "the English professors grading the essay test were insensitive to the writing errors made by black students, and, in effect, showed a bias towards these students when they graded the papers" (280). But they quickly dismissed this possibility, insisting that such overt racism was "unlikely for several reasons: readers would have had no way to distinguish the papers written by minorities from those written by the rest of the students, strict quality control measures would have led to high inter-rater reliability for EPT essay readings, and the criteria for scoring papers do in fact call for attention to grammar, syntax, and diction" (280). White and Thomas felt, in other words, that while minority students' lower competence scores may have been unfortunate, they were not indicative of racism per se: such racism could result from *intentional* bias on the part of assessors—that is, from blatant attempts to recognize and discriminate against minorities—but not from the racialized power latent within white mainstream standards, from assessors' perceptions of the value of such standards, nor from biases inherent in assessment concepts such as interrater reliability.

So while White and Thomas advocated a kind of racially sensitive and holistic approach to assessing student competence within the EPT at Cal State at many points within their text, they ultimately stressed the need to accept white mainstream standards without critique within the context of such assessment—standards upon which they insisted that "everyone can agree." These authors were apparently not inclined to question why, even under the auspices of their supposedly fairer and less racist assessment of student competence, minority students were routinely judged as less competent than their white counterparts.

Disciplinary Reconvergence amid Competence Concerns

These examples (again but a few of the many circulating at the time) suggest a disciplinary return to race consciousness during the late 1970s and early 1980s.[9] Texts like those from Hendrix espousing race-conscious activism continued to exhibit a clear interest in issues of race and racism as they theorized assessment of student competence. Meanwhile, others, like those from Brown and White and Thomas, agreed, at least up to a point, that race could and should play some role in determining who was or was not competent. But these latter texts nonetheless maintained that assessment of competence must be framed by students' facility with white mainstream standards; furthermore, they argued that two of the largest testing mechanisms of the time period, the WAT and the EPT, should rightly continue to view white mainstream standards as foundational to assessment activities. Thus, while disciplinary discussions of competence among high-risk/BW scholars during this period were in some ways more race conscious than their predecessors of the mid-1970s, they were once again limited in terms of the change for which they were ultimately able to advocate.

These examples also reveal an important dynamic of disciplinary interest reconvergence occurring within the high-risk/BW scholarship of this time. Scholars espousing race-conscious activism and those espousing more mainstream views saw their interests converge, at least to a point, around the idea that race could matter to high-risk/BW activity: disciplinary assessments of competence at this time were not completely color-blind. Nonetheless, this reconvergence was clearly limited by traditional mainstream linguistic standards in ways that condoned the sorting of students according to their perceived facility with Standard English. In an important sense, then, these mainstream *Bakke*-era disciplinary discussions had a fair amount in common with late-1960s and early-1970s bidialectical discussions: both tolerated some attention to race within larger assessments of students' purported needs even as they ultimately demanded adherence to white mainstream standards in general and Standard English in particular. But in another sense, these mainstream discussions were perhaps more linguistically and educationally conservative than even their bidialectical predecessors: the competence concerns that they articulated and the testing and assessment programs to which they gave birth were aimed at reducing the perceived institutional "risks" posed by minority students in ways not even imagined by bidialecticalists themselves.

Determining Competence in the EOP Rhetoric Program

In contrast to the rather staunch color-blind context of mid-1970s literacy crisis at UIUC, the late 1970s and early 1980s found both UIUC administrators and EOP Rhetoric administrators once again willing to view EOP, EOP Rhetoric, and the EOP Rhetoric writing lab as race-conscious entities. This willingness was especially evident in response to a new set of pressures being placed on UIUC by the Illinois Board of Higher Education (IBHE) that were very much in keeping with the *Bakke*-inspired logic of the age.

In 1979, the IBHE began expressing concern that there was "inadequate performance of the basic skills in the graduating high school student" in the state of Illinois ("Background" 1), as evident within "various forms for minimal competency testing" in use at the time (1). Consequently, in 1981, the IBHE mandated that all "remedial" programs at four-year state institutions within Illinois be eliminated within five years (9).[10] This mandate would effectively prevent all those students not already deemed competent by traditional measures from entering the four-year college and university environment in Illinois, relegating these students instead to the community college system (9).[11]

But the IBHE did allow for at least some measure of race consciousness by stating that its new definitions of competence did not apply to "special assistance programs," that is, those programs within four-year institutions that offered "distinctively organized educational and related support services designed to increase the number of, retain, and graduate those students who are educationally and/or economically disadvantaged" (8). The IBHE explained this exemption at some length:

> The clientele of special assistance programs is drawn from those populations which historically have been denied the opportunity for betterment through education. Special assistance is designed to integrate the educationally disadvantaged into the mainstream of university life. These programs are designed for students who, because of their backgrounds, have not received the educational opportunities commonly obtained by the more fortunate. In addition to remedial courses, these programs offer other services such as counseling, academic and career advisement, and financial assistance. In this respect, remedial efforts may be necessary as one of the integral components of special assistance programs which are designed to increase the probability of success for educationally and economically disadvantaged students in college. (9)

Even as it adopted a larger antiremediation stance, then, the IBHE granted that competence could be defined in at least somewhat race-conscious fashion within four-year institutional contexts.

The new competence concerns articulated by the IBHE had profound implications for both the larger EOP program and EOP Rhetoric during the late 1970s and early 1980s. By the late 1970s, EOP had actually entered a period of relative calm: EOP enrollments had been steadily averaging about 330 students or so since 1975 (Dean of OMSA, "Educational" 14), while none of the sweeping budget cuts feared by Dean B in the mid-1970s (see chapter 3) had actually come to pass. But these new IBHE mandates were nonetheless threatening: if "remediation" was now to be eliminated at UIUC, then many of the specific support services associated with EOP, including EOP Rhetoric itself, would be eliminated as well. This elimination would, in turn, undermine the extensive efforts of Director B, Director C, and others during the mid-1970s to transform EOP Rhetoric and the EOP Rhetoric writing lab into color-blind remedial entities (see chapter 3). Ironically, then, the campus was faced with the very real possibility that the IBHE could eliminate UIUC's efforts to offer "remediation" to students whom it deemed "deficient" writers. And perhaps even more ironically, the campus was faced with the possibility that stressing the race-conscious roots of EOP Rhetoric—that is, returning to some measure of programmatic race consciousness—might constitute the only possible way to gain an exemption from the IBHE for EOP Rhetoric and the kind of remediation that it provided.

Unsurprisingly, the IBHE's mandate prompted an immediate administrative response from UIUC. A 1981 letter from the vice-chancellor of academic affairs noted with alarm that "according to current law and IBHE policy we are supposed to be doing all possible to reduce remediation activities for regularly admitted students" ("Remediation Activities" 1). Then, in 1982, the VCAA asked that UIUC faculty begin immediately to "develop a persuasive argument that Rhetoric 103 and Rhetoric 104 are indeed college-level courses. . . . I will appreciate receiving other suggestions from any of you for strengthening our arguments to the IBHE. I am sure that we will have to have a very strong case in order to get a favorable response from the IBHE" ("Remedial Courses" 1). In response to this request, administrators and faculty with an interest in preserving EOP Rhetoric began formulating a "very strong case." One group of administrators wrote a detailed response to the IBHE arguing that EOP Rhetoric philosophy and structure should qualify it as precisely the sort of for-credit "special admissions" program that was ostensibly exempted from the IBHE's concerns about competence. Meanwhile, the director of EOP Rhetoric at the time ("Director D") conducted a comprehensive assessment of EOP Rhetoric students' language and literacy competencies that was designed to illustrate the specific work of the program and the specific competencies of the students enrolled in it. Both responses were intended to recharacterize EOP Rhetoric as a race-conscious entity that was populated by competent minority students. Both responses also ended up, however, reifying white mainstream standards in the process.

Defending EOP Rhetoric as a Support Mechanism for Competent Minority Students

The first means through which UIUC attempted to defend EOP Rhetoric against the IBHE mandate was a document titled "Responses to IBHE on Questions on Remedial Courses," which stressed that there remained many connections between EOP Rhetoric and minority recruitment and retention on the UIUC campus. It began by asserting that the EOP in general tried to "attract students from groups which because of educational or socio-economic circumstances traditionally have not enrolled at UIUC" (UIUC, "Responses" 1), noting in particular that "minority" students were a special focus of the program (5, 6). It then insisted that in order to recruit minority students for this program, UIUC necessarily defined competence somewhat differently than it did in the case of mainstream students: "UIUC does relax its admissions requirements with the understanding that it must then provide the necessary remediation support to ensure that the incoming students have an opportunity to succeed in attaining their goals while attending the University. The same rationale can be extended to those additional 'special admissions' categories that include athletes, General Assembly Scholars, and students with special skills in the performing arts" (1). Finally, the response warned that failure on the part of IBHE to recognize EOP Rhetoric as a for-credit enterprise serving minority students would be dire: in the event of such a failure, "no one should be surprised if undergraduate minority enrollment begins to wane at this university and the numbers of students in the Educational Opportunities Program decline" (5); nor should they be shocked to realize that "the adoption of the IBHE's policy would adversely impact UIUC's 'special admissions' students, minority enrollment, and the Educational Opportunities Program" (6).

Throughout much of this response, UIUC defended EOP Rhetoric as the embodiment of very much the sort of race-conscious "special admissions" program for which race-conscious administrators such as Director A, the NCTE liaison, and the writing lab codirectors had originally argued during the late 1960s and early 1970s (see chapter 2). The response stressed that there existed various historical ties between EOP Rhetoric and an institutional desire to serve "those populations which historically have been denied the opportunity for betterment through education," populations that needed "special assistance" in acclimating to the "mainstream of university life." It also insisted that EOP Rhetoric had long played an important role in campus desegregation efforts past and present, declaring that EOP Rhetoric had been a primary factor influencing whether or not "students from groups which because of educational or socio-economic circumstances traditionally have not enrolled at UIUC" came to the campus in the first place. And it finally concluded by warning that any attempt on the part of the IBHE to tamper with either the EOP Rhetoric program or its for-credit status would have a "chilling effect" upon minority recruitment and retention, as well as a negative effect on minority students' ability to negotiate their course requirements successfully, trends that would result in a "wane" and "decline" of minority student enrollment at UIUC. This defense of EOP Rhetoric thus seemed like a far cry from the institutional color blindness regarding the program espoused during the mid-1970s era of literacy crisis.

Even while it made such claims, however, this response repeatedly stressed the value and importance of traditional mainstream standards across the campus in general and within the EOP Rhetoric program in particular. It asserted, for instance, that "it is a recognized fact that the academic abilities of the general student body [at UIUC] . . . are, on the whole, a cut above those at other public institutions of higher education in the State of Illinois. . . . The quality of the general student [at UIUC] has achieved a level comparable to that of the very best schools in the nation" (4–5). As evidence of this "cut above" quality, it also included an appendix listing a variety of standards-oriented statistics and figures: ACT scores of the whole UIUC student body that were anywhere between five and seven points higher than the state average in a given year, percentages of UIUC students drawn from the top 10 percent of their high school class, and the number of incoming UIUC students scoring above 30 on the ACT (UIUC, "Responses . . . Attachment 1" 1). The response thereby implied that by even the staunchest traditional standards, all UIUC's students—including its EOP Rhetoric students—were in fact "a cut above" those in the rest of the state.

The response also praised the IBHE for its statewide concerns regarding competence. In particular, it asserted that "UIUC's resistance to the IBHE's proposed policy should not be misconstrued as a lack of interest in the writing . . . skills of the students in the state" ("Responses" 6). As well, it asserted that UIUC would itself try to enforce "minimum competence in English . . . at all admission levels" (1) through the development of a "large-scale multi-national assessment of achievement in writing to determine program effects, student effects, and cultural effects on achievement"(6).[12] In this way, UIUC indicated that it actually saw nothing wrong with the competence concerns of the IBHE, at least not as long as these concerns were directed toward other state institutions.

And finally, the response even reversed some of its own earlier race-conscious arguments as it described the basic function of EOP Rhetoric on the UIUC campus. It insisted that while EOP students might be viewed as competent according to more general state criteria, these students nonetheless needed significant help in meeting standards that most mainstream white students at UIUC purportedly already possessed. In particular, it argued that "the gap between regularly admitted students and specially admitted students is widening at UIUC. They see the competition as tougher than ever and their chances for survival as growing smaller. It is clear to students entering UIUC special assistance programs that they will have to work harder and to sacrifice more if they select UIUC instead of other public institutions of higher education in the State of Illinois" (5). The response therefore cautioned that any IBHE interference with EOP Rhetoric (e.g., by refusing to allow EOP Rhetoric to be offered for credit) would make this "gap" even more apparent, thus rendering it "extremely difficult to convince EOP students to take the course in question. Many would attempt to skip these courses and would undoubtedly opt to take courses beyond their abilities. . . . Therefore it is very likely that specially admitted students would pay the least attention to those courses that should form the foundation for their future academic endeavors" (5).

By making these particular claims, this response posited that EOP students were deficient with respect to the standards already being met by their white mainstream peers. It further posited that this deficiency threatened the very "survival" of EOP students on a demanding UIUC campus by forcing them either to enroll in various for-credit courses at Illinois that were simply beyond their ability level or to attend some lesser institution in which they would not be expected to work as hard or sacrifice as much. In either case, while UIUC minority students were competent as far as the state was concerned, they were not deemed fully competent with respect to UIUC's own mainstream population.[13]

By repeatedly referencing standards in these ways, UIUC clearly limited its earlier race-conscious pronouncements regarding EOP Rhetoric and the competencies that it fostered: it championed apparently color-blind scores on objective tests like the ACT, it praised the IBHE for its interest in promoting competence and upholding standards across the state, and it openly denigrated the abilities of EOP students themselves with respect to their white mainstream counterparts. In this sense, it appeared that the UIUC administration was not advocating a full-blown race-conscious view of EOP

Rhetoric as it considered issues of competence; instead, it was offering a limited emphasis on race consciousness aimed first and foremost at reversing this specific IBHE mandate.

Defending EOP Rhetoric through
Assessment of Student Competence

A second example of the effects of IBHE concerns regarding student competence at UIUC can be found in the assessment of the EOP Rhetoric program conducted under Director D, an individual who served in this role from 1981 through 1983. In the midst of these other deliberations with the IBHE, Director D had been asked by the English Department head ("Head B") to compile data regarding "what specifically [EOP Rhetoric] does for the undergraduate student" (letter to Director D, 4 January 1982, 1). In explaining this charge, Head B noted that Illinois upper administration had been weighing various options, including retaining "EOP Rhetoric with some format changes" (1), in the event that the IBHE chose to eliminate EOP Rhetoric and its for-credit status.[14] In other words, UIUC needed a backup program in the event that EOP Rhetoric was to be dismantled, and Director D's assessment would be foundational to any such program that was subsequently built.[15]

In response to this request from the head, Director D submitted a report concerning the nature of EOP Rhetoric and the competencies that it sought to foster in its students. This report attempted to answer two fundamental questions: "How does the entering E.O.P. student differ from the entering non-E.O.P. student?" and "What happens to both sets of students in the course of one semester's instruction?" ("Report" 1). In the hopes of answering such questions, this report employed six different measures: three qualitative measures of student ability (i.e., instructor commentary regarding student strengths and weaknesses, a brief qualitative description of students' written work and course projects, and a brief discussion of student performance on a pre- and post-test holistically graded writing sample) and three quantitative measures of student ability (i.e., students' scores on the ACT, an assessment of the number of words per T-unit and number of words per clause produced within these pre- and post-test exercises, and student scores on a grammar and usage test).

Much like the "Response to IBHE on Questions on Remedial Courses," Director D's report seemed decidedly race conscious at many points. For instance, after noting that "these minority students arrive as new freshmen in a community [i.e., the UIUC campus] where for the first time in their life they may feel that they are really in the minority" (9), the report insisted that EOP Rhetoric students' work was every bit as interesting and compelling as that of their mainstream white peers: "That the E.O.P. students are capable of very sophisticated work is obvious from what some of them are doing with the research paper assignment. . . . Some of them are doing original research that might be considered sophisticated for an upperclassman" (9). The report further mentioned a long list of individual research topics that focused on race and racism: "unequal police protection in different parts of Chicago," "the history of Latin gangs in Chicago," "the racism involved in the Zoot Suit riots of 1943 in Los Angeles," "the effects of capitalism in Kenya," "the day to day resistance of blacks during slavery," and the "history of the Black Baptist Church" (10). After offering this litany of work, the report concluded that "these E.O.P. students are approaching the research paper in the right spirit—with an active desire to know about their subjects" (10).

Director D's report also presented quantitative data to support its claims concerning EOP Rhetoric student competence. In referencing a holistically scored pre- and post-test essay given to all EOP and non-EOP students, for instance, it noted that EOP students' scores (averaging a 6.47 on a scale from 2 to 12) at the end of their first semester of rhetoric instruction were roughly equivalent to scores (averaging 6.21 on this same scale) achieved by mainstream students entering the Rhetoric 105 course for the first time. In light of this data, the report asserted that "by the end of the 104 semester, E.O.P. students have arrived at the level of skill . . . shown by entering 105 students" (4). Furthermore, it noted that two measurements of "syntactic maturity" were roughly equivalent between EOP Rhetoric students exiting EOP Rhetoric 104 and mainstream students entering Rhetoric 105.[16] These scores indicated that "1) our E.O.P. students are ahead of many specially admitted students elsewhere, [and] 2) that they have in some respects reached the same level of syntactic complexity as their non-E.O.P. counterparts at Illinois" (6).

As in previous examples from this chapter, we see much in the way of race consciousness here. Director D's report praised EOP Rhetoric students' rhetorical and research abilities as equal to or in some cases better than those of their mainstream peers. It further praised EOP Rhetoric students for their interest in a variety of research topics, many of which appeared directly related to issues of race and racism. It even stressed that these students seemed to have achieved more or less the same level of competence by the end of EOP Rhetoric that their mainstream counterparts did in terms of "syntactic maturity." EOP Rhetoric students were apparently competent on many levels, and they ought to be recognized as such.

But despite these many seeming race-conscious assertions, Director D's report nonetheless asserted that EOP Rhetoric students were less competent with respect to their mainstream counterparts in at least one fundamental sense: namely, in their ability to adhere to typical standards of mainstream language and literacy use, especially Standard English. In discussing the questionnaire issued to EOP Rhetoric instructors, for instance, the report noted with some concern that "the T.A.'s consistently describe E.O.P. students as having more problems with syntax, usage, organization, and rhetoric than their non-E.O.P counterparts. E.O.P. students are perceived also as requiring more individual help on syntax and usage, rhetorical concepts, diction, and organizing their workload" (3). The report also mentioned that TAs "still perceived E.O.P. 105 students . . . as having more problems using standard English grammar and usage than non-E.O.P. students in Rhet 105" and that "E.O.P. students require more effort from their teachers—more individualized help on grammar, rhetoric, self-pacing, diction, and therefore more time spent by T.A.'s commenting on papers" (3). Still further, it stressed that when it came to "mastering of standard written English usage . . . it should be no surprise to find that E.O.P. students have more trouble with the fine points of written English than non-E.O.P. students because language habits of a lifetime cannot be expected to change suddenly" (8). The report raised this point in concluding as well, asserting that "many of the [EOP Rhetoric] students doing highly intelligent, original research, however, will turn in papers whose surface features will, in other classes, mark them as below average writers at this highly competitive university" (10). This report thereby concluded that, while students may have been competent from a number of vantage points, their errors with respect to Standard English still marked them as incompetent at this "highly competitive" university with respect to their white mainstream peers.

Ultimately, the report from Director D made a number of initial race-conscious pronouncements concerning minority students' competencies, but it undercut them at some level through its emphasis on white mainstream standards. It argued that these EOP Rhetoric students were capable of effectively analyzing their place in a predominantly white school, of effectively writing about racial issues, and even of scoring in ways equivalent to their white peers on assessments of syntactic maturity. Nonetheless, it insisted that these same students produced many "errors," had "more trouble with fine points of written English" than their white counterparts as a result of their "language habits of a lifetime," and otherwise wrote papers with problematic "surface features." Such difficulty, so this report concluded, was the primary trait that served to "mark [EOP Rhetoric students] as below average writers at this highly competitive university." My point here, of course, is not that Director D's report should have simply ignored the importance of "error" in students' lives, especially when such error likely did mark even the strongest EOP Rhetoric writers as "below average" in a mainstream context such as UIUC. Rather, my point is that, even in its attempts to be race conscious, this report never questioned the negative attitudes of TAs or other faculty regarding students' language use at this "highly competitive" university, nor did it raise critical questions concerning how best to recognize or cultivate students' "language habits of a lifetime" in ways that were positive rather than punitive. The ultimate purpose of EOP Rhetoric remained, in this sense, to continue fixing students' errors with respect to Standard English, not to cultivate students' existing linguistic and literate strengths.

The Institutional Outcomes of UIUC's Responses

The two primary responses from UIUC presented here met with some degree of success: the IBHE decided in the summer of 1983 to continue allowing credit for EOP Rhetoric, although it remarked that "the University [should plan] to upgrade the context of the Rhetoric courses by Fall Semester 1983 so that they will no longer be remedial" (IBHE, "Update" 94). In practice, this translated into a compromise within EOP Rhetoric: both semesters of EOP Rhetoric (i.e., both EOP Rhetoric 104 and 105) were preserved in their full for-credit form; meanwhile, work in the writing lab (i.e.,

EOP Rhetoric 103) would no longer receive credit (Director of Rhetoric, letter to VCAA, 22 February 1982, 1). But even in the wake of this victory, one institutional decision was made that began to call the long-term future of a race-conscious EOP Rhetoric program into serious question—namely, the decision to develop an "experimental" writing instruction program known as Rhetoric 199 (and later retitled Special Options Rhetoric).

Designed and discussed somewhat secretively during the entirety of Illinois's discussions with the IBHE, Rhetoric 199 constituted a version of the backup program earlier mentioned by the English Department head in his discussion with Director D. Its development was overseen by an administrative entity known as the Ad Hoc Committee on Rhetoric and Composition that was developed to imagine new courses that the campus might create in the event that the IBHE abolished EOP Rhetoric. This committee stressed that Rhetoric 199 was not "remedial": "We are aware of the concerns expressed by the IBHE relating to remedial courses and their desire to phase out such programs. The programs we describe here are not remedial, and are not subject to the statements of policy expressed by the Board on this issue. . . . Unlike remedial courses, the rhetoric courses described in this report are not designed to prepare students to take a conventionally-required course, but represent an alternate route to meeting requirements; the credit earned in them is used to satisfy degree requirements" (Ad Hoc Committee on Rhetoric and Composition, "Report" 7). Instead, this committee argued, the course was actually rooted in an "experimental" new pedagogy that featured multiple means of cultivating student competence: "intensive writing and re-writing in class, along with individualized, immediate feedback from the instructor and possibly peer reactions from small groups within the class. Since the least skilled students are those most likely to be unacquainted with the conventions of writing, we will attempt to help them understand the contexts, audiences, purposes, strategies, and formats of specific kinds of writing" ("Course Proposal for Rhetoric 199: Writing Workshop" 2–3). Crucially, even as it touted such experimental activity within this course, this committee rendered Rhetoric 199 decidedly color-blind and standards oriented in terms of both its placement and its assessment activities. Placement was determined solely by either ACT English subscore or timed essay exam (2); meanwhile, overall assessment of program effectiveness was determined via a "pre-test and post-test essay (like that administered to E.O.P. sections and to several sections of Rhet 105 for comparison), a course-satisfaction questionnaire, and a writing anxiety test" (3).

The development and implementation of Rhetoric 199 ultimately resulted in the operation of a two-tiered EOP Rhetoric structure by 1983: EOP Rhetoric 104/105 served high-risk minority students in the EOP program, while Rhetoric 199 served all other high-risk students (i.e., low-scoring white students). It is certainly possible to read this resulting dual programmatic structure as something of a "best of both worlds" scenario: UIUC effectively retained a race-conscious EOP Rhetoric program dedicated to ensuring the competence of specially admitted minority students while at the same time building a new program designed to ensure the competence of white low-scorers. But this dual structure nonetheless housed a second writing program that defined competence by only the most traditional of color-blind standards. Furthermore, as I will discuss at some length in the next chapter, this dual structure would soon be perceived by many mainstream UIUC administrators as both unnecessary and exceedingly expensive, prompting them to ask a number of pointed questions: Why does the campus need two expensive one-on-one programs serving students who do not possess writing competence according to traditional measures? Why not imagine some alternative that ensures the competence of all students regardless of race? The dual operation of EOP Rhetoric and Rhetoric 199 was, in this sense, a harbinger of fierce institutional battles to come—battles that would eventually result in the complete reconfiguration of the EOP Rhetoric program.

Institutional Interest Reconvergence in the Age of Competence

The history of debate and struggle surrounding EOP Rhetoric during the late 1970s and early 1980s indicates at least something of a reemergence of race consciousness at UIUC in the midst of competence concerns. Administrators stressed the need to support minority students at UIUC, and they touted students' race-based skills as strengths in ways that they had not done since the late 1960s and early 1970s. Nonetheless, these administrative responses to the IBHE ultimately stressed standards in ways that called such apparent race consciousness into serious question. Indeed, even as EOP

Rhetoric students were being described as minority students who were in some ways "a cut above" all others in the state, they were also being described as deficient with respect to standards and thus in danger of flunking out of the university. Furthermore, even as the campus was seemingly interested in continuing to offer EOP Rhetoric as a kind of exception to standards concerns on the campus, it praised the IBHE for its enforcement of standards (as long as that emphasis was directed elsewhere) and promised to mirror this enforcement in programs outside of EOP Rhetoric. And finally, even as UIUC built a backup Rhetoric 199 program in order to preserve EOP Rhetoric–type programmatic activity, this backup plan made absolutely no mention of race. So while the philosophies of the EOP Rhetoric program during the late 1970s were somewhat more race conscious than they had been in the mid-1970s, the program nonetheless remained rooted in status quo notions of students and competence and the white mainstream standards undergirding them.

These changes thereby demonstrate a clear dynamic of institutional interest reconvergence emerging during the late 1970s and early 1980s. The interests of those espousing race-conscious activism and those espousing more mainstream views of the program did converge, at least to some extent, toward the idea that EOP Rhetoric should serve as a program designed explicitly to support the language and literacy needs of high-risk minority students. But this reconvergence was, yet again, limited by a stress on mainstream standards and their relationship to UIUC's larger interests in defending itself against the IBHE. UIUC's approach to EOP Rhetoric at this time may have promoted some pursuit of racial justice, but only to the degree that this pursuit helped it in defending its larger interests against the IBHE's unwelcome intrusion.

Competence, Reconvergence, and the Ethos of the Age

Race-conscious activists working during the late 1970s and early 1980s in the wake of the *Bakke* decision clearly encountered a range of individuals and groups espousing mainstream perspectives, including the Supreme Court, key disciplinary figures, key UIUC administrators, and many others who were at least somewhat amenable to recognizing race at some level while considering the kinds of competencies that high-risk programs and their high-risk/BW components tried to foster. The interests of activists and of the mainstream therefore did begin to reconverge during this time: high-risk programs grew nationally, disciplinary discussions of competence blossomed, and EOP Rhetoric at UIUC was defended from IBHE attack. The late 1970s and early 1980s constituted, in this sense, a high-risk renaissance of sorts. Nonetheless, such reconvergence was also limited by the interests and needs of the white mainstream: national student aid paradigms shifted their focus toward "merit" in ways affecting high-risk students, disciplinary discussions embraced standards within various testing programs, and UIUC developed new standards-oriented programs to accompany EOP Rhetoric even as it stressed race consciousness. This renaissance, then, was a partial and limited one.

But as conflicted as these dynamics of reconvergence might be, they would actually mark one of the final periods in the history of high-risk discussion in which any vestige of 1960s-style race consciousness would be recognized as even potentially legitimate within mainstream four-year institutions. By the late 1980s and early 1990s, such recognition was largely gone, fueled by a combination of conservative-leaning and progressive-leaning theorists who believed strongly (although for very different reasons) that 1960s-style race consciousness was both outdated and ultimately unnecessary. This shift would promote a new period of interest redivergence that marked an important beginning of the end for much high-risk/BW activity.

The Late 1980s and Early 1990s

CULTURE WARS AND THE POLITICS OF IDENTITY

PREDOMINANTLY WHITE mainstream four-year colleges and universities in the United States found themselves grappling with yet another host of important issues related to racial and cultural diversity during the late 1980s and early 1990s. These institutions were encountering widespread demands that they prepare students more effectively for the challenges presented by an increasingly diverse and global populace—a future in which "ethnic minority persons will numerically dominate in U.S. society and U.S. higher education" (Cheatham 17) and in which "the workforce and workplace, whether office, factory, or school, will be more diverse" (LaBelle and Ward 59). They were also encountering "a frightening rash of racial incidents on college and university campuses" (Walker 129), including a controversy occurring between reporters and editors at the *Dartmouth Review* and an African American professor of music over the professor's purported lack of standards and desire to give "'affirmative action' kids . . . a course they can handle" (qtd. in McMahon 194–95); an incident at Brown University when a white undergraduate student was expelled after drunkenly screaming a series of racial slurs and threats under Brown's first attempt to enforce its "Standards of Student Conduct" for hate speech (Hower 156); and a host of other related incidents occurring on campuses including Wisconsin, Michigan, Purdue, Stanford, and Smith (Walker 129).

The racial issues and tensions of the late 1980s and early 1990s served as the backdrop for what would become known as the "culture wars," fought on many mainstream campuses and in the mainstream media over the nature of "multicultural" curriculum and other related efforts that were said to "make students aware of Western civilization in a context that includes exploration of other sources of thought, culture, history, political and social organization, music and art . . . to develop thinking and communication skills that extend beyond a single perspective, point of view, or manner of discourse . . . and [to recognize] the distinctive contributions and backgrounds, as well as the shared characteristics, of students and faculty from different cultural groups" (Schoem et al. 2). The context of the culture wars would find many conservative-learning critics achieving fame, even bestseller status, for scathing critiques of multiculturalism and of the 1960s-era programmatic initiatives that gave birth to them. However, this context would find many progressive critics calling for radical reconfiguration of 1960s-era multiculturalism and its manifestations as well.

One especially well-known example of a conservative-leaning culture wars argument of this time was Allan Bloom's best-selling 1987 book *The Closing of the American Mind.* Bloom lambasted what he called the "new curriculum" of multiculturalism, insisting that it had created a kind of present-day educational chaos whereby, "when a student arrives at the university, he finds a bewildering variety of departments and a bewildering variety of courses. And there is no official guidance, no university-wide agreement, about what he should study" (338). The only guiding principle that this student was sure to encounter, Bloom claimed, was the admonition that "we should not be ethnocentric. . . . We should not think that our way is better than others" (30). Bloom was adamant that this problematic manifestation of pluralism was actually the product of 1960s-era programs, particularly those related to minority recruitment and retention—that is, EOP, "black studies," and "Black English" (95). These efforts, he argued, had always been firmly rooted in the erroneous notion that "integrationism was just an ideology for whites and Uncle Toms. Who says that what universities teach is the truth rather than just the myths necessary to support the system of domination? Black

students are second-class not because they are academically poor but because they are being forced to imitate white culture" (94). Bloom finally
concluded that both contemporary multiculturalism and its problematic
1960s-era foundations should be rejected and replaced with the "good old
Great Books approach" to education (344), one demanding the reading of
"generally recognized classic texts, just reading them, letting them dictate
what the questions are and the method of approaching them—not forcing
them into categories we make up, not treating them as historical products,
but trying to read them as their authors wished them to be read" (344).

At the heart of Bloom's arguments (arguments echoed by a number of
others at the time) were three basic assertions: (1) that contemporary multicultural curricula were ignoring the "basics" in favor of problematic attention to "political" issues such as race and racism; (2) that these contemporary
multicultural curricula had roots in highly problematic 1960s-era programmatic structures that long encouraged this sort of unnecessary attention to
race and racism; and (3) that these curricula should be abandoned and replaced with a return to standards.[1] These arguments obviously shared a great
deal with their mid-1970s literacy crisis predecessors in the way that they
demanded a clear move away from race consciousness and back to the color-
blind "basics."

This type of conservative critique of multiculturalism was not the only
one being expressed within this context of the culture wars, though. There
was also a strong critique of 1960s-style multiculturalism emanating from
many progressive-leaning scholars at this time. This critique insisted that
multicultural programs were not political *enough*—that is, not willing enough
to confront and deconstruct essentialist political categories like race in light
of contemporary thinking about issues of power and not willing enough to
develop new programs rooted directly in progressive political thought. One
example of such work was Gerald Graff's well-known 1992 book *Beyond the
Culture Wars*. Graff argued that, within the contemporary multicultural university, "all sides [have become] comfortable preaching to the already con-
verted. We get clashing forms of political correctness that become ever more
entrenched the less they are forced to speak to one another. In a vicious
circle, opposing viewpoints are so rarely debated that on the rare occasions
when they are, the discussion is naturally hostile and confused, and this result then seems to prove that reasoned debate is not possible. Here, as I see

it, is the essence of problems of 'Balkanization,' separatism, and particularism that have come so to worry us: not the lack of agreement but of the respectful disagreement that supposedly is the strengths of democracies and educational institutions" (13). Graff did concede that there had been some value derived from the legacy of 1960s-era "non-Western courses" (13) and other multicultural efforts: these efforts had certainly "resulted in a far more culturally representative academic culture than had existed in the past (and, for that reason, a more candid acknowledgement by some of the place of politics in the academy)" (136). He concluded, nonetheless, that both contemporary "non-Western" courses and their Western counterparts were now outdated and needed to be dismantled and replaced with a curriculum dedicated to "teaching the conflicts" (15). Such a new curriculum would be properly dedicated to helping students "see the connections between the different interpretations, ideas, and values . . . if they are to enter actively into academic discussions" (14), thereby giving "academic culture a chance to work by connecting its dissociated parts" (172).

Graff's frustration with 1960s-style multiculturalism and the politics undergirding it was echoed by others of the time as well. Henry Giroux, for instance, expressed concern in 1993's *Living Dangerously: Multiculturalism and the Politics of Difference* that the basis of contemporary multiculturalism in 1960s-style identity politics was problematic because "the history of identity politics is not one that has moved unproblematically from resistance to a broader politics of democratic struggle. While identity politics was central to challenging the cultural homogeneity of the 1950s and providing spaces for marginal groups to assert the legacy and importance of their respective voices and experiences, it often failed to move beyond a notion of difference structured in polarizing binarisms and an uncritical appeal to a discourse of authenticity" (92). Giroux advocated, therefore, that contemporary multicultural curricula move away from 1960s-style identity politics as "an exclusive focus on subordinate groups" (61) and toward new kinds of race and power consciousness, examining "how racism in its various forms is produced historically, semiotically, and institutionally at various levels of society" (61). Mary Louise Pratt made a similar claim in 1991's "Arts of the Contact Zone." Although she was in some ways less worried than either Graff or Giroux about the negative aspects of 1960s-era identity politics and the programs that these politics helped to spawn, she nonetheless argued that the ideal multicultural curriculum was one that moved beyond 1960s-era notions and instead placed all students into a kind of "contact zone" in which they could "meet, clash, and grapple with each other, often in contexts of highly asymmetrical relations of power, such as colonialism, slavery, or their aftermaths as they are lived out in many parts of the world today" (34).[2] The resulting contact zone could, she felt, more profitably foster a space for students to share in a common encounter with difference writ large rather than difference narrowly defined in 1960s terms.

By making such arguments, Graff, Giroux, and Pratt (themselves working alongside a number of others of the time) offered their own three-part critique of multiculturalism: (1) that multiculturalism relied on outdated notions of racial identity in ways that promoted "clashing forms of political correctness," "'Balkanization,' separatism, and particularism," "polarizing binarisms," and/or "uncritical appeal to a discourse of authenticity"; (2) that while the 1960s-era roots of such multiculturalism in racial identity politics may once have been useful, they were no longer so; and (3) that contemporary multicultural curricula and programs must be dismantled and reconfigured in light of contemporary political thinking that explicitly highlighted and theorized differences between and among various racial, cultural, and social groups rather than simplistically valorizing "separatism" or "identity politics."[3] This three-part progressive critique emanated from a very different place than the more conservative critiques previously mentioned: if anything, it reflected a profound frustration with what it saw as the inability of contemporary multiculturalism to combat the deep roots of racism (and of classism, sexism, heteronormativity, and a range of other problematic expressions of hegemonic power) in ways that might truly reshape the social order. Nonetheless, it arrived at the same basic endpoint that more conservative critiques did: that those concerned with higher education ought to dismantle 1960s-era multicultural curricula and the programs that housed them, replacing them with more politically desirable curricula and programs. This more progressive critique thereby threatened to dismiss the potential historical and political power of 1960s-era multicultural programs, including high-risk programs themselves. It further dismissed the ways in which these programs had long served as institutional spaces from which racialized standards, especially racialized standards of language and literacy, could be critiqued. As a result, even this apparently progressive critique threatened to promote a kind of institutional color blindness and reification of linguistic standards in the name of promoting reform.

The late-1980s and early-1990s context of the culture wars within the U.S. academy thereby witnessed a rather peculiar agreement between conservative and progressive critics of multiculturalism—a sense on both "sides" that 1960s-style high-risk programs needed to be dismantled and replaced. This agreement also began to affect high-risk program operation in various contexts. For instance, in response to more conservative calls for stronger standards during the late 1980s and early 1990s, CUNY developed a new set of admissions criteria in 1992 as part of what would become known as the College Preparatory Initiative (CPI): the CPI articulated "competency statements" for various high school subjects, particularly math, science, and English, designed to ensure that students came to CUNY only after having demonstrated minimum competencies according to traditional measures (Renfro and Armour-Garb 40). CUNY also began administering its FSAT exams to interested high school students so that they could "begin addressing their academic underpreparation prior to their enrollment in CUNY" (41). As well, the school began enforcing stricter penalties for those at CUNY who did poorly on these exams and/or in their "remedial" classes—for example, expelling students who failed the same remedial course twice (41)—in the hopes of reviving "CUNY's pre-open-admissions standards" to as full a degree as possible (41). At the same time, however, self-proclaimed liberals such as James Traub were also insisting that Open Admissions at CUNY had proven a failure despite any good intentions that might have undergirded it. Traub claimed in the introduction to his own best seller, *City on a Hill: Testing the American Dream at City College,* that he actually "wanted City College to work" (18), as a function of his own particular brand of "sixties liberalism": "I had grown up with the civil rights movement and the war on poverty. . . . I believed in government activism, and I took it as a premise that a humane society focuses an important part of its energy on bringing the poor into the mainstream. I believed in the old-fashioned meritocratic principle that City College had arguably abandoned with open admissions, but I was also committed to the idea of equal opportunity" (18). Nonetheless, Traub insisted that Open Admissions at City College and throughout CUNY had failed—a point that he says even the most stalwart liberal must concede. City College had allowed its "remedial undercollege" (including its BW program, where he spent a good deal of time observing the students of

Marilyn Sternglass) to "[threaten] City's upper stories" of liberal arts and professional education (343). It should, therefore, be abandoned: "the only way to ensure that [City College] flourished as a fine professional and liberal arts institution, as it once did, is to recognize the limits of its social mission. City, and any other college that aspires to high academic standards, cannot be asked to educate large numbers of deeply disadvantaged students" (204).[4] CUNY was clearly under siege from right and self-proclaimed left.

A related two-sided dynamic also appeared to be affecting federal high-risk initiatives such as SSS during this time. The largest national study of the SSS program of the 1990s, the two-part *National Study of Student Support Services* (initially issued in 1994, with a follow-up in 1997), highlighted what it saw as two serious challenges confronting SSS. First, it cautioned that the SSS programs must do a much more effective job of responding to an increasingly conservative political climate of "fiscal stringency" and concern with "efficient service delivery strategies" (Calahan and Muraskin 9-2). In particular, it recommended that SSS programs carefully and systematically measure "student outcomes that reflect the SSS program's main goals," as well as retention and graduation statistics (9-27), in order to convince skeptical audiences of its value. At the same time, the report cautioned that SSS projects needed to do a better job of demonstrating to their current supporters that their services were "non-supplanting"—that is, not duplicating the many other student support services typically available to non-SSS students (e.g., tutoring services, smaller "remedial" classes, and the like). It warned that SSS programs must be prepared to offer a "clear definition of the term 'disadvantaged student' at each grantee institution that limits the target group for additional services" (9-1), especially given that, "when the SSS program began, it may have provided a unique and additional set of support services for a distinct population, but today, especially in larger institutions, it is likely to be one program among many for at-risk students" (9-5). In this way, the report argued that even those predisposed to support SSS-type programs were questioning these programs' continued value: while these programs had certainly been needed in the past, they might not be needed in the present within a context where considerable student support of many types was available.

Finally, the dual pressures being placed on high-risk programs such as SSS programs at the time also seemed to resonate with a slowing of high-risk program growth during the late 1980s and early 1990s. For instance, even though actual funding for SSS increased significantly, from roughly $91 million in 1988–89 to $143.5 million in 1998 (Chaney et al. 4-3), the overall number of SSS programs was frozen at 706 from 1988 until 1996 (Carey et al. 8). Furthermore, availability of need-based aid of the sort required by so many SSS students was continuing to be outpaced by the availability of merit-based aid: in 1988–89, while state-level need-based aid across the United States increased only 8 percent over the previous year, state-level merit-based aid increased 17 percent (Reeher and Davis 1); five years later, in 1993–94, need-based aid increased by about 12 percent over the previous year, whereas merit-based aid itself increased by 18 percent (Davis, Nastelli, and Redd 1). These aid trends, unfortunately, continued "shifting funds from blacks, Latinos, and Native Americans to whites and Asians, from city residents to suburban residents, from children of one-parent families to those who have two parents" (Orfield xiii). These trends also paralleled some important demographic changes within mainstream higher education at this time. Overall enrollment figures for whites, blacks, and Hispanics ages eighteen to twenty-four within higher education actually increased during the late 1980s and early 1990s: in 1988, these figures were 33.2 percent, 21.2 percent and 17.0 percent respectively, while in 1993 they had climbed to 37.3 percent, 25.2 percent, and 21.3 percent (Snyder, Dillow, and Hoffman 296). But these increases for minority students occurred disproportionately in two-year institutions: indeed, by 1995, two-year institutions served 42.1 percent of all black college students and 55.6 percent of all Hispanic college students, but served only 36.7 percent of white students (Carter and Wilson 18, 76). Taken together, these statistics indicate that one of the initial goals of high-risk program development—namely, the integration of mainstream predominantly white four-year institutions—had begun to change significantly by the early 1990s. Racial diversity was now less the concern of four-year institutions and more the concern of their two-year counterparts.[5]

Culture Wars and the Dynamics of Interest Redivergence

The situation of high-risk instruction within the late-1980s and early-1990s culture wars context clearly prompted movement away from even the rather limited race consciousness of the *Bakke* era (see chapter 4) and toward a kind of two-sided color blindness. Some individuals and groups espousing activism did continue to support the operation of race-conscious high-risk programs during this time. However, they faced simultaneous pressure from conservative-leaning critics, who argued that contemporary multicultural-ism and its politics be abandoned entirely, and from progressive-leaning critics, who argued that contemporary multiculturalism and its politics must be fundamentally reconfigured and updated. Consequently, high-risk programs such as Open Admissions at CUNY were being subjected to both to increasing regulation through conservative measures such as the CPI and attacks from self-proclaimed liberals such as Traub. Meanwhile, programs such as SSS were encountering cost-cutting and accountability pressures at the same time that even longtime supporters were questioning the continued need for their services. And all of this took place as shifts from need-based to merit-based aid continued with important consequences for higher-education demographics. In this sense, high-risk instruction was entering yet another dark age.

These trends also reveal a rather complex dynamic of interest rediver-gence taking place within the culture wars climate. The interests of those espousing race-conscious activism were diverging not only from those on the political and educational right but from those on the political and edu-cational left as well. This redivergence called the long-term future of high-risk instruction into serious question, especially as white mainstream support for high-risk instruction declined precipitously. It further underscored once again the important power of the white mainstream to dictate the path of race-based institutional change within the culture wars context. The main-stream apparently no longer had an interest in promoting 1960s-style diver-sity within undergraduate populations as it had even in the wake of *Bakke;* instead, it had a two-sided interest in dismantling and replacing such views of diversity with more purportedly "contemporary" approaches. As a result, any hope for continuing the work of race-conscious high-risk instruction into the mid-1990s and beyond was fading—and it seemed to be fading fast.

Debating the Disciplinary Legacy of 1960s-Era High-Risk/BW Programs

The debates regarding multiculturalism and the legacy of 1960s-era pro-grammatic activity that were so common within the larger context of the culture wars also strongly influenced composition discussions during this period of time. Composition and English studies scholars and teachers of the late 1980s and early 1990s routinely encountered discussions of multiculturalism from more linguistically conservative scholars and theorists such as former CCCC chair Maxine Hairston, who insisted in 1992 that composition courses in the multicultural age had become "too political" in a way that "puts dogma before diversity, politics before craft, ideology before critical thinking, and the social goals of the teacher before the educational needs of the student. It's a regressive model that undermines the progress we've made in teaching writing, one that threatens to silence student voices and jeopardize the process-oriented, low-risk, student-centered classroom we've worked so hard to establish as the norm" (180).[6] These scholars and teachers also encountered arguments from more linguistically progressive scholars and theorists who insisted that extant multicultural curricula in English studies ought to be radically reconfigured in light of something like Pratt's contact zone.[7] Patricia Bizzell argued in 1994, for instance, "I think we need a radically new system to organize English studies, and I propose that we develop it in response to the materials with which we are now working. Instead of finagling the new literatures and the new pedagogical and critical approaches into our old categories, we should try to find comprehensive new forms that seem to spring from and respond to the new materials. Instead of asking ourselves, for example, 'How can I fit Frederick Douglass into my American Renaissance course?' we need to ask, 'How should I reconceive my study of literature and composition now that I regard Douglass as an important writer?'" (164). In these ways, both conservative-leaning and progressive-leaning scholars were asking direct questions about the future relationship between multiculturalism and composition/English studies.

In turn, scholars and teachers working with high-risk/BW programs had a strong stake in these culture wars era discussions, especially because they were facing significant pressure to justify their work in this period of frozen high-risk-program support and shrinking institutional budgets. Writing in 2001, Gerri McNenny noted this pressure as it was manifested throughout the 1990s: "What many writing program administrators and other decision makers are faced with [in terms of the continued operation of their high-risk/BW programs] . . . is the decision of what to do about existing basic writing programs that may now or in the future be threatened, either by legislative mandate, budget constraints, or political pressures" (5). In response to this pressure, two types of work during the early 1990s attempted to theorize the history and legacy of existing high-risk/BW philosophies, practices, and structures in the hopes of determining a clearer path for the future. One type focused specifically on the legacy of iconic figures and programs and their import for contemporary instruction, what high-risk/BW scholar Donna Strickland described as a growing interest throughout the 1990s in understanding "the circumstances under which 'basic writing' emerged both as a college course and a field of study. Understanding these circumstances should begin to illumine the functions of basic writing" in the present (22).[8] Another type focused on high-risk/BW program "mainstreaming"—that is, the means through which long-standing programs should or should not be reconfigured both theoretically and programmatically according to new thinking about the needs of students within a multicultural age. High-risk/BW scholar Peter Dow Adams noted that mainstreaming scholars of the time period were increasingly concerned that "if what we are doing in the basic writing classroom is no longer significantly different from what we do in college-level writing classrooms, then the justification we once had for segregating basic writers may have evaporated" (24).[9] Together, these two types of scholarship marked an active effort during the late 1980s and early 1990s to revisit the history of high-risk/BW as a means of charting its future course. They also served as a backdrop against which scholars who were interested in actively promoting race-conscious high-risk/BW work encountered significant opposition from others making both conservative-leaning and progressive-leaning arguments about the need to radically reconfigure 1960s-era high-risk/BW efforts within this culture wars context.

Race-Conscious Praise for the Historical Legacy of High-Risk/BW

As was the case in each previous era discussed in this book, at least some of the scholars contributing significantly to high-risk/BW discussions during the culture wars era maintained a strong sense of race consciousness within their work. One example of this was Min Zhan Lu's 1992 *College English* (*CE*) essay "Conflict and Struggle: The Enemies or Preconditions of Basic Writing?"—an essay notable for generating a great deal of debate about the future of high-risk/ BW. Debate was so vigorous, in fact, that *CE* published a follow-up 1993 issue, the "Symposium on Basic Writing," dedicated to discussing issues that Lu raised; meanwhile, Lu herself published a 1994 follow-up article in *CCC* titled "Professing Multiculturalism: The Politics of Style in the Contact Zone" that attempted to clarify some of the pedagogical issues originally raised within "Conflict."[10]

Lu began her discussion by insisting that high-risk/BW discussions had, since their initiation in the mid-1970s, tended to avoid issues of race and class struggle rather than confronting them directly. She insisted that many of the key figures responsible for founding the contemporary BW movement, including Kenneth Bruffee, Thomas Farrell, Mina Shaughnessy, and other "teachers influenced by the work of these pioneers" (889), tended "to view all signs of conflict and struggle as the *enemy* of basic writing instruction" (889). In so doing, she said, these scholars ignored the profound ways in which high-risk/BW grew out of the "immediate, intense, sometimes violent social, political, and racial confrontations" of the late 1960s and early 1970s (907); they also ignored the "'psychic woe' that [non-white and non-mainstream students] experience as a result of the dissonance within or among cultures, their ambivalence towards cultural bleaching, and their interest in racial/class politics" (904).

Despite the problematic past of high-risk/BW instruction, Lu believed that contemporary instruction could be reclaimed through overtly embracing a version of race consciousness that blended 1960s-era insights with poststructural understandings. In particular, she argued that high-risk/BW programs could be reimagined as contemporary sites where the "possible uses of conflict and struggle" (907) within language and literacy instruction were acknowledged and even encouraged. One way to engage in such reimagining of high-risk/BW, she argued, was to "re-read" the work of its pioneering scholars "in the context of current debates on the nature of language, individual consciousness, and the politics of basic skills" (909). Another way was to "gather more [contemporary] oppositional and alternative accounts from a new generation of students, those who can speak about the successes and challenges of classrooms which recognize the positive uses of conflict and struggle and which teach the processes of repositioning" (910). Still a third way involved interrogating white mainstream standards and their hegemonic effects within these programs: "Most of all, we need to find ways of foregrounding conflict and struggle not only in the generation of meaning or authority, but also in the teaching of conventions of 'correctness' in syntax, spelling, and punctuation, traditionally considered the primary focus of Basic Writing instruction" (910).

Throughout her comments, Lu offered both a race-conscious critique of the historical legacy of high-risk/BW programs and a race-conscious plan for how this legacy might be usefully reclaimed. She insisted that many iconic figures within the past history of high-risk/BW had tended to downplay or even ignore cultural and racial conflict within writing instruction, along with the "psychic woe" that such conflict and struggle was likely to foment. But she did not despair. Instead, she argued that those in the discipline could gain new insights into how conflict and struggle could be positively utilized within contemporary programs by critically revisiting this history, by talking to students directly about their struggles, and (especially) by continuing to challenge notions of standards in ways that highlighted their ties to mainstream power.

Another important example of race-conscious work from this time period, one focusing more directly upon the institutional legacy of 1960s-era high-risk/BW programs, was William Jones's 1993 *Journal of Basic Writing* article "Basic Writing: Pushing against Racism." Although Jones's piece did not necessarily generate the same level of critical discussion that Lu's article had, it was nonetheless noteworthy for its explicit praise of the race-conscious programmatic legacy of high-risk instruction and its roots in 1960s-era activism.

Jones opened his argument with as direct a race-conscious statement as one was likely to find within the literature at this time: "I begin with the assumption that racism is a core feature of American life, that White supremacy is a central tenet, that efforts to maintain White privilege and power spring naturally from its assumption, and that it posits intelligence as innate, unequally distributed among individuals, and by easy extension, hierarchically arranged among races" (72–73). But Jones did not condemn past or present-day high-risk/BW programs in light of the racism and white supremacy that he identified. He argued, instead, that these 1960s-era programs had long possessed the race-conscious roots and orientation necessary to combat such racism. Toward this end, he pointed directly to two 1960s-era high-risk programs: the Academic Foundations Department and the Educational Opportunity Fund (EOF) Program at Rutgers University in New Jersey (78), arguing that they (and others like them) were worthy of praise because they had been premised upon "an ethos that influences educational policy and decisions that counterstate the deficit mode of minority student functioning" (76). Jones further argued that such 1960s-era programs tried to "encourage Black and Latino students to use the intuitive and generative linguistic powers available to them as native speakers of English and as competent bilinguals" (77), while, at the same time, prompting critical questions regarding the role of "grammar" within language and literacy instruction: "What is the nature of the evaluation that situates grammar instruction as a central feature in a [typical] basic writing program? In what way does grammar instruction focus on remediation instead of on literacy, on the complex acts of reading and writing? When grammar instruction is a feature, does it deepen and increase existing linguistic competence or does it hold students hostage until they master the minutiae of workbook grammars?" (77). Jones finally concluded that other contemporary high-risk/BW programs should try to emulate these exemplary race-conscious 1960s-era programs at Rutgers. Contemporary programs should require instructors "whatever their color or ethnicity" to continue "noting the contradictions between the public image of minority students and [their own] actual moment-to-moment interactions with their youth charges" (78). In addition, they should emulate the ways in which exemplary 1960s-era programs "foster competence, balancing and juxtaposing course work, faculty mentoring outreach, and academic advising and individual support that may include peer tutoring and counseling by both professionals and peers" (77).

Throughout his article, Jones insisted that high-risk/BW programs could and should embrace their race-conscious legacy as it had been embodied in programs like these two 1960s-era high-risk/BW exemplars at Rutgers. He felt strongly that such programs had long utilized race consciousness as a means to cultivate students' extant linguistic and literate strengths, especially by asking important questions regarding standards and their effects as part of their larger writing instructional experiences. He concluded, therefore, that contemporary programs had a great deal to gain from recognizing and extending the rich histories of these 1960s-era high-risk/BW efforts.

These two brief arguments from Lu and Jones (two of several articles circulating at the time) demonstrate that high-risk/BW instruction was in fact being theorized in race-conscious ways throughout the late 1980s and early 1990s.[11] But race-conscious arguments of this sort were typically met with one of the two responses common within this climate of the culture wars: responses from conservative-leaning scholars, which contended that the race-conscious legacy of high-risk/BW needed to be soundly rejected and summarily abandoned, and responses from progressive-leaning scholars, which contended that the legacy of high-risk/BW now needed to be reconceived and reconfigured in light of contemporary theoretical and political thought.

Conservative-Leaning Critiques of High-Risk/BW

One important example of linguistically conservative and standards-oriented critique from this period was Patricia Laurence's response to Lu's "Conflict and Struggle," included in the aforementioned *College English* "Symposium on Basic Writing" issue.[12] Within her response, Laurence declared that Lu had grossly misinterpreted both the original historical conditions under which high-risk/BW began and the current role of these programs within the higher-education landscape. Laurence argued emphatically that "anyone who knows the history of Open Admissions (its stormy beginnings with the student takeover of the City College Campus and the burning of buildings in 1969) and the work of Mina Shaughnessy knows the stress in an institution that initiated an educational policy five years earlier than planned. Guiding institutional change, as Mina Shaughnessy did for years at City College, required a nuanced appreciation of this cultural dynamic, and in the early phases of this then-controversial educational movement there was a rhetorical strategy enacted in the classroom and public forums to employ indirection and a language that enhanced notions of cultural exchange and reciprocity" (881). In light of this history, Laurence insisted that Lu's ideological stress on "conflict" and "struggle" was highly problematic: "To have employed a metaphor of 'conflict' or 'struggle' (then or now) rather than the language of understanding, caring, exchange, and reciprocity would have been counterproductive, irresponsible, and explosive. This was not a 'methodology' that emerged from a pedagogical community in the field of composition as it exists now in the relative calm of a second generation of composition specialists, but the strategy of an embattled faculty that understood linguistic and cultural exchange and still struggles with this powerful subtext" (882).[13] Laurence further asserted that Lu had ignored the ways in which responsible high-risk programs have always embraced "the dream of a common language" (882)—that is, a clear (and apolitical) standard for language and literacy use—rather than a linguistic approach stressing "political polarization" (882). This was especially the case at CUNY since "students . . . for the most part, [have been] seeking an education that would enable them to join the mainstream" (882). Laurence concluded, therefore, that high-risk/BW programs ought to continue to operate, but only in the apolitical manner that she advocated. These programs needed to be guided by "teachers and leaders of balance like Shaughnessy, McQuade, Bruffe, and Lyons who understand cultural change, and politics and the English Language. We need those who can help us find clarity of mind and common ground in our institutions and classrooms . . . rather than language and theory that construct educational institutions as sites of political polarization" (882).

We see Laurence arguing across these passages that the history and legacy of high-risk/BW activity were absolutely not "political," at least not in the ways that Lu defined politics. Instead, Laurence's view of history meant that "cultural exchange and reciprocity" were the only high-risk/BW politics that really mattered in the past and, hence, remained the only politics that should continue to matter in the present and future. Laurence further insisted that there had clearly been a standard "majority language"—a clear apolitical version of Standard English—traditionally associated with the best high-risk/BW programs that responsible scholars and teachers must both acknowledge and embrace. Accordingly, she concluded that only "teachers and leaders of balance" who possessed "clarity of mind" and a profound belief in the "dreams of a common language" (as opposed to "political polarization") could be entrusted to oversee the future of such high-risk/BW efforts—not ideologues like Lu or others who unnecessarily dwelled upon problematic political issues.

Laurence's comments echoed certain strains of the mainstream conservative argument outlined previously: namely, that the high-risk classroom was no place for politics, particularly racial politics; that its pedagogies and practices needed to be premised upon integration rather than purported separatism; and that its long-term future was rooted in balance and calm rather than conflict or struggle. Although not motivated by the same overt rejection of high-risk activity as the ideas of someone like Bloom, these comments nonetheless revealed a related longing for an a past time when standards were clear, unambiguous, and the "natural" focus of all language and literacy instruction.

Progressive-Leaning Disciplinary Critiques of High-Risk/BW

In clear contrast to the more linguistically conservative approach of someone like Laurence, David Bartholomae's "The Tidy House: Basic Writing in the American Curriculum" offered a more progressive strain of high-risk/ BW critique. This essay, a version of Bartholomae's famous chair's address at the 1992 Conference on Basic Writing in Maryland, was a strong catalyst for the BW mainstreaming debates of the early and mid-1990s (McNenny 1). It also continues to stand as one of the earliest and most influential articles of the time to suggest that 1960s-era high-risk/BW programs were outdated and in need of fundamental reconfiguration.

Bartholomae's basic argument in "The Tidy House" was that the politics of high-risk/BW activity needed to be updated in order to reflect contemporary thinking about issues of difference and diversity. Bartholomae began his argument by insisting that high-risk/BW courses had long reflected outdated notions of multiculturalism, specifically a "grand narrative of liberal sympathy and liberal reform" (8) rooted in the "tidy distinction between basic and mainstream. In this sense, basic writers are produced by our desires to be liberals—to enforce a commonness among our students by making the differences superficial, surface-level, and by designing a curriculum to both insure them and erase them in 14 weeks" (11). Bartholomae insisted that the best way to counter this problematic liberal legacy of high-risk/BW instruction was to reconceive the entire enterprise in terms of Pratt's contact zone. Pratt, he felt, "rejects the utopian notion of a classroom where everyone speaks the same language to the same ends; she imagines, rather, a classroom where difference is both the subject and the environment. She gives us a way of seeing existing programs as designed to hide or suppress 'contact' between cultural groups rather than to organize and highlight that contact" (14). For Bartholomae, Pratt's work offered a useful heuristic for scholars and teachers, while reimagining high-risk/BW philosophies, practices, and structures:

One could imagine the current proportion of students in basic writing courses and mainstream courses redistributed by an exam that looked for willingness to work, for a commitment to language and its uses, for an ability to produce a text that commands notice, or (in Pratt's terms) for the ability to produce opposition, parody, unseemly comparisons, to work outside the rhetoric of authenticity, to produce the autoethnographic text. Or we could imagine not tracking students at all. We could offer classes with a variety of supports for those who need them. These might be composition courses where the difference in students' writing becomes the subject of the course. The differences would be what the course investigates. We would have, then, a course in "multiculturalism" that worked with the various cultures represented in the practice of its students. (14)

As he made these arguments, Bartholomae did not demand that all existing high-risk/BW structures be immediately dismantled: "Would I advocate the elimination of courses titled 'basic writing' for all postsecondary curricula beginning next fall? No. I fear what would happen to the students who are protected, served in its name" (20). But he did assert that high-risk/BW programs should be rethought and retooled according to a new politics like that of the contact zone—and he felt that such work needed to begin as soon as possible.

We can see much potential for race consciousness within Bartholomae's proposed ideological, pedagogical, and institutional reformulations of high-risk/BW as a kind of contemporary contact zone. He was certainly concerned with developing programs to investigate the power relationships enacted by the "dominant other," with contrasts between "elite and vernacular cultural forms," with investigation of "rhetorics of authenticity," and with "cultural mediation." He also seemed quite committed to rethinking placement and program decisions such that "difference" could be interrogated more thoroughly.

Despite these assertions, however, Bartholomae made it clear that he did not see traditional 1960s-style race consciousness as a remedy to this problematic grand narrative of liberal reform. He stressed this point in particular during his analysis of the work of critical race theorist Patricia Williams, work that he also saw as a useful model for the stance toward race that he felt high-risk/BW discussions ought to consider adopting. He praised Williams for eschewing "Black power" politics (10) and other related political orientations premised upon the idea that "a writer must remember, discover her blackness, to let race define who, as a writer, she essentially is" (10). Instead, he said, Williams rightfully asserted that "subject positions [are] produced, not essential, and . . . strategic. Williams' book thinks through what it is like to write, think, live, and practice law as a Black woman—that is, to occupy positions that are White and Black, male and female all at once" (10). Bartholomae further argued that high-risk/BW should be willing to reconceive itself and its work "in Patricia Williams' terms" (15) by viewing issues of race and racism "as rhetorical gestures, useful for certain purposes but also breaking down at the very moment we need them" (15). Toward this end, he even highlighted a passage from Williams's *The Alchemy of Race and Rights* in which she questions "the supposed purity of gender, race, voice, boundary; [this questioning] allows us to acknowledge the utility of such categorizations for certain purposes and the necessity of their breakdown on other occasions. It complicates definitions in its shift, in its expansion and contraction according to circumstance, in its room for the possibility of creatively mated taxonomies and their wildly unpredictable offspring" (Williams, qtd. in Bartholomae 10–11). By highlighting this passage, Bartholomae implied that Williams's questioning of long-standing identity categories should serve as an inspiration for high-risk/BW scholars to reconfigure their programs: rather than allowing their programs to rely on simplistic categories of "white" or "black," "male" or "female"; high-risk/BW reformers should instead require their programs to conceptualize identity within their program as malleable, socially constructed, and open to multiple negotiations of "creatively mated taxonomies and their wildly unpredictable offspring."

Bartholomae used his particular reading of Williams's work to advocate that high-risk/BW programs abandon 1960s-era notions of racial politics in favor of more updated contact-zone-oriented approaches to instruction. However, in the course of making this argument, Bartholomae ignored some of the key ways in which labels like "black" and "woman" could and did matter profoundly to Williams and her central arguments throughout *Alchemy*. Williams stressed, for instance, a number of her own explicitly racialized feelings of anger and frustration when she was not allowed to enter a Benetton store by a young white clerk because she was a black woman. She wrote, "I was enraged. At that moment I literally wanted to break all the windows of the store and take lots of sweaters for my mother. In the flicker of [the young white clerk's] judgmental gray eyes, that saleschild had transformed my brightly sentimental, joy-to-the-world, pre-Christmas spree to a shambles"

(45). She also noted that, while she wrote about this incident for various legal journals, she became even more troubled by the color-blind ways in which her story was being read and retold by her editors: "Two days after [my writing] was sent to press, I received copies of the final page proofs. All reference to my race had been eliminated because it was against 'editorial policy' to permit descriptions of physiognomy. 'I realize,' wrote one editor, 'that this was a very personal experience, but any reader will know what you must have looked like when standing at that window.' In a telephone conversation to them, I ranted wildly about the significance of such an omission. 'It's irrelevant,' another editor explained in a voice gummy with soothing and patience; 'It's nice and poetic,' but it doesn't 'advance the discussion of any principle. . . . This is a law review after all'" (47–48).[14] In these passages, it is clear that Williams did feel that categories such as "black" and "woman" had profound physical, emotional, intellectual, and professional effects: race was "rhetorical" on one level, but it was very "real" on many others. In his reading, however, Bartholomae chose not to recognize this crucial dimension of Williams's work or to dwell upon its potential importance for his own thinking about high-risk/BW. He did not acknowledge that, just as Williams herself had problems with the real-life consequences of racism, so too might high-risk/BW programs and the minority students whom they served. Nor did Bartholomae acknowledge that, just as Williams found some value in thinking about race in strategically essentialist 1960s-era terms, so too might high-risk/BW programs and their students.

Within the work of Bartholomae, then, we see a second and ostensibly more progressive strain of disciplinary color blindness taking shape. His work assumed that reconfiguring existing high-risk/BW efforts in accord with progressive politics such as Pratt's contact zone or Williams's view of race and racism would make these programs more egalitarian. But in so doing, he ignored the power that race-based 1960s-style identity politics had long afforded programs for establishing official institutional spaces for minority support activity. He also ignored the possible benefits of continuing to use explicit 1960s-style discussions of race and racism within these programs as tools with which to critique mainstream white standards, especially those related to white mainstream Standard English. In these ways, Bartholomae's work threatened to dismantle institutionally sanctioned spaces of race-conscious activity in the name of saving them.

The Disciplinary Dynamics of Redivergence

Scholarly discussions concerning high-risk/BW issues during late-1980s and early-1990s debates about the culture wars indicate an important disciplinary movement away from race consciousness and toward a kind of color blindness. While the examples offered by Lu and Jones certainly demonstrate that important strains of race-conscious disciplinary discussion of high-risk/BW were circulating during this time period, examples from Laurence and Bartholomae demonstrate that such race consciousness was frequently rejected by other influential theorists, both conservative leaning and progressive leaning, who agreed that high-risk/BW programs rooted in 1960s-era thinking about issues of race and racism needed to be replaced. From this perspective, to defend 1960s-era high-risk programs was to be either wrongheaded or outdated, while to replace them was a sign of willingness to embrace needed change.

Discussions of the time also demonstrate that, while those espousing race consciousness in high-risk/BW maintained clear interest in preserving programs, their interests diverged simultaneously from both conservative-leaning scholars and more progressive-leaning scholars. Such divergence thereby helped to create a disciplinary context in which two groups both asserted independently that high-risk/BW programs needed to be dismantled—a trend observed and critiqued by Karen Greenberg in 1993. Greenberg argued that, for many in high-risk/BW at the time, it seemed as though "reactionary political academics and budget-minded administrators and legislators" were "join[ing] forces with composition 'stars' like David Bartholomae to attack basic writing programs" ("Politics" 66). In the face of such attacks, Greenberg worried, high-risk programs might well be "doomed" (66), while students themselves might be left to "sink or swim" (66).

The Reconfiguration of EOP Rhetoric

In chapter 4, I noted that the late 1970s and early 1980s saw many predominantly white institutions across the United States emphasizing the need to recruit high-achieving minority students—that is, those with test scores and educational backgrounds more akin to those of their white mainstream peers

—rather than high-risk minority students. By the mid-1980s, UIUC was following suit. In 1984, it established a program called the President's Award Program (PAP) to attract 300 new minority students per year (again mostly African American and Latino) who possessed strong scholastic profiles—"students who were valedictorians or who had a certain class rank or ACT score [of 24 or higher]" (Dean A, interview, 15 April 2002). PAP was designed to increase an overall UIUC minority enrollment that had dropped to about 220 or so new freshman students per year by 1984 (Dean of OMSA 14). And in fact, it was successful in doing so: by 1988, the number of black and Latino freshman had risen to 614—an increase of nearly 75 percent over 1984 levels (vice-chancellor for student affairs 1).

PAP was notably race conscious in many of its philosophies and practices, a point that the dean of the Office of Minority Student Affairs (OMSA) emphasized in a 2002 interview:[15] "Some people thought [throughout the 1980s and 1990s] that, 'Oh, we have these bright students. All we need to do is give them the money, and they'll get by on their own and blend in.' But there were still institutional issues in America where not everyone just blends in to this wonderful melting pot. Now some students did ['blend in'], but people deal with this climate in different ways" (27 March 2002). The dean of OMSA insisted, in other words, that because even the well-prepared minority students recruited by PAP faced issues of racism on a campus like UIUC, they were strongly encouraged to take advantage of various race-conscious support mechanisms on campus.

One of these race-conscious mechanisms was EOP Rhetoric. With its smaller class sizes, sense of student community, and potential at some points in its history for race-conscious attention, EOP Rhetoric was perceived by OMSA as a program that could help its students to "deal with this climate" of UIUC successfully. And indeed, the director of EOP Rhetoric at this time ("Director E") shared this view, espousing race consciousness frequently from the time that he was hired in 1984 as the first full-time director of EOP Rhetoric until the time that he left in 1997.[16] Director E's 1991 description of EOP Rhetoric, for instance, stressed that the program tried to be race conscious in terms of its hiring and teaching efforts, striving specifically to "hire those who have experience with minority students" ("To the EOP Rhetoric Review Committees" 1) and who possess "sensitivity to and awareness of issues involving minority students on this campus, including an appreciation of the cultural diversity mission of the [EOP Rhetoric] program" (1). His description also insisted that experience with and awareness of minority students' needs on the part of teachers should be translated into pedagogy within the program: successful teaching candidates typically possessed an "orientation toward writing problems on the part of minority students which allows the candidate to understand EOP students' problems as language use problems not as social or mental problems" (1). Director E asserted, finally, that the English Department must diversify its own graduate student population so that EOP Rhetoric might have a more racially and culturally diverse pool of competent graduate instructors from which to draw: "The English Department has only 3 African American grad students: 2 are on fellowships and one is teaching literature. The only U.S. Hispanic grad student teaches in EOP Rhet but she is returning to Puerto Rico in the summer" (1–2). In the eyes of Director E, at least, the EOP Rhetoric program of the late 1980s and early 1990s clearly possessed some important race-conscious dimensions.

This type of race-conscious thinking about PAP and EOP Rhetoric was being challenged directly, however, by at least two strains of institutional discussion circulating within this culture wars context that paralleled those circulating nationally and at the level of the discipline. The first and ostensibly more conservative strain of such administrative thought stressed that EOP Rhetoric was both too expensive and too politically outdated with respect to its views of student ability and standards to be preserved. Meanwhile, the second and ostensibly more progressive strain of this thought stressed that EOP Rhetoric needed to be brought into better alignment with progressive thinking about multicultural writing instruction. Despite their different motivations, both strains ended up recommending that the existing EOP Rhetoric program be dismantled and rebuilt as a new color-blind remedial program.

Conservative-Leaning Administrative Critiques

Arguments expressing concern about the combined expense and outdated political orientation of EOP Rhetoric appeared across a number of administrative documents generated during the mid- and late 1980s, especially as the overall size of the EOP Rhetoric program had grown by 30 percent to almost ninety sections per year by the end of the 1980s (dean of LAS, letter to VCAA, 18 May 1987, 1). Administrators routinely mentioned that, by the end of the decade, the cost per student in EOP Rhetoric was "somewhat over 3 times the cost of the per student costs in other rhetoric courses" (1). This increased size and cost led administrators to wonder about where funding for the EOP Rhetoric program might be found. It also led them to wonder whether such funding was even prudent, given the supposedly "better" EOP Rhetoric student entering UIUC during the PAP era.

The first inkling of this combined argument about cost and student ability actually appeared in 1984: the dean of LAS at the time wrote to the VCAA to argue that "the long term future of the EOP Rhetoric program" and its funding status should be discussed in light of the fact "the quality of the students in the program is increasing. Indeed, the average ACT scores are well above the national average" (11 June 1984, 2). This argument was articulated even more forcefully, however, by the associate dean of LAS in 1990. After having conducted her own fiscal analysis suggesting that the actual cost of EOP Rhetoric might be "almost five times the cost in regular rhetoric sections" (letter to associate vice-chancellor, 16 March 1990, 1), she requested that the VCAA's office provide about $96,000 in additional recurring campus-level funds for the EOP Rhetoric enterprise—a new budget totaling nearly $200,000 per year (6). However, in another letter, from 1989, this associate dean had expressed serious concern about this request to the English Department head at the time ("Head C"). When asking for these funds, she admitted, "I find myself in the position of needing to be able to answer questions about why the placement policy [for EOP Rhetoric] exists in its current form. For example, our admissions policies for the EOP program and certainly the profiles of EOP students have changed over the last fifteen years, while the placement policies have not. Would it be appropriate to review rhetoric placement policy now as we discuss the magnitude of EOP Rhetoric underfunding?" (22 September 1989, 1).

Implicit across these arguments, first from the dean of LAS in 1984 and then from the associate dean of LAS in 1989–90, was the idea that "better" minority students did not require the sort of expensive EOP Rhetoric support that they were currently receiving: students' scores on standardized measures of language and literacy—for example, ACT English scores—were higher than those of previous EOP students, such that these students did not require extensive extra support. So even while administrators such as the dean of OMSA and Director E were supporting the race-conscious dimensions of the program, other key mainstream administrators remained adamant that EOP Rhetoric was both increasingly expensive and unnecessary given the changing nature of the minority population at UIUC.

Progressive-Leaning Administrative Critiques

The second common strain of discussion regarding EOP Rhetoric circulating at this time emerged most fully in the wake of initial arguments about cost and importance outlined above—or, more precisely, in the wake of the particular response to these complaints by the VCAA of this time period. In 1990, this VCAA actually agreed to provide $37,000 in additional recurring funds for EOP Rhetoric, roughly a third of what the associate dean of LAS had requested, for a new permanent EOP Rhetoric budget of about $135,000 (letter to dean of LAS, 20 June 1990, 1). But the VCAA made one very significant demand in doing so: namely, that the EOP Rhetoric program undergo a detailed series of internal and external reviews designed to determine which aspects of EOP Rhetoric were ultimately necessary, given its overall cost. In articulating this demand, the VCAA insisted that "a thorough evaluation of the program and its several aspects is needed to ascertain what its most important ingredients are and which students need what ingredients. I believe that we must look to cost containment measures. I simply do not have $96,000 to spend on this program, nor do I expect to have it in the foreseeable future" (1). This VCAA further defined "cost-containment measures" as follows: "1) Hold 1990–1991 enrollment in EOP Rhetoric by non-EOP students to no more than 1988–1989 levels; 2) Increase average section size to 16; 3) Reduce the number of students enrolling in the two semester sequence" (1).[17] And finally, the VCAA concluded his comments with a rather ominous note for EOP Rhetoric: "During the coming year we [must] evaluate the program and the effectiveness of its components and . . . look at other ways to support the needs of EOP students. I want to be sure that we do what is needed to help these students, but that we do so as cost-effectively as possible" (1).

The demand from the VCAA for a full-scale review of the EOP Rhetoric program actually generated three related program reviews during 1990 and 1991: an "external" evaluation conducted by two outside composition reviewers; an "internal" evaluation conducted by Illinois faculty outside the English Department; and an assessment and analysis by members of the

English Department, the EOP Rhetoric program (including Director E), and members of UIUC's newly emerging graduate composition program, the Center for Writing Studies. Collectively, these reviews concluded that EOP Rhetoric needed to be reconfigured in keeping with a new and purportedly more progressive vision of program politics that reflected a second and more progressive-leaning strain of program critique.

Overall, these three reviews were quite positive regarding many aspects of the EOP Rhetoric program. The internal review noted, for instance, what it called "the positive educational contributions of the program and the dedication and commitment of its director [Director E] and staff that made these achievements possible" ("Report of Internal Review Committee" 1). It also insisted that "the EOP Rhetoric Program is now functioning well. It is very good. . . . It could well become a model of its kind in the nation" (6). The external review concurred, noting both that "our general reaction is that the EOP Rhetoric Program is serving students and the University well" ("External Review" 1) and that "we are impressed by the quality of students in the Program. Our conversations with them as well as their papers reveal interesting people capable of and committed to pursuing undergraduate degrees. Their retention records and their grades in subsequent writing courses confirm this impression. . . . The students we talked to were eager to succeed and seemed likely to make it" (2). And finally, the English Department found the program to be, at its core, both "effective and well-run" ("Departmental Response" 1).

Furthermore, all three of these reviews were openly critical of the economic motivations prompting the actual review process, each going so far as to insist that the EOP Rhetoric program must be retained in some form or another as a minority support mechanism in spite of its cost. The internal review argued, for instance, that "the EOP Rhetoric program is a valuable and indispensable part of the University's efforts to serve its minority students (and others with special needs) effectively and well. The program should be supported financially at an adequate level with recurring funds" ("Report of Internal Review Committee" 5). The external review elaborated on this sentiment:

> We recognize the issue of cost. Small classes with effective tutorial components are relatively expensive, and the university does not wish to spend resources needlessly. At the same time, the University has committed itself

to minority student recruitment and can ill afford to admit these students, take their tuition money for a year, and allow them to flunk out. Some people have the impression that this review of the EOP Rhetoric program signals a decreasing commitment to minority students: "Minority Admissions are fine unless they cost the University too much." We reject this cynicism. The students themselves are proof that spending some monies on specialized writing instruction during the first year repays itself many times over in higher retention rates, in creating greater diversity in the student population (which is beneficial to all students), and in ensuring productive careers for a generation of the state's citizens. ("External Review" 2)

Finally, the English Department review argued that, despite its cost, EOP Rhetoric should remain part of larger efforts to "coordinate the various offices dealing with minority students" ("Departmental Response" 5).

But even as each of these reviews heaped seemingly race-conscious praise on the program, all three nonetheless concluded that EOP Rhetoric needed to be dismantled and reconfigured in keeping with more contemporary and progressive disciplinary thinking about issues of race and culture as they shaped writing instruction. Each argued that the best way to enact EOP Rhetoric reform was to revise its placement mechanism fundamentally such that the program was opened to white mainstream students on a more regular basis. Such program "updating" was thought to create a kind of multicultural contact zone between low-scoring minority students and low-scoring whites.

The internal review argued for this updating by insisting that EOP Rhetoric needed to rid itself of programmatic "stigma" attached to issues of race and racism: "By linking admission primarily to race, the University is—unwittingly—stigmatizing a group of students whose skills may actually be quite adequate" ("Report of Internal Review Committee" 5). It further contended that, through this race-based placement mechanism, "the University is also failing to recognize the needs of those non-minority students whose writing skills, for whatever reason, have not been nurtured in the high school" (5). In something of a contrast, the external review initially rejected the notion of racial "stigma," insisting that students whom it interviewed during the review process "were not particularly worried about any 'social stigma' attached to the course, certainly not in the same way that some faculty members seemed to worry about 'segregating' these students. In fact, these minority students seemed grateful for the chance to be in a class where they were a majority" ("External Review" 2). Nonetheless, the external review agreed that the placement mechanism for the program ought to be changed, asserting that "we see no *instructional* advantage to groupings based on non-academic criteria (though we recognize political reasons for keeping separate courses for minority and non-minority students)" (3) and that "placement procedures [should] be revised so that students who need a semester of basic writing instruction, whether minority students or not, gain access to this instruction" (4). Finally, the English Department review reaffirmed this notion of "stigma" originally raised by the internal reviewers, insisting that "although EOP Rhetoric is regarded very favorably by students in the program, we believe that it is important to do everything possible to decrease the perception of isolation and difference on the part of EOP students and in the eyes of the university community. . . . The goal of reducing the stigma of EOP Rhetoric should . . . be aided by opening the basic writing program to non-minority students, a practice followed by some of our peer institutions" ("Departmental Response" 2). In these ways, all three reviews ultimately recommended that the race-based placement mechanism within the program be abandoned such that the program no longer performs an official minority support function. Instead, they argued, it should revert to a more typical view of color-blind standards—those supported by test scores and placement mechanisms only. Any bias inherent in these standards would presumably be eliminated once this stigma was removed.

These three reviews clearly demonstrate that the second strain of color blindness common within the culture wars context was also being manifest within the EOP Rhetoric program. Race-conscious proponents of EOP Rhetoric were already faced with mainstream administrative complaints about cost and a "better" student body; now they were also faced with the assertions of three separate committees that the program should be updated and rendered more "contemporary" in keeping with mainstream racial thinking. Each committee insisted directly that the current program was far too "separate" and too "isolated" in the ways that it conceptualized issues of race and racism; each also argued that the 1960s-style race consciousness upon which the program had long been based was outdated, leading to problematic instructional "stigma" and "isolation." In this important sense, the double-sided pressure that minority support efforts in general seemed to be facing during this period of the culture wars was also being confronted by the EOP Rhetoric program of the late 1980s and early 1990s. And this dou-

bled pressure directly threatened the operation of a program that had func-
tioned at UIUC for nearly a quarter of a century.

The Reconfiguration of EOP Rhetoric and the Birth
of the "Academic Writing Program"

In the wake of these numerous administrative complaints and subsequent
reviews, the English Department decided to alter dramatically both the placement mechanism and the institutional structure of EOP Rhetoric even as it
maintained its new program budget of $135,000 per year ("Departmental
Response" 1). The EOP Rhetoric program was renamed the Academic Writing Program (AWP) and reconstituted with two separate no-credit tracks: a
full-year course sequence with tutorial (i.e., Rhetoric 101 and 102 with the
no-credit tutorial course Rhetoric 103) and a full-year course sequence without tutorial (i.e., Rhetoric 103 and 104). Placement within this new program
was determined only by placement score, which combined ACT English
score (range 1–36) and placement exam score (range 1–9). All students scoring 24 and below on this mechanism would be placed into the new AWP
Rhetoric 101/102 sequence with tutorial; students scoring either 25 or 26
would be placed in AWP Rhetoric 103/104 without tutorial; and students
scoring 27 or higher would be placed in some level of "regular" rhetoric (i.e.,
105, 108) or granted an exemption from the course sequence entirely. AWP
would, in this way, be able to serve about 280 students per year with tutorials and about 244 more per year without tutorials ("Working Report" 1).
This two-tiered system was also thought to create a kind of contact zone
between and among poor writers: indeed, the English Department review
insisted directly that "by eliminating the tutorial sequence for students less
at risk, the program would, without any increase in funding, free up additional places for non-minority students in need of special assistance" (3).[18]

Herein lies an important irony. By changing the institutional structure
and function of the program in these two ways—both purportedly "updating" the program in accord with contemporary multicultural thinking—the
new AWP program actually ended up decreasing its material support for
minority students on the campus. Under the old EOP Rhetoric regime, placement was reserved for minority students; furthermore, all minority students
in the program were guaranteed tutorials as part of the EOP Rhetoric expe-

rience. For some students, this arrangement provided one semester of EOP Rhet 105 with a guaranteed tutorial, while for others it meant two semesters of EOP Rhet 104 and 105 with a tutorial. In either case, the tutorial was part of the larger EOP Rhetoric package and therefore guaranteed to all minority students who wanted it. Under the new AWP program, placement was conducted on the basis of ACT/placement score only, and the total number of tutorials offered in the program was dramatically reduced. This decision meant both that fewer spots in AWP overall were offered to minority students and that still fewer one-on-one tutorial spots were guaranteed to minority students who did still enroll in this new program.

A brief analysis of enrollment numbers immediately before and after the change from EOP Rhetoric to AWP further reveals the extent of this diminished material support for minority students at UIUC. In the four years previous to the conversion of the EOP Rhetoric program to the AWP program, the population of minority students within EOP Rhetoric fluctuated anywhere between about 85 percent to about 90 percent. In contrast, after its transformation into AWP, the program served anywhere between 65 percent and 70 percent minority students (see table 5.1). In other words, the new AWP program began serving about 20 percent fewer minorities than it had in the past—and it did so despite the extra $37,000 provided yearly by the VCAA. Furthermore, if we look at the total number of slots in the program featuring one-on-one tutorial support, we see another decrease. Whereas the EOP Rhetoric program averaged about 445 tutorial slots (again, about 90 percent of which went to minority students) in the four years previous to this conversion, it averaged only 290 total tutorial slots (about 70 percent of which went to minority students) after this conversion to AWP (UIUC, "Underrepresented Groups" 1991–94). In other words, AWP both served far fewer minority students than EOP Rhetoric did and offered less guaranteed one-on-one tutorial support to the fewer minority students that it did still serve.

This newly constituted AWP program presented an interesting paradox. As all three reviews note, AWP was still regarded as a de facto "minority support" mechanism. Yet it actually served fewer total minority students each year, while simultaneously reducing the overall amount of tutorial support available to these fewer students. The real winners in the transformation of EOP Rhetoric into AWP were, therefore, not the minorities who were ostensibly still served under its auspices, but rather low-scoring whites, who now received more official UIUC support than at any point perhaps since

5.1 Racial/Ethnic Demographic Data for EOP Rhetoric/AWP Rhetoric, 1991–98

Fiscal Year	No. Black	No. Latino	No. American Indian/ Alaskan Native	No. Asian Pacific Islander	No. Minority		No. White		No. Unknown	Total
1991	304	119	1	21	445	(89.3%)	52	(10.4%)	1	498
1992	194	73	1	16	284	(89.3%)	31	(9.7%)	3	318
1993	279	150	2	28	459	(85.3%)	70	(13.1%)	9	538
1994	243	117	2	26	388	(90.4%)	35	(8.1%)	6	429
1995	148	87	4	50	289	(68.8%)	128	(30.4%)	3	420
1996	175	66	1	47	289	(66.4%)	140	(32.2%)	6	435
1997	N/A									
1998	141	56	5	39	241	(69.4%)	106	(30.5%)	182[a]	529
1999	N/A									
2000	148	60	4	49	261	(69.6%)	114	(30.4%)	54	429
2001	125	40	0	43	208	(73.5%)	75	(26.5%)	130	413
2002[b]	125	40	0	43	208	(73.5%)	75	(26.5%)	130	413
2003	114	46	0	41	201	(68.1%)	93	(31.9%)	165	459
2004	138	64	0	28	230	(79.3%)	60	(20.7%)	142	432
2005[c]	150	72	1	105	328	(82.5%)	70	(17.5%)	9	407

[a] In 1998, the program began relying on instructor reports to gather racial demographics, but apparently instructors in a number of sections refused to gather this data. Thus, the number of "unknown" entries radically increased at this time and remained comparably high until 2004. However, if we assume that the racial distributions in classes that were not reported were roughly the same as those that were reported, then rough overall percentages of minority versus white students can still be estimated.

[b] The repeated figures from 2001 and 2002 are taken verbatim from each year's report.

[c] The reason for the rather sharp increase in the overall number of minority students during 2004 and 2005 is unclear. Also unclear is the reason that UIUC stopped collecting this statistic in 2005.

Sources: University of Illinois, "Underrepresented Groups at the University of Illinois: Participation and Success," fall 1991–fall 1998, and *A Report on the Participation and Success of Underrepresented Students and Staff,* fall 2000–fall 2005

the abolition of the English Qualifying Exam in 1968 (see chapter 2). Still further, this transformation placed remaining minority support activity on the campus in a rather precarious financial position in the eyes of administrators such as Director E. In a 1998 interview, Director E expressed his concern that, as a result of this transformation, "the program [would become] no longer officially by statute, on the books, a safety net program for minority students," such that "we'll suffer the budget axe cuts the next time they come from Springfield" (1 November 1998). He further suggested that even while serving as part of the English Department review committee, he had traveled "all around trying to talk to all the people in the power structure whom I thought would be friendly to this argument, that they should be very careful to make sure that if the program is changed, or when the program is changed, that it should be kept a safety net program for minority students. They decided not to do that, I'm sorry to say. Many people thought that it would [remain a minority support program] de facto anyway." For Director E, then, the transformation of EOP Rhetoric into AWP marked a profound change in UIUC's commitment to race-conscious writing instruction—and clearly a change for the worse in his view.

Ultimately, the programmatic transformation from EOP Rhetoric to AWP might be read as in keeping (to reference the language of the internal review committee) with "the latest models in composition and writing studies"—at least if these latest models were mandating the creation of a kind of mainstreamed contact zone that abandoned explicit focus upon issues of race and racism in the vein of recommendations from someone like Bartholomae. From this point of view, instead of supposedly "stigmatizing" and "segregating" students into courses based on race, the new AWP program successfully "integrated" weak students from all racial and ethnic backgrounds into remedial courses in which they would be able to learn alongside each other. But this change to AWP can also be read as violating the latest models in composition being offered by Lu, Jones, and others who demanded explicitly the preservation and maintenance of 1960s-era spaces for race-conscious high-risk language and literacy instruction. This change effectively eliminated a long-standing program and diminished actual support in measurable ways, and it reified certain standards once again in the process.

I can certainly imagine some readers responding here that if AWP was actually little more than a "remedial" program, then high-scoring minority students should not have been held back by making them take classes that they did not need. I agree that high-scoring students should not have been forced to take "remedial" courses on the basis of their race. But I would also point out that this new view of AWP constituted a significant break with the past history of minority student support at UIUC—or at least portions of this past history—as embodied within EOP Rhetoric. In the eyes of its more race-conscious administrators, EOP Rhetoric had never been first and foremost a "remedial" program; rather, it had been a minority support program that served a range of students, both stronger and weaker with respect to language and literacy skills, to create a kind of race-conscious support community. AWP changed this perception at an institutional level, effectively dismantling an institutional space in which the possibility of such change was routinely debated and discussed in favor of furthering the cause of "remedial" education.

The Dynamics of Institutional Interest Redivergence

EOP Rhetoric's transformation into AWP within the culture wars era signified a crucial and rather permanent shift toward color-blind writing instruction at UIUC. Some administrators like the director of OMSA and Director E tried to maintain race consciousness within the program. However, they encountered fiscally conservative upper administrators espousing a kind of standards-oriented challenge to the continued value of an EOP Rhetoric program that they felt was aimed at the students of twenty years ago rather than the students of the present; at the same time, they also encountered theoretically progressive writing program administrators and others insisting that the 1960s-era racial politics of the program were both outdated and "stigmatizing" in ways that demanded their reconfiguration. In this sense, those desiring the long-term preservation of race consciousness within EOP Rhetoric faced strong opposition from right-leaning and left-leaning institutional forces, which eventually abolished EOP Rhetoric as an official minority support mechanism at UIUC.

The transformation from EOP Rhetoric to AWP thus illustrates crucial institutional dynamics of interest redivergence in action. Clearly, the interests of those espousing race-conscious activism diverged from the interests of others in power who stressed the need to reconfigure EOP Rhetoric in keeping with more "acceptable" educational, financial, and/or political orientations, whether rooted in cost-cutting measures or in the need to bring the program in line with more contemporary thinking. This redivergence helped to dismantle a program that had been operating on the campus for more than twenty-five years as an institutional space where race-conscious reform and resistance were, if not always achieved, at least routinely discussed and debated.

Culture Wars and Interest Redivergence

The culture wars climate of the late 1980s and early 1990s clearly posed significant challenges to those with an interest in theorizing, enacting, or institutionalizing race-conscious high-risk language and literacy instruction. While this era saw some continued articulation of important race-conscious arguments regarding multiculturalism in general and high-risk/BW activity in particular, it also saw both conservative-leaning and progressive-leaning scholars demanding that these 1960s-era programs be dismantled and replaced. And as the interests of race-conscious activists rediverged from those of the mainstream nationally, at the level of the discipline, and institutionally, profound changes to minority student support in mainstream four-year institutions occurred. In the wake of these changes, the value of 1960s-era programmatic activity was routinely questioned, programs themselves were dismantled, and the standards circulating within mainstream four-year spaces were ultimately preserved—all indicative of a new dark age for high-risk programs and their high-risk/BW counterparts.

Unfortunately, as will become clearer in the next and final chapter of this book, this prolonged dynamic of redivergence would prove to be the beginning of the end for much high-risk programmatic activity across the United States. Indeed, in the time period since the early 1990s, it has been increasingly difficult to sustain any sort of explicit high-risk activity or other race-conscious student support effort. In this sense, the late-1980s/early-1990s period of the culture wars initiated a direct challenge to high-risk/BW activity that has only grown increasingly intense over time.

The Late 1990s to the Present

THE END OF AN ERA?

FROM THE LATE 1990s through the present day, mainstream four-year colleges and universities in the United States have been forced to respond to a powerful pressure to pursue institutional "excellence." Greene and McAlexander characterize this pressure as prompting four-year institutions to begin "raising admissions standards, downsizing or eliminating remedial programs, and placing more emphasis upon research—all while paying close attention to . . . rankings in the media" (15).[1] They further assert that this pressure has created a contemporary context in which institutions are restratifying in ways that more clearly differentiate responsibilities between four-year and two-year institutions: "Postsecondary institutions are being differentiated into hierarchical categories according to, theoretically, the academic merit of the students. . . . The lower-ranking students are increasingly channeled to the less selective two-year institutions, which are also often attended by students for financial or family reasons" (14–15).

In turn, contemporary pressures toward excellence and institutional stratification have been exacerbated by growing contemporary anti–affirmative action sentiment during the last fifteen years or so. At the state level, the

1996 *Hopwood v. Texas* decision involving white law school applicants struck down the use of race-based affirmative action within the state of Texas; meanwhile, California's 1996 passage of Proposition 209 (an initiative initially spearheaded by University of California regent Ward Connerly and later replicated in other states) banned considerations of race, ethnicity, and sex in hiring by all public institutions, including state colleges and universities.[2] At the federal level, the Supreme Court decided *Grutter v. Bollinger,* a case concerning law school admissions at the University of Michigan, in 2003: while the court did uphold a limited notion of race-conscious admissions in *Grutter,* it did so by clearly privileging traditional "standards" in ways echoing *Bakke.*[3] In 2007, the court decided *Parents Involved in Community Schools v. Seattle School District No. 1,* a case involving race-conscious K–12 school-districting policies in Washington State. The court's decision in the case was decidedly color-blind, with the majority decision penned by Chief Justice Roberts declaring that the only real way to "stop discrimination on the basis of race is to stop discriminating on the basis of race" (40–41).

Still further, the present situation is being compounded by skyrocketing higher-education costs. The price of public four-year tuition has increased an average of 5.6 percent beyond the general rate of inflation for each of the last ten years, with tuition at four-year public institutions having risen on average 7.9 percent for in-state students and 6.0 percent for out-of-state students from 2009–10 to 2010–11 alone (College Board, "Trends in College Pricing" 1).[4] Institutional appropriations per full-time equivalent (FTE) from state and federal sources have simultaneously decreased, with figures from 2009–10 19 percent lower than 1999–2000 levels after being adjusted for inflation (3). In light of these trends, higher-education scholar Michael Polliakoff argues that "at many colleges and universities, these are times of crisis. Endowments have shrunk, and fundraising is significantly more difficult. Reductions in state funding for higher education have been massive. And a *Chronicle of Higher Education* survey of chief financial officers reveals that 62% believe the worst is yet to come" (1).

In the face of these pressures toward excellence, stratification, anti–affirmative action, and cost-cutting, the future of high-risk programs in four-year institutions seems to be in serious jeopardy. These programs are increasingly viewed as antithetical to contemporary definitions of excellence and therefore outside the purview of the four-year institution. They are increasingly perceived to reflect 1960s-style affirmative action mandates now assumed to be both outdated and unnecessary. And they are typically regarded as far too expensive to be supported during a time when institutions are looking to cut costs whenever and wherever possible. It is unsurprising, then, that higher-education scholars Lara Couturier and Alisa Cunningham worry that "college outreach/early intervention and preparatory programs that serve low-income [and underrepresented minority] students are frequently [being] targeted for elimination" (viii). Greene and McAlexander express a similar sentiment, noting that the high-risk movement that "sprang up so vigorously in the late 1960s and 1970s is coming to an end in many of these [four-year] institutions" (14).

One important example of the disappearance of high-risk programs on four-year campuses is CUNY, where all senior colleges were required in 1999 to abolish their previous Open Admissions policies. This decision was motivated in part by a mayoral task force report insisting that Open Admissions had failed miserably: "The City University of New York is adrift. An institution of critical importance to New York and the nation, potentially a model of excellence and educational opportunity to public universities throughout the world, CUNY currently is in a spiral of decline. . . . Its extensive remediation efforts proceed haphazardly, and there are no objective measures of which remediation efforts are or are not succeeding" (Schmidt et al. 5). In place of Open Admissions, CUNY has adopted a rather complicated two-step process for admission to its senior colleges. In the first step, all students applying to a four-year CUNY campus under normal (i.e., non-SEEK) admissions guidelines are "conditionally" admitted on the basis of "minimum criteria" for high school coursework and grades (Parker and Richardson 12).[5] In the second step, conditionally admitted students are reevaluated in terms of either their SAT or their state regents' exam scores, with only those meeting minimum scores admitted outright (12). Students not meeting second-step criteria are required to take either a series of noncredit "free skills immersion workshops" on a four-year campus or noncredit remedial courses on a CUNY community college campus before retaking and passing their entrance exams (12). In their 2003 study of the effects of the changes of this new admissions policy on the CUNY system, Tara L. Parker and Richard C. Richardson Jr. note that absolute percentages of African American, Latino, and white students admitted to the CUNY system as a whole had actually increased, although gains for African Americans (6.7 per-cent) and Latinos (12.9 percent) were far lower than those for whites (29.1 percent) (9). But Parker and Richardson also note that only 45.5 percent of African American applicants and 50.8 percent of Latino applicants were ad-mitted to a BA program in comparison with 69.9 percent of white applicants (7–8). In light of these changes, Parker and Richardson conclude that "African American and Latino students [have been] disproportionately affected in terms of preparation and participation" by this change in admissions policy (18), creating a "growing gap between the proportion of Whites and students of color in CUNY freshman cohorts . . . [that] suggests the need for con-tinuing vigilance in a post-remediation era" (19).

High-risk programs such as SSS have also been facing significant contem-porary challenges within four-year institutions. Admittedly, the most recent federal report on SSS program activity from 2010 is quite positive, high-lighting the beneficial effects of SSS on students' GPA, total credits earned, overall retention, overall degree completion, and transfer between two-year and four-year schools (Chaney 71). Furthermore, this positive assessment of SSS activity has been accompanied by a spike in SSS program growth since the late 1990s, with 90 new programs emerging during 1997–98 (Carey et al. 3) and nearly 150 more new programs emerging during 2001–2 (Zhang et al. 2). As a result, the total number of SSS programs has remained around 950 for the past decade (with the number of program renewals changing slightly from year to year), supported by a budget of just over $300 million per year as of FY 2009 (U.S.D.E., "Student" par. 2). Importantly, though, roughly two-thirds of the newest SSS programs introduced in 2001–2 emerged within two-year institutional contexts (Zhang et al. 2), creating a situation in which two-year institutions now account for just over 50 percent of all SSS initiatives (U.S.D.E., "TRIO" 2). This shift toward SSS programs in two-year contexts marks a significant change from 1992, when two-year in-stitutions accounted for about 40 percent of all SSS programs (Calahan and Muraskin 5-4), and 1975, when two-year institutions accounted for about 20 percent of SSS programs (6-3). Furthermore, this shift in SSS activity from four-year to two-year contexts has been accompanied by the continued ero-sion of need-based aid made available to those wishing to attend four-year institutions. Even though Pell Grant funding increased significantly in re-cent years (by 58 percent overall in 2008–9 alone [College Board, "Trends in

Student Aid" 22]), these grants cover only 34 percent of the total tuition costs at all public four-year institutions in 2010–11 (22)—a far cry from the mid-1970s, when they covered 99 percent of these costs (Cook and King 5).[6]

Clearly, then, the problems facing contexts such as CUNY and SSS are contributing to a larger U.S. trend in which four-year institutions are remaining majority-white, while two-year colleges are hosting disproportionately high numbers of underrepresented minority students: in 2008, black students composed 11 percent of the public four-year student body, but 14 percent of the public two-year student body, while figures for Latinos were 10 percent and 17 percent respectively (Aud et al. 117); in contrast, whites composed 67 percent of the four-year public student body and 59 percent of the two-year student body, while figures for Asian/Pacific Islanders were 7 percent and 7 percent respectively (117). Statistics like these prompt Couturier and Cunningham to remark that "students from traditionally underserved populations [remain] less likely to be enrolled in certain types of institutions, such as private, four-year, and selective institutions" (7) in ways that negatively affect their chances at BA attainment, postgraduation earnings, and other related measures.

The Dynamics of Continued Interest Divergence

Contemporary higher-education dynamics indicate that race-conscious high-risk instruction at four-year institutions is currently under serious threat: famous programs like those on CUNY's four-year campuses have been dismantled outright, programs such as SSS are increasingly being built and supported less in four-year and more in two-year institutional contexts, and the value of the need-based aid necessary to cover costs at four-year institutions is continuing to decrease. In the wake of these threats, underrepresented minorities are less and less likely to be found on four-year campuses than on two-year ones. In an important sense, the original vision of high-risk programs—that is, as race-conscious desegregation mechanisms for mainstream four-year campuses—is disappearing.

These contemporary dynamics further indicate that the interests of race-conscious activists and the mainstream regarding high-risk activity in four-year institutional contexts are perhaps more distant than at any time in the last four decades. While there certainly remains some contemporary interest among activists in preserving race-conscious high-risk instruction, this interest is increasingly at odds with mainstream desires to promote four-year institutional excellence and stratification. This contemporary climate is thereby prolonging the interest redivergence dynamics first introduced in the late 1980s and early 1990s. In turn, these prolonged dynamics of interest convergence suggest that the power of white mainstream racism to dictate the path of high-risk programs may be stronger now than it has ever been. As this mainstream pursues excellence and stratification ever more vigorously, it has less and less use for high-risk activity of any kind within the boundaries of the four-year institution. As a result, high-risk programs in the four-year context appear to be on the brink of extinction.

Contemporary Disciplinary Effects
of Prolonged Interest Divergence

At the level of the discipline, our contemporary climate has prompted the dismantling of a number of well-known sites of high-risk/BW instruction, including CUNY, the University of Minnesota, the University of Cincinnati, Cal State Fullerton, the University of Louisiana–Lafayette, and others.[7] But one particularly striking loss in terms of overall disciplinary impact is the Studio program at the University of South Carolina (USC), discussed by Rhonda Grego and Nancy Thompson in their recent book *Teaching/Writing in Third Spaces: The Studio Approach.* Grego and Thompson's "Studio" has been widely praised by many eminent figures within high-risk/BW as a disciplinary paradigm of sorts for what contemporary high-risk/BW mainstreaming efforts ought to look like. Unfortunately, however, even this widely respected program has proven unable to survive within our difficult contemporary climate.[8]

Grego and Thompson originally designed and implemented the Studio program at USC in the early 1990s as an alternative programmatic and institutional space in which high-risk students from all backgrounds could receive extra institutional support without being labeled as high-risk/BW. In terms of programmatic structure, the Studio program saw to it that high-risk/BW students were placed in "regular" sections of courses but supported by weekly small-group instruction (10–14). In terms of overall philosophy, the Studio encouraged students to respond to the demands being placed on them within the space of the university—that is, to think explicitly about not only particular assignments in particular courses but also where those demands came from, how best to respond to them, and how to gauge both the costs and the benefits of responding to them within their given institutional situation. These authors remark that the Studio was designed to provide "a space/place where [the] relations among students and teachers and institutions can be attended to, thus stimulating an external, metarhetorical analysis to illuminate the problems that student writers face and to provide a sense of possibility and potential empowerment" (23–24). Grego and Thompson also comment that while the Studio at USC was never officially defined as a minority support mechanism, it nonetheless served as a de facto support mechanism for many minority students on the campus. They highlight, for instance, the support that the Studio offered to African American students such as Carson, the first-year writer struggling to understand instructor expectations (104–8), and Lavinia, the engineering student negotiating the tricky world of scientific presentation and publication (134–40).

Despite its many virtues, the Studio program at USC survived only until 2001. In chronicling the program's demise, Grego and Thompson observe that

- The USC Writing Studio was abolished in 2001 as its initial grant expired and as institutional concerns about research excellence at USC grew (208);
- The administration of the Studio program at USC was folded into the Writing Center, an entity whose new director (an individual without composition training) rejected the Studio model and its goals (209–10);
- Author Rhonda Grego was denied tenure in 1995 despite having developed the program, securing funding for it, and coauthoring numerous articles about it (207–8).

The demise of the Studio program at USC constitutes a troubling story both for Grego and Thompson and for the USC campus: the care, the hard work, and the effort that went into creating this program were clearly dismissed. Given the disciplinary status of the Studio, however, this demise also constitutes a troubling story for the discipline of high-risk/BW more generally, illustrating vividly that even one of the most well-conceived and widely heralded mainstreaming programs of its kind was unable to stave off extinction in the midst of contemporary antiremedial and anti–affirmative action pressures. The Studio example therefore prompts those of us involved in theorizing and implementing these programs to confront a rather tough question: If even a widely praised program like Grego and Thompson's Studio has been dismantled, then what hope is there for the rest of our programs within our vexing contemporary climate?

Contemporary Institutional Effects of Prolonged Interest Divergence

In comparison with events at a place such as USC, the institutional effects of prolonged interest divergence at UIUC have been in some ways less dire. I say this because the AWP program that was born in the wake of the EOP Rhetoric program (see chapter 5) still exists on the UIUC campus. In fact, AWP has remained on UIUC's official list published each year of programs "that have a primary purpose to serve underrepresented students and that have a budget allocation from the institution for this purpose" (UIUC, *Report . . . 2006* B-1).[9] AWP has, therefore, continued to play at least some sort of role as a de facto minority support mechanism on the UIUC campus—no small feat within a larger national climate that is less and less amenable to such activity. It also served roughly 400 students in FY 2005 (the last year for which statistics are publicly available), approximately 325 of whom were African American, Hispanic, Native American, or Asian/Pacific Islander (B-1).[10]

Nonetheless, the operation of AWP has coincided with a more general dynamic of continued divergence on the UIUC campus operating during the last fifteen years or so. This is especially evident in what appears to be a freeze in overall minority student enrollment rates at UIUC since 1994. Table 6.1 shows that, during the ten years before the EOP Rhetoric program was reconstituted, African American enrollment at UIUC had increased roughly 3 percent, Latino enrollment had increased 3.5 percent, Asian/Pacific Islander enrollment had increased 7.1 percent, and Native American enrollment remained quite small at .2 percent.

In contrast, table 6.2 shows that in the more than fifteen years following the transformation of EOP Rhetoric into AWP Rhetoric, the African American population at Illinois has actually shown a slight decrease of .4 percent, the Latino population has increased only 1.3 percent, the Asian/Pacific Is-

6.1 UIUC Undergraduate Enrollment Percentages by Race/Ethnicity, FY 1985–94

Race/Ethnicity	1985	1986	1987	1988	1989	1990	1991	1992	1993	1994
American Indian/Alaskan Native	.2	.2	.2	.2	.1	.2	.1	.1	.2	.2
Asian/Pacific Islander	5.5	6.0	6.9	7.8	8.5	9.7	10.5	11.3	11.9	12.6
Black	4.0	4.4	5.1	5.8	6.7	7.1	7	6.9	7.0	7.0
Hispanic	1.9	2.1	2.5	3.1	3.8	4.3	4.6	5.1	5.3	5.4
White	86.6	85.4	83.6	81.2	78.9	76.6	75.6	73.9	72.6	71.8
International	.8	.8	.9	1.0	1.1	1.2	1.4	1.6	1.7	1.7
Unknown	1.0	1.0	.8	1.0	.9	1.0	.8	1.1	1.3	1.4

Source: University of Illinois, *University of Illinois Student Data Book: Fall Term 1993 with a Ten-Year Overview;* University of Illinois, *Profile of Students, Faculty, and Staff by Racial/Ethnic Group, Gender, and Disability, Fall 2009*

6.2 UIUC Undergraduate Enrollment Percentages by Race/Ethnicity, FY 1995–2009

Race/Ethnicity	1995	1996	1997	1998	1999	2000	2001	2002	2003	2004	2005	2006	2007	2008	2009
American Indian/Alaskan Native	.2	.2	.2	.2	.2	.2	.2	.2	.2	.2	.3	.3	.3	.3	.3
Asian/Pacific Islander	12.6	12.6	12.7	13.0	12.9	13.2	12.9	12.7	12.4	12.7	12.6	12.3	12.8	13.3	13.2
Black	7.0	7.1	7.3	7.3	7.3	7.0	6.7	6.9	7.3	6.9	6.6	6.8	6.7	6.7	6.6
Hispanic	5.5	5.3	5.3	5.3	5.4	5.7	5.7	5.9	6.2	5.9	6.4	6.8	6.9	6.8	6.7
White	72.1	71.7	71.2	70.7	70.8	70.1	68.0	67.2	66.2	67.2	67.5	66.5	65.6	63.6	61.3
International	1.6	1.8	1.9	2.0	1.9	2.3	3.0	3.3	3.9	3.3	4.7	5.2	5.6	7.2	9.0
Unknown	1.0	.8	1.4	1.4	1.5	1.4	1.4	3.8	3.7	3.8	2.0	2.2	2.1	2.2	2.8

Source: Compiled from University of Illinois, *Profile of Students, Faculty, and Staff by Racial/Ethnic Group, Gender, and Disability, Fall 2009*

lander population has increased only .6 percent, and the Native American enrollment has increased .1 percent.[11] These numbers suggest that the transformation of EOP into AWP in 1994 marked a period of general satisfaction at UIUC with minority student enrollment rates—rates that were apparently viewed as "good enough" by this Research I institution dedicated to pursing traditional excellence.

Further proof of this apparent satisfaction with rates of underrepresented minority students' enrollment at UIUC appears in the institution's 2009 *Profile of Students, Faculty, and Staff by Racial/Ethnic Group, Gender, and Disability* report. Here UIUC includes a highlighted graph indicating that UIUC has the highest combined population of black and Hispanic students within all Big Ten universities—a figure of 13.5 percent as of fall 2009 (5). This report does not acknowledge, however, that this statistic is far less than the overall percentage of African American and Latino high school graduates in the state of Illinois, a figure of roughly 27 percent as of 2005 (Kurlaender and Felts 128–29). Nor does this report acknowledge that its minority student enrollment ranks UIUC in the bottom half of state flagship institutions across the United States for both African American and Latino student enrollment relative to overall state minority population, at least as of 2005 (127–28). In other words, while UIUC may well perceive its own recruitment rates as the state flagship in Illinois as sufficient, other figures suggest that these rates could be significantly better. Of course, it would be wrong for me to say that there is a clear causal relationship between the development of AWP and the UIUC's complacency regarding race. Nonetheless, I do see a correlation between the introduction of an official color-blind stance embodied in a program like AWP and the larger sense of color-blind complacency that has pervaded UIUC since the mid-1990s.

The Past, Present, and Future of High-Risk/BW

Our present situation forces us to confront an important question: what can we learn from the history of high-risk/BW programs that will help us to preserve and perhaps even expand the important work of these programs in the present and future? In the hope of answering this question, three trends regarding the nature of high-risk/BW history offered by this book seem especially important to highlight.

First, this book has demonstrated that white racism has been both a powerful and a persistent influence over high-risk/BW discussion and activity across every significant time period during the last forty years. During some of these time periods, the influence of this white racism has been expressed somewhat subtly. For instance, during the late-1960s and early-1970s racial crisis, activists were able to promote some degree of egalitarian change to higher education with the help of race-conscious disciplinary statements such as the SRTOL and institutional advances such as the development of the EOP Rhetoric writing lab; nonetheless, these activists watched as their changes were substantially limited by bidialecticalists and others appealing to white mainstream standards and Standard English. In contrast, during other periods of time, the influence of white racism has been expressed quite overtly. For example, during the mid-1970s, race-conscious activists saw mainstream concerns with literacy crisis prompt important disciplinary and institutional attacks on fledgling high-risk/BW programs in the name of restoring standards and getting "back to basics." These examples of the power of white racism (along with the others highlighted throughout the late 1970s/early 1980s, late 1980s/early 1990s, and the present) therefore call to mind one of Bell's most dire pronouncements about the dynamics of race-based institutional reform: the idea that "our actions [toward reform] are not likely to lead to transcendent change and, despite our best efforts, may be of more help to the system we despise than to the victims of that system we are trying to help" ("Racial" 308).

Second, and in something of a contrast to the first point above, this book has demonstrated that at least some measure of change has occurred within the context of high-risk/BW activity *despite* the power of white racism. Activists have certainly managed to discuss, develop, and implement at least some measure of change during periods such as the late 1960s/early 1970s and late 1970s/early 1980s. As a result, hundreds of high-risk/BW programs have served hundreds of thousands of non-white and nonmainstream students (even if limitations were ultimately placed on these programs). Still further, at least some of these programs have survived several periods of direct threat, including the mid-1970s, the late 1980s/early 1990s, and the present, in order to continue serving students. These important changes, all realized even in the face of powerful white racism, therefore bring to mind one of Bell's more hopeful assertions regarding our potential for imagining "policy positions and campaigns that are less likely to worsen conditions for those we are trying to help and more likely to remind those in power that there are imaginative, unabashed risk-takers who refuse to be trammeled upon. . . . Continued struggle can bring about unexpected benefits and gains that in themselves justify continued endeavor. The fight itself has meaning and should give us hope for the future" (308).

Finally, this book has demonstrated that lasting race-based change within high-risk/BW has been generated more effectively and with longer-lasting consequences within periods of interest convergence than within periods of divergence—largely because periods of convergence have been accompanied by white mainstream federal, state, and institutional support. Indeed, periods of convergence such as the late 1960s/early 1970s and late 1970s/early 1980s have been primarily responsible for creating enduring high-risk/BW change and reform, whereas periods of divergence such as the mid-1970s, the late 1980s/early 1990s, and the present have been primarily responsible for allowing these changes and reforms to erode. So while periods of convergence have not necessarily generated completely egalitarian change—at times, they have even seemed to be "of more help to the system we despise than to the victims of that system we [were] trying to help" (308)—they have nonetheless served as what Bell describes as an important "gateway to obtaining a more meaningful status" (308) for those oppressed by racism.

In turn, these three specific trends regarding the history of high-risk/BW—that is, the consistent power of white racism over time, the fact that some level of change has been achieved at times despite this white racism, and the fact that periods of interest convergence have been more amenable to change than interest divergence—prompt us to think carefully about the future. More specifically, they challenge us to acknowledge the power of white racism and its problematic effects on attempts to cultivate race-conscious high-risk/BW programs, even if this acknowledgment is difficult. They also challenge us to recognize that reform can be achieved even in the face of this racism. But perhaps most important, they challenge us to imagine new ways that we might actively promote interest convergence in the hopes of creating the longest-lasting and furthest-reaching change possible. Indeed, these trends demand that we demonstrate the many specific ways in which race-conscious high-risk/BW programs benefit not only underrepresented minority students but the mainstream predominantly white institutions that house them. Of course, attempting to promote interest convergence in this manner is not without risks: if it ends up simply perpetuating the idea that minority students are nothing more than commodities to be traded by mainstream institutions as these institutions pursue their goals, then this strategy could certainly end up being "more help to the system we despise than to the victims of that system we are trying to help." Nonetheless, if promoted carefully and critically, convergence offers us crucially important possibilities for promoting successful race-based change.

Creating Interest Convergence through "Story-Changing" Work

As a general framework through which to imagine promoting interest convergence in the present and future, I turn to the work of Linda Adler-Kassner, as presented within her recent book *The Activist WPA: Changing Stories about Writing and Writers*. In her book, Adler-Kassner offers us a powerful set of rhetorical strategies that she says are designed to "change the dominant story about the work of writing instruction" (2) in order to "have some voice in the frames that surround our work and the tropes that emanate from those frames regarding our classes and students" (37). These "story-changing" strategies, she says, can help us to "think about where we have the most influence and the loudest voices—at our local levels. We can think about who we can reach out to, learn from, and enlist as allies. And with them, we can develop a communication plan that helps all of us shape and communicate messages about writers and writing to audiences who might just attend to those messages—and change the stories that they tell" (163). Story-changing strategies offer us a useful framework through which to imagine emphasizing the specific value of race-conscious high-risk/BW instruction within our contemporary climate (what I will refer to as "RCBW" work during the rest of the chapter). They can help us both to alter old stories and to tell new stories demonstrating how and why RCBW programs remain relevant and important—even essential—to the success of both underrepresented minority students and mainstream institutions themselves in the present day. Toward this end, three possibilities for contemporary story-changing seem especially promising.[12]

*Story-Changing Possibility #1: We can stress that RCBW
has clear and unequivocally positive effects on the learning,
retention, and graduation of the students whom it serves.*

The first type of story-changing regarding RCBW that we might engage in
elucidates the specific value of RCBW spaces for the retention and graduation of underrepresented minority students within mainstream predominantly white institutions. The reason for performing this work is simple:
retention and graduation statistics are of supreme importance to contemporary administrators at mainstream institutions because they are seen as directly related both to enhancing institutional excellence and to cutting costs.
Education scholar Vincent Tinto writes, "Forced to cope with tight, if not
shrinking, budgets, institutions face mounting pressures to improve their
rates of student retention and graduation. In many cases, this pressure reflects the movement of states to include graduation rates in a system of institutional accountability. In other cases, this pressure reflects the impact of
widely publicized ranking systems that include graduation rates as one measure of 'quality.' In still other cases this pressure mirrors the reality that increased student retention is critical to the stability of institutional budgets"
(qtd. in P. R. Powell 667). Pegeen Reichert Powell adds that "the extent to
which retention efforts are funded by upper-level administrators is often
dependent on the extent to which such efforts will realize financial gains, in
the form of tuition dollars, state funding, or future graduates' support as
alumni" (667). If we can demonstrate how the work of RCBW is good both
for students of color and for the reputations and bottom lines of the mainstream institutions that house them, then we should go far toward promoting worthwhile convergence.

One important resource from which to draw as we try changing stories
about RCBW is contemporary higher-education research that investigates
what educational researchers Jennifer Engle and Colleen O'Brien call "High–
High" four-year colleges and universities in the United States—that is, institutions that achieve "higher than expected graduation rates and high graduation
rates relative to the national average" (2) for underrepresented minority students. As they outline the circumstances for success within high-high institutions, Engle and O'Brien note the contemporary presence of official
high-risk programs, including SSS, in each of them (24). They also note the
presence and importance of explicit race-conscious support mechanisms:

All of the High-Highs also have programs that target services to underrepresented minority students, such as separate programs for the largest minority groups on campus or an integrated Multicultural Student Services office. Such programs provide tutoring and mentoring by students and faculty of color as well as cultural programming. These programs provide a "home base" on campus for minority students, and the staff members in these programs often serve as "first responders" to students' needs by providing referral services to other offices and programs. Students participating in these programs said they feel more comfortable going to program staff than to academic advisors or faculty when problems arise with their coursework or financial aid. As a result, special programs and their staff serve an important role in helping at-risk students navigate and succeed in these large institutions. (24)

Finally, Engle and O'Brien highlight the operation of teaching-intensive, small-section, and carefully constructed first-year courses on these campuses, including:

- "Well-developed first-year programs, such as freshman orientation programs, freshman success courses, freshman interest groups, and first-year learning communities, in which student participation is mandatory or high" (3);
- "Efforts to improve instruction in 'gatekeeping' introductory courses, particularly in mathematics, such as reducing class sizes or keeping class sizes 'small' through supplemental instruction" (3); and
- "Early warning and advising systems in place to monitor student progress and to intervene when student performance is low" (4).

In these ways, Engle and O'Brien (alongside a number of other contemporary scholars) outline programs and practices that contribute to institutional success in terms of retention and graduation rates—programs and practices that those of us who work in effective and well-run RCBW programs already know a good deal about.[13] Our RCBW programs frequently offer a kind of "home base" for students as we act as "first responders" to their needs. Our programs frequently provide support in the form of "success courses" and well-conceived "'gatekeeping' introductory courses" that enhance students' chances of graduating. And our programs also frequently feature a kind of "early warning system" that can identify and address student difficulties before they become insurmountable. In these ways, our

RCBW programs are likely already doing the sorts of things that Engle and O'Brien identify as contributing to successful retention and graduation rates. We need to make sure that we engage in specific story-changing activities that demonstrate our work in each of these areas.

Fortunately, some contemporary scholarship specific to RCBW programs is already beginning to engage in exactly this story-changing work. Greg Glau, for instance, has recently examined enrollment, pass rates, and retention rates for various groups involved in the mainstreamed *"Stretch"* program at Arizona State University (ASU), focusing in particular upon these rates among "under-represented groups"—that is, "students who identify as African American, Asian American, Hispanic, or Native American" (37). Glau notes that students enrolled in the *Stretch* course "consistently pass" their later freshman composition courses "at a higher rate than do their counterparts who take traditional [freshman composition]" (38) and that "when ASU implemented *Stretch,* our retention rate immediately improved" (38). He also notes that disseminating knowledge about these successes has helped him and others concerned with the fate of high-risk/BW at ASU and elsewhere to counter last-minute administrative proposals to raise class sizes or otherwise compromise the kind of important work that *Stretch* performs (44).

Matthew Killian McCurrie has similarly analyzed the value of the Summer Bridge program at Columbia College in Chicago. McCurrie notes that over "half the Bridge students [at Columbia] are minorities and many come from a troubled, urban public school system" (36). He also stresses the ways in which Columbia's Summer Bridge program is explicitly race conscious in its attempts to "use students' experiences as opportunities for reading and writing in personally meaningful ways" (36), while at the same time fostering an "urban, multicultural environment" (36) that offers "a bridge between mostly urban, minority students and the more middle-class, white first-year students" (36). His preliminary work with retention among the Bridge population indicates its students have a freshman fall-to-spring retention rate that has improved from 61 percent in 2004 to 68 percent in 2008 (although he also notes that this rate still lags behind the 84 percent retention rate for regularly admitted students) (44). From this work, McCurrie concludes that "summer bridge programs can play an important role in improving the learning experiences of at-risk students when they give prospective students a challenging college experience that prepares them for real college-level work and thus builds confidence" (44).

These examples of contemporary scholarship suggest that we can success-fully highlight the ways in which RCBW programs promote the retention and graduation of underrepresented minority students. But they also sug-gest that we should continue to investigate other important questions re-lated to retention and graduation that are designed to change stories about RCBW in ways that continue to promote convergence:

- What exactly is the relationship between RCBW instruction and minority student retention and graduation trends? How can we most accurately describe and measure this relationship?
- How might we partner with other educational research groups, both outside the discipline (e.g., the Pell Institute) and inside the discipline (e.g., the Conference on Basic Writing, WPA, CCCC), as we conduct new research concerning RCBW and its effects on retention and graduation?[14]
- How can we use our new research to change stories in ways that promote interest convergence as fully as possible?

Story Changing Possibility #2: We can demonstrate that RCBW successfully supports and enhances the work of other programs and initiatives currently valued by the contemporary mainstream—especially ESL programs and academic support programs within athletics departments.

In the concluding chapter of their recent book *Basic Writing,* coauthors George Otte and Rebecca Mlynarczyk offer the following observation about the future of high-risk/BW: "Basic writing . . . may once again exist in a new century, but not as a unified project. Coherence, if it ever exists in academic research or its application, is a property of beginnings. Maturity breeds complexity" (163). Given my strong belief that RCBW programs must try to sustain themselves as race-conscious institutional spaces in one form or an-other, I am not quite ready to concede that RCBW *cannot* exist as a "unified project." But I do agree that there lies a degree of future "complexity" that necessitates careful thinking about how we might forge new kinds of part-nerships between RCBW and other programs that attempt to meet the lan-guage and literacy needs of students within mainstream institutions. We need to imagine what these partnerships might look like, and we need to imagine what kinds of story-changing activities we might enact with their help in order to promote convergence. Two potential partnerships seem especially promising in this regard.

The first of these partnerships involves contemporary English as a Second-Language (ESL) programs at mainstream institutions. ESL scholars note that many mainstream four-year institutions are currently facing strong pressure to recruit international students, both undergraduate and graduate, as part of their pursuit of excellence. ESL researcher Angela M. Dadak describes a strong recent push at her home institution of American University to become a "premiere global university" through a number of initiatives, including "increasing the presence of international students at the university" (94). ESL researchers Ryuko Kubota and Kimberly Abels similarly note that their home institution, the University of North Carolina (UNC)–Chapel Hill, has been increasingly expected to engage in "internationalization" by integrating "global issues and perspectives into graduate and professional experiences and the university's overall research enterprise" (77). These contemporary scholars also point out that new ESL programs are currently being created in response to these pressures. Dadak notes, for example, that American University has recently created new instructional relationships between the ESL program and the writing program, including a new WAC-style model for developing ESL teaching skills among faculty across departments and new one-on-one and small group tutoring arrangements (Dadak 101–2). Kubota and Abels similarly point out that UNC–Chapel Hill has recently developed a teachers of English to speakers of other languages (TESOL) graduate program and teaching component that strives to "create a cadre of ESL professionals on campus who [can] teach international students, lead others to develop appropriate, informed support programs, and provide an academic nexus for research and learning around English language learning issues" (Kubota and Abels 88).

Those of us working in RCBW programs should be thinking carefully about ways in which we might contribute to the creation and support of these new ESL programmatic formulations—especially since these programs are doing so much to promote convergence with mainstream interests. In this sense, I agree strongly with Steven Accardi and Bethany Davila that our RCBW programs have much to offer ESL concerning specific ways in which to "recast difference as an advantage that offers additional opportunities for learning and engagement" (57); to foster "an open and honest pedagogy that honors students' home languages, dialects and cultures" (58); to "teach multi-lingual and multidialectical students that they are, in fact, at an advantage for knowing more than one language as opposed to a disadvantage for not know-ing standard edited English" (58); and to "allow, and even encourage, the use of home languages and dialects" within writing activities and assignments (58). At the same time, I agree with Paul Kei Matsuda that our RCBW pro-grams also stand to gain a great deal from this type of partnership by helping us to recognize "the increasing diversity of students who come to basic writing classrooms . . . [such that] it is no longer possible to define basic writers in terms of abstract and ultimately unreliable criteria such as their writing place-ment test scores, language backgrounds or immigration status. Rather the general definition of basic writers needs to include all students who are subject to the disciplinary and pedagogical practices of basic writing" (84).

Possibilities for partnerships, as well as for effective story-changing activi-ties involving these partnerships, are many. In terms of teaching philosophy and practice, we can offer new ESL programs our RCBW expertise in fac-ulty and TA training, especially by sharing our strategies for dealing with difference. We can also begin codeveloping training programs and methods that integrate those who teach ESL with those who teach RCBW into groups of race- and culture-conscious teacher-scholars who seek to cultivate students' existing linguistic and literate abilities even as they strive to help them develop new ones. In terms of programmatic structure, we can consider new ways to merge (and perhaps even streamline) budgets, administrations, staffs, and locations in ways that capitalize on this expanded mainstream interest in globalization and internationalization, while at the same contributing our part to cutting unnecessary institutional costs. Obviously, the goal in advo-cating for careful and strategic programmatic merging is not to dismantle either ESL or RCBW as important autonomous institutional spaces. Rather, the goal is to strengthen both programs by stressing their shared sense of purpose and their centrality to the interests that mainstream institutions currently hold. In light of these possibilities, we should continue to grapple with the following kinds of questions:

- What kinds of relationships currently exist between ESL and RCBW programs?
- How might ESL and RCBW programs forge new and mutually beneficial relationships, both philosophically and programmatically?

- In what specific ways might ESL programs be enhanced by race-conscious and culture-conscious RCBW work (and vice versa)?
- How might we engage in story-changing work that highlights these partnerships and their specific impacts on mainstream institutions while promoting explicit convergence?

A second potentially worthwhile partner for RCBW story-changing work is the mainstream athletic program. Although many athletic programs are criticized for being concerned more with money or winning than with student learning, they remain tremendously powerful influences over the stories that many major institutions tell the general public and their own campus constituencies.[15] Athletics program researcher J. Douglas Toma reminds us that

> spectator sports are commonly portrayed as the front door to the university; they are what many people on the outside see and what eventually gets them inside. . . . They are the aspect of the university that is most visible to those outside of the academic community. . . . High-profile sports assume an often substantial role in the personal identity of individuals—particularly students—within the university community. They are also an essential part of the personal identity of a large group of external constituents who associate with the institution primarily—if not exclusively—through teams and games. The often intense institutional identification that results from engagement with spectator sports provides the university with a critical tool in garnering support. At schools with high-profile teams, administrators involved in external relations—admissions, advancement, alumni relations, community affairs, development, governmental relations—orchestrate through college sports the involvement in campus life of key constituents that is so important in advancing various institutional ends. (81)

Athletics programs play a profoundly important role in defining what a mainstream university is, both to outside constituencies and to those on campus. As a result, these programs are often perceived by the mainstream as immensely valuable.

Also valuable are the academic support programs that help student-athletes to preserve their academic eligibility to compete. Keith Carodine, Kevin F. Almond, and Katherine K. Gratto note that these academic support programs provide students with assistance related to study skills, time management, and students' college reading and writing activities (26). Jason Storch and Matthew Ohlson add that these programs frequently offer both "group and individual services" that "augment the academic performance of student athletes" through "a holistic approach that assists [their] total academic and personal development" (81–82). Finally, Dawn R. Person, Marcella Benson-Quaziena, and Ann Marie Rogers emphasize that many programs even offer what they describe as "a culturally responsive approach to working with student athletes" (59), advocating "a holistic perspective in serving students . . . [that] includes knowledge of cultural dynamics and knowledge of how ethnicity, race, and power influence human functioning" (59).[16]

I see much that RCBW programs can bring to the crucial work of athletic academic support programs. To begin, we can provide these programs with tutor training and support—especially when it comes to issues of writing, difference, and sentence-level "error." We can also develop new kinds of informal and formal programmatic partnerships with these programs designed to bridge the gap between the worlds of athletics and academics more directly. Two quick examples from my current institution, the University of Colorado (CU)–Boulder, illustrate this. For several years now, I have been able to work alongside several of my colleagues to provide tutor training and support for our CU-Boulder athletics program, focusing in particular on the ways in which its staff can recognize linguistic difference and work with student "error" effectively. Those with whom we have worked have generally been pleased with our training and support, highlighting its importance to the success of their program on a campus where the racial and cultural backgrounds of many (though certainly not all) athletes are quite different from their largely white, affluent peer group. Meanwhile, our own "directed self-placement" BW courses (which are not officially race conscious but nonetheless tend to attract instructors with interest in and experience with issues of linguistic diversity) have typically enrolled a high percentage of athletes, thereby allowing those who play together to work and study together in the same class as freshmen and/or sophomores. In this sense, we have been able to host unofficial "learning communities" for athletes at CU-Boulder. We have also been challenged to help student-athletes who clearly possess high levels of literacy outside of traditional academic contexts to draw on these literacies within our classrooms.

Even these brief personal examples suggest that there is strong potential for more productive partnering and story-changing between athletics departments and RCBW, especially within our sports-hungry U.S. mainstream culture. Developing and publicizing these partnerships will help us both to engage in story-changing and to promote new kinds of interest convergence —a point raised explicitly by sports program researcher Shaun R. Harper. Drawing directly on Bell's notion of interest convergence, Harper insists that race-conscious athletic support programs should attempt to create awareness among "many white college faculty, administrators, and coaches" concerning "the overall benefit to the institution (and in some instances, to themselves)" afforded by the success of athletes of color within predominantly white environments.[17] Harper's words ring true for RCBW as well: we need to focus on how we can build these sorts of partnerships and publicize the specific ways in which they can help both student athletes and their host institutions. Toward this end, we need to continue grappling with the following questions:

- What current relationships, whether formal or informal, currently exist between college athletics programs and RCBW programs?
- What new sorts of mutually beneficial relationships between these entities might we develop? How might these relationships operate, and why?
- How can we stress the value of the convergence promoted by these partnerships to as many mainstream constituencies as possible—especially given the profound importance of sports programs to mainstream institutional life—through new types of story-changing work?

Story-Changing Possibility #3: We can illustrate that RCBW programs are helping to revive race-conscious instructional programs on campuses where they have previously been abolished.

A third way in which we can promote meaningful story-changing work relevant to race-conscious RCBW is by analyzing the growing number of institutional sites where race-conscious instruction has been dismantled in the past but is now reappearing. One important site of this sort is CUNY: approximately five years after its official Open Admissions program was disbanded, the CUNY system initiated a program called the "Chancellor's Initiative on the Black Male in Education," or the Black Male Initiative (BMI) for short. The BMI describes its overall mission in decidedly race-conscious terms: "It is a well-established fact that institutions of higher education in the U.S. do not successfully recruit, retain and graduate . . . African-American and Caribbean men. Myriad statistics discuss the disproportionately low percentages and numbers of young black men within higher education, public higher education and even at CUNY. [Accordingly, over] the next four years, Chancellor Matthew Goldstein will oversee the development and implementation of a new University-wide program [i.e., the Black Male Initiative] aimed at implementing some of the most effective practices in this area" ("CUNY Black Male Initiative: Task Force Report" 1).[18] The BMI also characterizes its overall return to race consciousness in ways that directly stress convergence with mainstream CUNY goals and interests: "Increased access to higher education is critical for black males. Access to an education at a CUNY campus, for those in New York City, is an imperative. CUNY's mission, to provide equal access and opportunity for *all* its current and prospective students, is consistent with the philosophy that education is a means to advancement" (5). Especially noteworthy, however, is the fact that a number of the twenty-eight programs operating under the auspices of the BMI in 2010–11 identify writing and literacy programs within their overall efforts ("CUNY Black Male Initiative: Campus Involvement" n.p.). Three schools (Brooklyn College, College of Staten Island, and the CUNY law school) support specific writing programs, while at least three more (Baruch College, City College of New York, and Hunter College) mention race-conscious student-support programs that would appear to involve some sort of writing or literacy component.

In an important way, the BMI is helping to resuscitate race consciousness within a number of four-year CUNY campuses, even after Open Admissions had been abolished. Furthermore, RCBW-type writing instruction is contributing directly to this race-conscious resuscitation—and hence to promoting interest convergence at CUNY. This fact should prompt us both to conduct more research into the nature of these new RCBW-type programs at CUNY and to envision specific new story-changing activities that can allow us to make this important RCBW work more recognizable.

Another important example can be found at UIUC. Although I argue earlier in this chapter that UIUC has promoted a general climate of interest divergence during the last fifteen years or so, the past several years have seen resurgence of interest in issues of race and racism on campus through

UIUC's Ethnography of the University Initiative (EUI). The EUI is composed of "a group of faculty, staff, and students at the University of Illinois interested in research on universities as institutions" ("Ethnography of the University Initiative: From the Directors" par. 1). One of the EUI's most important recent projects has been "Race and the University," an effort to understand how and why race works as it does on mainstream campuses: "Whether spoken of in the context of 'diversity' or 'multiculturalism,' race is at the heart of the American university—its history, its contemporary challenge, and its futures. This project examines the ways in which the U.S. university and the American college experience are indelibly racialized. In particular, this project examines longstanding U.S. debates and discussions on affirmative action" ("Ethnography of the University: Cross-Campus Initiative" 4). In this way, the EUI initiative has been allowing race-conscious activist researchers to tie their interests to the goals and values of a prestigious university research program.

Especially noteworthy is the fact that this EUI initiative has afforded AWP instructors specific opportunities to remake their individual course sections into race-conscious "Race and the University" sections. For instance, one instructor for AWP Rhetoric 101 (the first semester of the current two-semester first-year composition sequence with tutorial) offered the following race-conscious writing course in fall 2008: "This course will engage issues of race, diversity and representation at the University of Illinois. We will think about what the university is, as well as about race and ethnicity as phenomena within the university's narratives. The readings in the course will interrogate U.S. race politics as a way to contextualize our understanding of the relationship between race and the U of Illinois" (Rhetoric 102 instructor 1). Course readings (e.g., Omi and Winant) and assignments (e.g., journal entries, interview assignments, course projects) also reflected the theme of race and racism.[19] Furthermore, one publicly available sample student research project demonstrates how a student from this actual course grappled with these issues as they impacted her and other students in the Bridge/Transition program at UIUC:[20] "The primary reason for this research paper is to explore the answers to three questions, which are; does the Bridge-Transition Program own up to what is was designed to accomplish, is the transition to college through Bridge-Transition easier academically speaking, does this program targets minority and if so why" (Rhetoric 102 student 1). This project offers analysis of interview data from program students and staff, virtually all of whom describe the program as an explicit (although not exclusive) minority support program on the UIUC campus. As one current student remarked when asked, "Do you think Bridge-Transition targets minorit[ies]?": "Yeah. That's what it's supposed to do offer equal opportunity to minorities. . . . Look at our university. . . . It's just giving us a chance" (9).

The EUI has thereby allowed for an important new return to race consciousness at UIUC. Furthermore, it has allowed teachers and students in the AWP program to engage in important new RCBW-type activity. While I do think that these contributions are likely to be longer lasting if they are formally coupled with other institutional programs and activities (e.g., OMSA or UIUC's Bridge/Transition program), this partnership between EUI and AWP nonetheless offers significant hope for more widespread institutional story-changing in the future that is aimed at promoting interest convergence. More research about this contemporary activity within the AWP program at UIUC certainly seems justified.

The examples of revitalized race consciousness at CUNY and at UIUC demonstrate that even contexts that have recently been rendered color-blind have the potential to change their stories. They also demonstrate that RCBW work can be fundamentally important to this process. Both contexts suggest, therefore, important possibilities for new story-changing work, especially if we keep the following questions in mind:

- What specific types of race-conscious work are being reintroduced within institutional contexts across the country that have recently abolished high-risk instruction? What kind of research related to these programs is being and/or should be conducted?
- How exactly have RCBW programs contributed to revitalized race consciousness within these institutions? What specific stories have these RCBW programs told, and what specific kinds of convergences have they promoted as a result?
- What do we stand to learn from these examples that might be applicable story-changing across other institutional contexts and situations?

Changing Stories at a National Level

By focusing upon story-changing at the disciplinary and institutional levels, I am not trying to dismiss the value of national story-changing work—work that is obviously critical to the preservation of high-risk/BW instruction in the long term. But I do see wisdom in Adler-Kassner's assertion that story-changing work needs to begin locally:

> Story-changing work is most effectively enacted at the local level. It's easy to become concerned about actions that have the potential to substantially affect WPA work at the national level. . . . But an individual WPA, or even a group of WPAs collaborating together, is but a fly on the windscreen of this approaching steamroller. On the other hand, working at the local level, we can develop assessment strategies within our own programs that reflect what *we* value, that ask questions and implement procedures that reflect what we know about best practices within our own courses and discipline. We can then use these assessments as bases for conversations beyond our programs—with our department chairs, our provosts, our university press officers, assessment coordinators, and presidents. Working bottom-up from our programs and top-down with our administrators, we can hope to provide alternative frames for these conversations that reflect our values and interests. (184)

Adler-Kassner reminds us here that changing stories in ways that will immediately promote national interest convergence is immensely difficult. In contrast, if we can begin changing local disciplinary and institutional stories, then we can likely also build momentum toward national changes in ways that can eventually produce meaningful results.

Convergence, Divergence, and the Lessons of History

The history of high-risk/BW discussions during the last forty years, particularly as revealed through the dynamics of interest convergence and divergence upon which I have focused throughout this book, demonstrates the difficulty of achieving egalitarian race-based change within writing instruction. In one important sense, this history has shown that well-intentioned efforts to promote race-based institutional change have been profoundly limited by the power of white mainstream racism at nearly every turn. Acknowledging this power is important, especially if we want to offer an honest assessment of what has or has not been accomplished by the high-risk/BW movement. But in another important sense, this history has highlighted important opportunities for race-based change by demonstrating that egalitarian improvement has occurred despite the power of white racism. It has further suggested that we do have the ability to promote contemporary interest convergence that, while certainly not perfect, can still help us to secure the present and future of RCBW activity.

By changing stories about the value of RCBW programs that will demonstrate their importance both to the students whom they serve and to the many mainstream stakeholders who also stand to benefit directly from their success, I believe that we can successfully begin to promote interest convergence. If we promote convergence uncritically, of course, we run the risk of merely offering the appearance of hope while actually reinforcing a racist status quo. However, if we promote this convergence critically and thoughtfully, we can cultivate an important means of imagining and implementing new forms of race-conscious change—and thereby of providing the sort of egalitarian educational reform toward which high-risk/BW has long worked within the mainstream four-year institutional environment.

NOTES

Chapter 1. The Development and Evolution of High-Risk Writing Instruction

1. For further discussion concerning the proliferation of high-risk programs, see Douglass; Lavin and Hyllegard.

2. I use the term "high-risk/BW" here and in chapters 3 through 6 in order to reflect the complex racialization of these programs since their inception. Whereas most high-risk programs were originally conceived as race-conscious programs, many were reconceived in partially or fully color-blind terms as they were transformed into BW programs during the mid-1970s (see chapter 3). The term "high-risk/BW" serves as my attempt to capture this complicated history, especially since the mid-1970s.

3. See, e.g., Horner and Lu; Mutnick; McNenny; Grego and Thompson, *Teaching/ Writing;* Greene and McAlexander; Otte and Mlynarczyk.

4. In *Talkin' and Testifyin',* Geneva Smitherman similarly argues that racialized appeals to Standard English in the context of high-risk/BW programs were intended to reify the idea that "speech that conforms to white, middle class standards of etiquette is better and more logical" than all other forms (211).

5. Writing in the early 1970s, James Sledd contended that those advocating for race-conscious change within high-risk/BW programs were not necessarily advocating against instruction in Standard English: "There is not . . . and there never has been, a serious proposal [among those advocating for race-based change] that standard English should not be taught at all, if for no other reason than because its teaching is inevitable. Most teachers of English speak it (or try to speak it); most books are written in it (somnigraphy being sadly typical); and since every child, if it is possible, should learn to read, schoolchildren will see and hear standard English in the schools as they also see and hear it on TV. Inevitably their own linguistic competence will be affected" ("Doublespeak" 455). Instead, Sledd argued, individuals espousing race-conscious change insisted that focusing on Standard English must never eclipse the larger need to "know and respect our children's language as we demand that they know and respect our own. And we should make no harsh, head-on attempt to change their language, to make them speak and write like us. If they value our world and what it offers, then they will take the initiative in change, and we can cautiously help them" (456). Sledd's arguments thus share much in common with those of Rose today: i.e., the goal of race consciousness is not to deny the value of standards entirely, but rather to investigate standards and their effects with an intensely critical eye.

6. Bell does not view race as a fixed or static social category, but rather as "an indeterminate social construct that is continually reinvented and manipulated to maintain domination and enhance white privilege" (*Race* 9). But Bell nonetheless does use the terminology of "white" and "black" to denote the racialized dimensions of "relative so-

cial status" (10), particularly those related to dynamics of racialized "domination and exploitation" (11).

7. See, e.g., L'Eplattenier and Mastrangelo; Soliday; DeGenaro; Tassoni; Hoogeveen; Greene and McAlexander.

8. See, e.g., Grabill; Grego and Thompson, *Teaching/Writing.*

9. See also Lavin and Hyllegard; Bastedo and Gumport; Parker and Richardson.

10. For a number of other projects with a similar focus, see Ritter; Stanley; Grego and Thompson, *Teaching/Writing;* Otte and Mlynarczyk.

11. Parks notes numerous times that the SRTOL was developed through the racialized activism and agitation of students of color during the late 1960s and early 1970s. He even dedicates an entire chapter of his text to describing "Black Power/Black English" as a catalyst for this change, arguing that in order to "understand the SRTOL's relationship to the 1960s . . . it is important to understand the competing images of Black English during the period in which Black Power originated" (91). But Parks ultimately concludes that race is less useful than class as the primary lens through which to understand the history of the SRTOL: he wonders openly, in fact, whether the CCCC might not have "too quickly appropriated African American struggles for social and economic justice into educational paradigms that reinforced hegemonic understandings of how race and class work in the United States" (5) as it conceptualized and implemented the SRTOL. What the CCCC should have aimed for instead, he says, is a more systematic examination of "the economic aspects of discrimination based on race, gender, or sexual preference" in ways that might contribute to "broad-based social justice that goes beyond classroom and university practices" (6).

Similarly, Soliday acknowledges that basic writing in CUNY's Open Admissions program was clearly affected by issues of race and racism, suggesting that perceptions regarding "the decline in literacy skills and the consequent need for remedial writing instruction [became] attached to students of color" (60) within the context of the program. But she nonetheless concludes that by overemphasizing issues of race and racism within such programs, well-intentioned analysts and critics may inadvertently contribute to a situation in which "agency is assigned to students' underclass status" such that it becomes "difficult to build coalitions between groups who may have shared economic interests" (136).

Finally, even as Greene and McAlexander also acknowledge the roots of high-risk/BW in the Civil Rights Era 1960s, they nonetheless argue that it is an "oversimplification" to view high-risk/BW as a minority domain or to analyze it as such, especially in light of the fact that contemporary programs often "cut across race, ethnicities, and class" (7). They conclude that "although the basis for hostility to basic writing programs in the early years might have involved racism, that hostility was later more strongly fueled by intellectual elitism" (8).

12. See also Gilyard, *Race;* Villanueva, "On the Rhetoric"; M. Powell; Kynard; Young, *Minor Re/Visions;* Kirklighter, Cardenas, and Murphy.

13. Smitherman worked with other authors, including Richard Lloyd-Jones, Darnel Williams, Myrna Harrison, and Ross Winterowd, on the earliest drafts of the SRTOL (Parks 161).

14. Carmen Kynard's 2007 article "'I Want to Be African'" makes some of these same points as it directly criticizes Parks's *Class Politics* for its discussion of race within the

SRTOL. Kynard insists that Parks's analysis of the SRTOL features an unfortunate tendency to "reduce (Black) English(es) and their urban allies (all those other 'nonstandard' varieties from people of color) to incorrect grammar from hoodrats who know no better but can be rescued from it when their class oppression is wiped out" (381).

15. Greene's focus here is interesting given that her coauthored introduction to the *Basic Writing in America* volume seems somewhat dismissive of race. See note 11 for more discussion of this dismissal.

16. See Mutnick; Tassoni; Davi.

17. In the early program, most EOP Rhetoric students were African American. By the late 1970s, EOP Rhetoric students were mostly African American and Latino.

18. From 1968 to 1971, the two-semester EOP Rhetoric sequence was known as Rhet 101 and 102, with Rhet 103 serving as the tutorial. In 1972, however, course names were changed to EOP Rhet 104 and 105 (while EOP Rhet 103 retained its original name) as part of a larger restructuring of English Department curricula.

19. This is not to say that all students necessarily appreciated this separation: some early students actually saw it as a sort of race-based segregation within the writing classroom (Dean A, "Role" 5). However, a 1991 review of the EOP Rhetoric program conducted by two outside reviewers in the field of composition (see chapter 5) found that most students "were not particularly worried about any 'social stigma' attached to the course, certainly not in the same way that some faculty members seemed to worry about 'segregating' these students. In fact, these minority students seemed grateful for the chance to be in a class where they were a majority" ("External Review of the EOP Rhetoric Program" 2). In other words, concerns about the racial stigma attached to the program may have been occasionally articulated by students, but they were articulated much more frequently—and for very different reasons—by mainstream administrators who were interested in redirecting EOP Rhetoric resources away from race-conscious writing instruction.

20. The racially egalitarian legacy of EOP at UIUC continues to be celebrated by contemporary administrative entities such as the Office of Minority Student Affairs (OMSA), the current home of EOP. The historical section of the OMSA Web site from early 2010 reads as follows: "The Office of Minority Student Affairs (OMSA) was created as a result of campus leadership, local community support, and the activism of African American law students. After the 1968 'Project 500' initiative to increase campus enrollment by 500 African American students was successful, Latino/a, Caucasian, and Asian American students also began matriculating through the project. As a result of these increasing numbers, students and staff felt that a permanent campus program was needed to increase retention and provide services for the enrichment and development of current and future underrepresented students at the University of Illinois at Urbana-Champaign. Their vision and persistence resulted in the development of the Educational Opportunities Program (EOP)" (par. 1). OMSA clearly stresses here that the "leadership" and "activism" exhibited by EOP students and their race-conscious allies over time has left an enduring legacy at UIUC, one marked by both "vision" and "persistence."

21. I did obtain informed consent to quote from the interviews that I conducted with several key program administrators past and present.

22. I suspect that virtually all of these actors saw themselves as having students' best interests in mind—whether espousing race-conscious or mainstream standards-oriented

discourses—in ways that clearly render simplistic judgments of "good" or "bad" on my part to be problematic.

23. See my *College English* article "'What's in a Name?' Institutional Critique, Writing Program Archives, and the Problem of Administrator Identity" for detailed discussion of these methodological issues.

Chapter 2. The Late 1960s and Early 1970s

1. See also Schulman; LaBelle and Ward.

2. See especially Egerton, *Higher Education* and *State Universities;* McDaniel and McKee; Gordon, "Programs"; *Opportunity.*

3. SSS operated in tandem with two other K–12 efforts, Upward Bound and Talent Search, to comprise the TRIO program.

4. These evaluators would offer a rather negative assessment of SSS in 1975—a point to which I will return in chapter 3.

5. For more discussion of early federal sponsorship of high-risk programs, see Zhang and Chan; Engle and O'Brien; Muraskin and Lee.

6. The racial categories "white," "black," and "Hispanic" have been and remain the sole three used by the *Digest of Education Statistics* to map college enrollment by high school graduates ages eighteen to twenty-four since 1972.

7. Furthermore, as Bruce Horner points out, the board managed to "oppos[e] ethnic integration to academic excellence" ("'Birth'" 11) through these assertions, thereby implying that racial justice and excellence were binary opposites rather than complementary goals.

8. The Southern Education Reporting Service described itself at this time as a "non-profit agency established in 1954 by a group of Southern Newspaper editors and educators to gather and publish information on school desegregation and education for minorities and low-income groups" (qtd. in Egerton, *State Universities* 3).

9. See Berlin; Connors; S. Miller; Crowley; Shor.

10. I use the term *high-risk writing instruction* in this chapter rather than *high-risk/BW* because the BW movement would not become widely known until later in the decade through the work of scholars such as Mina Shaughnessy.

11. See also Meyers.

12. Smitherman's early work was mostly concerned with the needs of African American students, but her later work encompassed linguistic and cultural differences more broadly.

13. The SRTOL was first circulated as a paragraph-long disciplinary resolution in 1972 and as then as a thirty-plus-page disciplinary position statement and teaching guide in 1974.

14. For other discussions of the importance of the SRTOL, see Parks; Kinloch; Wible; Kynard.

15. The SRTOL also speaks at some length about race-conscious issues beyond the immediate writing classroom, particularly standardized testing (13), writing in "courses other than English" (13), writing in the workplace (14), and teacher training (18).

16. See especially Sledd, "Doublespeak," "Bi-Dialecticalism"; Kochman; O'Neill.

17. Allen also wrote several other bidialectical texts during the early 1970s, for *TESOL Quarterly, Modern Language Journal,* and the 1973 NCTE edited collection *Teaching English as a Second Language and as a Second Dialect.*

18. For bidialectical responses to and critiques of the work of Sledd, see Eskey. For other bidialectical responses to the original 1972 and 1974 SRTOL resolutions, see Hendrickson; Pixton; Cannon; Faggett; Ruble.

19. The reason that the overall EOP Rhetoric program of the late 1960s and early 1970s is so sparsely documented remains a mystery. However, several administrators with whom I spoke informally suggested that one disgruntled administrator in the late 1970s may have set fire to a box of materials related to EOP Rhetoric in order to protest higher-level administrative decision making regarding the program. (I have never been able to confirm or refute this story.) I can say, though, that extensive documentation related to the EOP Rhetoric writing lab was preserved in large part through the efforts of the chair of the Senate Committee on Student English (SCSE). This individual (about whom I have much to say in the latter part of this chapter) left all of his administrative correspondence to the main UIUC archives before his death, including a folder of memos and letters chronicling the operation of both the SCSE and the writing lab.

20. The lab was budgeted for $78,000 during its first year of operation and for $60,000 during its subsequent years (Director A, letter to dean of LAS, 9 Dec. 1968, 1).

21. It should be noted that some members of the SCSE had become skeptical of the overall value of the EQE as then being employed. Several even went so far as to propose that the EQE be abandoned in favor of a new upper-division writing requirement at UIUC (SCSE, Minutes, 7 Nov. 1967, 2–3). But no official plans to abolish the EQE were implemented, at least not until after the EOP program was announced in May 1968.

22. Some readers might argue that "ghetto Blacks" are not necessarily singled out in this passage as in need of "survival" skills; after all, underprivileged whites and rural students are mentioned here as well. However, I would argue that because the demographics of EOP were overwhelmingly black during this time period, this statement refers most obviously to black students.

23. As I will note later, the use of the term *remedial* would remain prominent within the final version of the lab mission statement approved by the SCSE.

24. This subcommittee was made up of the director of EOP Rhetoric, the NCTE liaison, and two other individuals whose institutional roles were not specified (NCTE liaison 1).

25. This reference to "attitudinal change" is of a different sort than that advocated by the chair: whereas the chair used this notion to urge linguistic and literate assimilation on the part of EOP students in the ways outlined previously, the subcommittee used this term as part of a larger emphasis upon "the personal, on the writer finding his own voice, on expression as a self-creative act" (2).

26. This new director of assessment was assisted by a part-time assistant director with expertise in writing (director of assessment for the EOP writing lab 1). This assistant director eventually became "Director B" of the EOP Rhetoric program from 1972 to 1975 (see chapter 3).

27. The tenure of this director of assessment was short-lived for a number of reasons that I will discuss in chapter 3.

Chapter 3. The Mid-1970s

1. For other examples of literacy-crisis discourse at the time, see Armbruster; Tibbetts and Tibbetts.

2. Open Admissions was never actually open to all students who applied: there were always some sort of minimum standards for admission.

3. This marked significant change from the previous Open Admissions policy requiring students to obtain a minimum GPA of 2.0 after sixty credits (Lavin and Hyllegard 211).

4. In 1976, CUNY also began discussing plans to subject all incoming freshman students to a "far-reaching, centralized policy of skills assessment" for the purposes of placement into and exit from remedial courses (Lavin and Hyllegard 211). This testing regime, one eventually encompassing both the set of general CUNY placement exams and its Writing Assessment Test (WAT), was implemented in 1978. This regime will be the subject of extended discussion in chapter 4.

5. Vincent Tinto and Roger M. Sherman's 1974 *The Effectiveness of Secondary and Higher Education Intervention Programs: A Critical Review of the Research,* another important federally sponsored study of the time, drew similarly negative conclusions. It granted, on the one hand, that high-risk programs might be having some sort of positive effect on students' perceptions of higher education, what Tinto and Sherman describe as "some impact . . . in the attitudinal and motivational orientations of program students, changes perceived as positive consequences of the program" (vii). However, it concluded that these programs have had "little impact on the cognitive academic achievements of targeted populations (e.g., reading and mathematics achievements)" (vii). It also advocated that future funding be granted only to those programs demonstrating "sufficient information to indicate that [they] can effectively deal with the problems of disadvantaged youth" (67): as these authors concluded, "it would seem unwise . . . to increase funding to those programs . . . [because] we are unsure as to their effectiveness" (67).

6. For other similar examples of race-conscious responses to literacy crisis at the time, see Elgin; Smitherman, *Talkin'.*

7. Wagner's work from this time period continues to stand as one of the more widely known and strident critiques of Open Admissions at CUNY to be issued by one of its own faculty members (see Lu, "Conflict").

8. This article was also noteworthy for the fact that it followed quickly on the heels of a 1977 *College English* piece that Guralnick coauthored with Paul Levitt, called "Improving Student Writing: A Case History," which detailed efforts at the University of Colorado at Boulder to reinstate written standards in the midst of literacy crisis.

9. For other examples of such overtly color-blind discussion, see Nauer; L. G. Heller.

10. See, e.g., Wiener; Perl, "Composing," "Look"; Lunsford, "What We Know," "Cognitive"; Bartholomae, "Study."

11. As noted in chapter 2, the university had offered a remedial rhetoric course for all those failing to pass the English Qualifying Exam from 1941 to 1960.

12. Director B extended this argument even further during a subsequent interview with the EOP program, insisting that EOP Rhetoric was "in fact, discriminatory. It's discriminatory in both directions. Most kids hear about it as a black course or a Latino course, and, of course, if we took all freshmen and tested them and took scores from them we would not have an all black course by any means. I don't think it would be even 50 percent black, I doubt if it would be. . . . There are some very low scores among regu-

larly admitted students who are not given the opportunity to take this particular course in rhetoric" (qtd. in Dean B, "Educational Opportunities Program" III-24). Evident in this quote are Director B's beliefs that any race consciousness on the part of the EOP Rhetoric program was tantamount to a kind of racial "discrimination" and that reconstituting the program was the only way to remedy this problem.

13. Head A did seem to offer a compromise of sorts in concluding his request: specifically, he suggested that if it gained full control over the lab, the English Department/ EOP Rhetoric program would endeavor to find and hire a "qualified Black, at the Professorial Rank" (letter to dean of LAS, 24 Sept. 1974, 2) for both the EOP Rhetoric program and the writing lab as a means to minimize any remaining racial "stigma" (2) within the program.

At first glance, it might appear that Head A was trying to ensure that administrators, instructors, and students would continue to share some sort of racial or ethnic background even within a newly reorganized writing lab. Importantly, however, Dean B expressed skepticism regarding Head A's suggestion, arguing that the main goal of EOP relative to the lab was "the delivery of the best possible services to our common clientele," not simply the hiring of a person of color to preside over a problematic program (memo to head of English Department, 11 February 1975, 2). Dean B further argued that he had only been granted "a cursory exchange of views and ideas" with the one candidate whom the English Department had in mind for this position and was not convinced from such "superficial interaction" that this person would be a good fit for EOP Rhetoric or the lab itself (2). In this way, then, Dean B underscored the important point that a black director would not necessarily be a race-conscious or effective one.

14. One writing lab tutor wrote to the director of undergraduate studies for the English Department to complain that Director B was being vehemently color-blind in her talk about the lab. In his letter, he attributed this quote to Director B.

Chapter 4. The Late 1970s and Early 1980s

1. In explaining this first decision, the Court wrote, "While the goal of achieving a diverse student body is sufficiently compelling to justify consideration of race in admissions decisions under some circumstances, petitioner's special admissions program, which forecloses consideration to person like respondent, is unnecessary to the achievement of this compelling goal and therefore invalid under the Equal Protection Clause" (*Regents . . . v. Bakke* 267).

2. Catherine Prendergast has further pointed out the ironic way in which the Court reified Harvard's status in its *Bakke* ruling as "the pinnacle of literacy attainment" (*Literacy* 39), rather than characterizing Harvard as an institution whose beliefs about language and literacy needed to be interrogated in race-conscious ways.

3. SSS was known at times during its earlier history as "Special Services for Disadvantaged Students," or SDSS.

4. I will have much more to say about the writing portion of these FSAT exams, the CUNY Writing Assessment Test (WAT), later in this chapter.

5. Much of this scholarship focused in particular upon the benefits of determining student competence via the logic of "holistic" assessment, a type of assessment that was typically thought to be more egalitarian than the more "objective" tests of student writ-

ing ability common before this time period. Kathleen Blake Yancey writes that such holistic approaches to determining student competence were typically thought to offer "a more valid, classroom-like assessment" of student writing (490) than objective tests that focused primarily on decontextualized issues of "grammar and usage" (486).

6. This volume constitutes one of the larger collections of race-conscious work on writing assessment circulating at the time: notable chapters include Farr Whiteman's "Dialect Influence in Writing"; Valadez's "Identity, Power, and Writing Skills: The Case of the Hispanic Bilingual Student"; Lewis's "Practical Aspects of Teaching Composition to Bidialectical Students: The Nairobi Method"; and Hoover and Politzer's "Bias in Composition Tests with Suggestions for a Culturally Appropriate Assessment Technique."

7. White also included a revised version of this "Racial Minorities and Writing Skills Assessment" article in his 1985 collection *Teaching and Assessing Writing.*

8. See chapter 3 for a discussion of Harvey Daniels's overtly race-conscious critique of the TSWE.

9. For similar examples of seemingly race-conscious work that ultimately promoted white mainstream standards at some level, see Odell; Matalene; White, *Teaching.*

10. The IBHE defined "remedial" programs as those offering a "freestanding attempt to bring unprepared students to a level of basic skills necessary to pursue college level work . . . most often a single course designed to elevate a specific skill competence—arithmetic, writing, or reading—and, as such, is seldom an integrated part of a total college curriculum" (9).

11. The IBHE declared that "community colleges have viewed and should continue to view the remedial function with equal priority to its [*sic*] other missions such as baccalaureate, vocational, and technical education. The community college should be recognized as the postsecondary institution where deficiencies in basic skills of adults will be addressed" (9–10).

12. Not all of the specific moves advocated here by UIUC as a means to assure student competence were draconian. For instance, UIUC said that it would offer a variety of required and elective writing courses that "focus on writing skills" ("Responses" 3); offer "substantial papers on issues relating to the subject matter of the course" (4); engage in the extensive training of "teaching assistants who are responsible for providing instruction in writing classes" (5); and assist in the development of teacher education programs "committed to educating teacher/scholars who are well-trained in the teaching of college English" (7). Nonetheless, even these worthwhile goals were couched within a larger framework of antiremediation and standards that was neither questioned nor interrogated in any significant way.

13. This response also stressed that these sorts of standards had long been a feature of UIUC's autonomous self-regulation, an autonomy that UIUC felt the IBHE was threatening. It insisted, for instance, that at Illinois "each college determines its own admissions and graduation requirements, with approval by the Senate and the Board of Trustees" ("Responses" 3). It also stressed that UIUC had long possessed "the right to establish its own curricula and to determine its own graduate requirements, subject to action by the Senate and the Board of Trustees" (4). Working from this premise, the response ultimately demanded that EOP Rhetoric be allowed to operate without IBHE interference in light of the fact that "in the past, campus administration has been extremely reluctant to dictate policy to colleges on curricular matters. It has respected the fact that disciplinary

expertise resides in the academic unit, which should, as a result, be the primary unit determining curricular matters. Now the IBHE is asking that the campus administration dictate policy on such matters to its colleges [with respect to the issues of credit for EOP Rhetoric], and the campus does not believe such action would represent sound academic policy" (4). In this way, UIUC argued that it was fully capable of enforcing EOP Rhetoric standards on its own and that any attempt by the IBHE to interfere with its power was both unwarranted and unappreciated.

14. In making this argument, the head was echoing a concern articulated by the current VCAA that the campus ought to develop a contingency plan in the event that the EOP Rhetoric program was effectively abolished by the IBHE: "Even if it is determined that [existing rhetoric courses] are remedial and cannot be offered for credit, will there be a need for such courses? I believe that the answer to that question is that there definitely will be a need that will have to be met" (letter to members of the English Department, 12 Oct. 1981, 1).

15. Head B apparently felt that this backup plan needed to be race conscious: he asserted explicitly that he did not want to do anything that might function to "[eliminate] most black undergraduates from this campus" (letter to Director D, 4 Jan. 1982, 1). The director of rhetoric at the time (who was, technically, the administrative superior of Director D) agreed: "If the EOP courses are not to carry credit toward graduation, it is altogether possible that the next step will be to discontinue the EOP Program in Rhetoric. To do so would be to reduce substantially the number of black students enrolled as undergraduates in this institution, a situation that I feel would be quite indefensible" (letter to VCAA, 18 Feb. 1982, 1–2).

16. On the first of these measurements, words per T-unit, the report noted roughly equivalent scores between EOP students exiting Rhetoric 104 (mean = 14.7; median = 14.5; SD = 3.5; Range = 17.6) and mainstream white students entering Rhetoric 105 (mean = 14.8; median 13.8; SD = 1.7; Range = 9.7). On the second of these measurements, words per clause, the report mentioned a similar result between EOP Rhetoric students exiting Rhetoric 104 (mean = 9.11; median = 9.45; SD = 1.68; Range = 6.6) and mainstream students entering Rhetoric 105 (mean = 9.86; median = 9.10; SD 2.07; Range = 7.6).

Chapter 5. The Late 1980s and Early 1990s

1. See also D'Souza; Schlessinger; Hirsch; Kimball; Douglas; Ravitch; Cheney.

2. Pratt wrote that actual 1960s-era programs should be at least temporarily preserved because "where there are legacies of subordination, groups need places for hearing and mutual recognition" (40).

3. See also Gitlin; Kanpol and McLaren; Aronowitz; Grossberg; various contributors to Berube and Nelson.

4. Of course, Traub's critique here was not identical to that of someone like Graff, Giroux, or Pratt: Traub's "liberalism" was one that dismissed multiculturalism in all forms. Nonetheless, his critique demonstrated that many scholars purporting to be on the mainstream left were openly disillusioned with 1960s-era initiatives such as high-risk programs.

5. I am not trying to be critical of two-year institutions or of the important work that they perform. Rather, I am arguing that these two-year schools were increasingly being held responsible for all diversity within the higher-education context, leaving four-year schools free to pursue color-blind "excellence." I will have a good deal more to say about this in chapter 6.

6. For debate regarding Hairston's claim, see the 1993 interchanges between and among Trimbur, Wood, Strickland, Thelin, Rouster, Mester, and Hairston in *CCC*.

7. For other detailed discussions of the "contact zone" in composition from this era, see R. Miller; Harris.

8. See especially Lu, "Redefining"; Gay; Laurence, "Vanishing"; Horner, "Rethinking."

9. See especially Bartholomae, "Tidy"; Shor; Greenberg, "Politics"; Grego and Thompson, "Repositioning."

10. This symposium issue also featured some discussion of an article by Paul Hunter titled "'Waiting for Aristotle': A Moment in the History of the Basic Writing Movement."

11. See especially Patthey-Chavez and Gergen; Fox; Gay.

12. Featured within this "Symposium" issue were Laurence, Rondinone, Gleason, Farrell, Hunter, and Lu. For other similar arguments being made outside this symposium, see Laurence, "Vanishing"; Maher.

13. Laurence even suggested at one point that such an emphasis upon "conflict and struggle" was better suited for predominantly white elite institutions than for diverse urban institutions like CUNY: "Perhaps . . . 'conflict' strategies are needed at predominantly white, and perhaps 'elite,' institutions in order to engender a certain awareness among the students, but I would contend that the use of polarizing language in our descriptions of pedagogy does not encourage the cultural and educational understanding that we wish to encourage in a diverse society. At City College, where 'difference' is structured into the institution in its 80 percent minority enrollment, there is a cultural subtext in every classroom. What surfaces are the linguistic and cultural questions and conflicts of our city and society, discussions of what Paulo Freire calls 'the majority language' and the value of having many 'voices' along with various cultural responses to the books we choose to read and the topics upon which we focus" (881).

14. Williams also noted that she was able to reinsert race explicitly into her account of these events only with great effort: "Ultimately I did convince the editors that mention of my race was central to the whole sense of the subsequent text; that my story became one of extreme paranoia without the information that I am black; or that it became one in which the reader had to fill in the gap by assumption, presumption, prejudgment, or prejudice. What was most interesting to me in this experience was how blind the application of principles of neutrality, through the device of omission, acted either to make me look crazy or to make the reader participate in old habits of cultural bias" (48).

15. OMSA was the new administrative home of EOP after 1986.

16. Director E's title after 1993 was "director of the Academic Writing Program" for reasons that will soon be discussed.

17. In his reference to "non-EOP students," the VCAA referred to PAP students, not to the white students already being admitted to the program under its Rhetoric 199/ Special Options moniker (see chapter 4).

18. The actual figures given in the English Department review were provided in enrollments per semester: 345 enrollments per semester in the old system and about 500 enrollments per semester under the new ("Departmental Response" 3). However, another document, entitled "EOP Ten-Year Enrollment History and Review of Placements," provided a formula for converting these enrollments into actual number of students being served: the per-semester number for enrollments should be doubled and multiplied by .57 (the average ratio of students to enrollments from the years 1988–93) to determine an approximate number of students served (2). I derive the figures in table 5.1 using this formula.

Chapter 6. The Late 1990s to the Present

1. For other discussions of this emphasis on excellence, see Hazelkorn.

2. For detailed discussions of Proposition 209, see Bell, *Race;* Marin and Horn; Bowen, Kurzweil, and Tobin; Douglass.

3. In his analysis of *Grutter,* educational critic Donald E. Heller argues that "echoing its ruling of 25 years earlier, the focus of the Court's decision in *Grutter* was once again on the benefits of diversity in the university, rather than on the use of affirmative action to help address the current issues of past discrimination and present inequities that linger because of that discrimination" (87).

4. Private four-year school tuition rose 4.5 percent during 2010–11 as well (College Board, "Trends in College Pricing" 1).

5. Notably, students applying for admission through SEEK are not subject to this two-step admissions process. But they are still expected to take noncredit skills courses, and they still need to pass the same battery of skills tests by the end of their first year in order to remain enrolled at a four-year institution (Parker and Richardson 16).

6. In contrast, reliance on merit-based aid has continued to grow, increasing nearly 300 percent from the mid-1990s to the mid-2000s across federal, state, and institutional levels (Couturier and Cunningham 19).

7. See Gleason, "Evaluating Programs"; Soliday; Gibson and Meem; Crouch; Greene; and other writers included in Greene and Alexander.

8. In his 1997 "Our Apartheid," Ira Shor praised the Studio program for being one of several "good mainstreaming experiments . . . [that] appear to require structural changes, thematic changes, different courses/credit/staffing structures as well as new student-centered subjects and methods" (100). In 2005, John Paul Tassoni and Cynthia Lewiecki-Wilson credited the Studio model with having "shifted our attention from merely working to change composition pedagogies to asking more productive questions about relationships: How do students understand the rhetorical situatedness of writing and academic culture more generally, and how do teachers communicate (or not) their objectives?" (69). There is even presently a CCCC "Studio Special Interest Group" dedicated to Studio development and implementation.

9. It is noteworthy that the official description of AWP remains color-blind. According to this description, AWP "offers a year-long alternative to Freshman Rhetoric in which students receive more intensive writing instruction than in the standard rhetoric course, Rhet 105. Successfully completing the first-year AWP rhetoric sequence is one way to

fulfill the Composition I requirement at the University of Illinois at Urbana-Champaign" (UIUC, *Report . . . 2007–2008* 34–35).

10. This figure from 2005, the last year for which UIUC has published systematic racial demographic data for AWP, reveals a minority population of just over 80 percent within the program—a figure somewhat higher than the 70–75 percent average within the programs from 1994 through 2004. (See also table 5.1.)

11. The population of Native American undergraduate students at UIUC has remained extremely small—between .2 percent and .3 percent—throughout this entire forty-year period.

12. I want to stress two additional things about the nature of this story-changing work. First, this work needs to be rooted squarely in the idea that RCBW programs occupy race-conscious institutional spaces that have been and continue to be essential to the pursuit of racial justice within U.S. higher education. Story-changing activity must reflect, in other words, Deborah Mutnick's assertion that "'basic writing' emerged at a particular historical moment" (71) to play "a vital role in increasing access to higher education, in particular for working-class people of color" despite some of its obvious problems and "internal contradictions" (71–72). Story-changing must also reflect contemporary insights from scholars who are interested in developing and maintaining contemporary race-conscious institutional spaces within a mainstream higher-education landscape dominated by white power and privilege. Hill Taylor, for instance, speaks of the need for race-conscious writing programs to continue developing philosophies, practices, and structures that are "place- and space-specific . . . that [acknowledge where] students are writing from, both materially and spatially" (102). In particular, he speaks of the need for institutional spaces that foster "*knowledges* and *uses* radically different than many other programs due largely to [their] spatial (and racial) context" (204). These kinds of race-conscious spaces, he insists, avoid simply "'fixing' problems with language . . . [and] 'fixing' identities and hegemonies in ways that run counter to projects of social justice and initiatives of opportunity" (102). Instead, they envision the "quintessential project of libratory education that hinges on the belief that the aims of education should be the pursuit and achievement of social justice, along lines of gender and race, with the ultimate goal being rearticulations of the gritty materialities of political economy and the construction of identity (and its perceived representations)" (103). Angelique Davi similarly argues that RCBW programs can serve as effective race-conscious spaces for students of color within mainstream predominantly white institutions. Through her analysis of the service-learning-oriented program at her home institution of Bentley College, Davi argues that RCBW programs should help students to "develop their reading and writing skills, recognize the contributions they make to their community and college, and understand how looking critically at issues of race, class, and gender can play a significant role in their intellectual growth" (73). These programs should also serve as a space where "many students of color . . . [can develop] not only a new vantage point for understanding positions of privilege in the education system and the role they have occupied within educational settings, but also a new appreciation for their untapped potential" (92). (For other examples of work related to issues of race and space, see Kynard and Eddy; Kirklighter, Cardenas, and Murphy; Mendez-Newman.)

Second, given our present anti–affirmative action climate, contemporary RCBW programs should explicitly try to serve students from all backgrounds even as they promote explicit race consciousness. As educational policy experts William Bowen, Martin Kurzweil, and Eugene Tobin argue, contemporary programs seeking to preserve race-conscious activity in the present must be explicit about the fact that they are not "racially exclusive" (156). But even as they serve all students, RCBW programs must retain an explicit focus on long-standing race-conscious goals of the sort originally articulated in the late 1960s and early 1970s—i.e., recognizing directly students' existing racial/cultural literacy abilities and practices, using these abilities and practices as the basis for effective writing instruction, and critically examining the power of mainstream standards in the process. (RCBW cannot assume, as AWP did in the early 1990s, that creating a de facto race-conscious space will necessarily result in long-term support for minority students.) RCBW programs must also strive to obtain additional resources with which to perform this service for all students rather than agreeing to stretch their already slim minority student support resources even thinner. (They cannot assume, as AWP also did in the early 1990s, that spreading their existing funding even thinner will result in satisfactory levels of support for minority students.) Obtaining additional resources at present will not be easy, of course, but it will perhaps be made easier by promoting convergence in some of the ways that I am about to outline.

13. See also Couturier and Cunningham; Engle and Tinto; Muraskin and Lee.

14. The Pell Institute for the Study of Opportunity in Higher Education, a primary sponsor of Engle and O'Brien's work, "conducts and disseminates research and policy analysis to encourage policymakers, educators, and the public to improve educational opportunities and outcomes for low-income, first-generation, and disabled college students" (par. 1).

15. See Seaman; Lawrence, Ott, and Hendricks; Sharp and Sheilley.

16. Among the specific approaches adopted within these programs are "acknowledging cultural differences and becoming aware of how these differences affect . . . many students of color" (Person, Benson-Quaziena, and Rogers 60), "fully appreciating cultural differences" (60), "understanding the dynamics of differences" (60), "understanding the meaning of behavior within a cultural context" (60), and "knowing where or who to obtain specific cultural information" (60).

17. Harper stresses that the two-year college can promote convergence by stressing its role in supporting athletes' transfer to (and eventually graduation from) four-year institutions: "For community colleges, transferring students to four-year institutions is among the areas in which accountability agents expect to see progress" (34). He says that promoting such convergence can result in "reputational gains for the community college" (34), gains in the reputations of coaches working with these students (34), and even praise and monetary donation from those athletes who go on to play professionally (35).

18. Race consciousness also pervades many of the specific goals espoused within the BMI program. Under "Recommendation #1: Establish Strong University Leadership," e.g., the task force charged with implementing the BMI argues that "the City University of New York has a public responsibility to provide critical leadership on the challenges facing black youth and men, and to raise its voice vigorously and unwaveringly to help mobilize efforts to achieve long overdue educational and social equity on their behalf" ("CUNY Black Male Initiative: Task Force Report" 2). Under "Recommendation #3: Increase Admission and Graduation Rates and CUNY Colleges," the task force offers some specific policy suggestions related to hiring activities: "In order to envision them-

selves as being successful in college, prospective and matriculated black male students must see role models of successful black male faculty and staff in the college community. Campuses must be more deliberate in their recruitment of qualified black males for all professional positions—at all levels of the professoriate" (2).

19. No information is provided, however, concerning whether or not this instructor adopts a race-conscious approach to student language or "error."

20. Bridge/Transition is an official UIUC support mechanism, affiliated with OMSA, that is designed specifically for at-risk students and that serves a predominantly minority population.

WORKS CITED

Aarons, Alfred C. "Linguistic-Cultural Differences and American Education." Spec. issue of *Florida FL Reporter* 7.1 (1969): 1–174.

Accardi, Steven, and Bethany Davila. "Too Many Cooks in the Kitchen: A Multifield Approach for Today's Composition Students." *Teaching English in the Two-Year College* 35.1 (2007): 54–61.

Adams, Peter Dow. "Basic Writing Reconsidered." *Journal of Basic Writing* 12.1 (1993): 22–35.

Ad Hoc Committee on Rhetoric and Composition. "Report of the Ad Hoc Committee on Rhetoric and Composition." 1 September 1981. University of Illinois English Department archives, Urbana.

Ad Hoc Committee on the Writing Lab. Minutes. 18 November 1968. Record series 9/5/33, box 1, University of Illinois archives, Urbana.

———. Minutes. 20 January 1969. Record series 9/5/33, box 1. University of Illinois archives, Urbana.

———. Report. April 1969. Record series 9/5/33, box 1. University of Illinois archives, Urbana.

Adler-Kassner, Linda. *The Activist WPA: Changing Stories about Writing and Writers.* Logan: Utah State University Press, 2008.

Allen, Virginia F. "Teaching Standard English as a Second Dialect." *Florida FL Reporter* 7.1 (1969): 123–30, 164.

American Historical Association. "Statement on Standards of Professional Conduct." *historians.org*. 2005. 29 February 2008.

Andersen, Paul V. "Simple Gifts: Ethical Issues in the Conduct of Person-Based Research." *CCC* 49.1 (1998): 63–89.

Armbruster, Frank. "The More We Spend, the Less Children Learn." *New York Times Magazine* 28 August 1977, 9–11, 53–56, 60.

Aronowitz, Stanley. *The Politics of Identity.* New York: Routledge, 1992.

Associate dean of Liberal Arts and Sciences (LAS). Letter to associate vice-chancellor for academic affairs. 16 March 1990. University of Illinois English Department archives, Urbana.

———. Letter to English Department head. 22 September 1989. University of Illinois English Department archives, Urbana.

Astin, Alexander W., Helen S. Astin, Kenneth C. Greene, Laura Kent, Patricia McNamara, and Melanie Reeves Williams. *Minorities in American Higher Education.* San Francisco: Jossey-Bass, 1982.

Aud, Susan, et al. *The Condition of Education 2010.* Washington, DC: National Center for Educational Statistics, 2010. *nces.ed.gov/pubsearch.* May 2010. 27 November 2010.

Baratz, Joan C. "Educational Considerations for Teaching Standard English to Negro Children." *Teaching Standard English in the Inner City.* Ed. Ralph W. Fasold and Roger W. Shuy. Washington, DC: Center for Applied Linguistics, 1970. 20–40.

Bartholomae, David. "The Study of Error." *CCC* 31.3 (1980): 253–77.

———. "The Tidy House: Basic Writing in the American Curriculum." *Journal of Basic Writing* 12.1 (1993): 4–21.

Bastedo, Michael N., and Patricia J. Gumport. "Access to What? Mission Differentiation and Academic Stratification in U.S. Public Higher Education." *Higher Education* 46.3 (2003): 341–59.

Baum, Sandy, and Kathleen Payea. *Trends in Student Aid.* Washington, DC: College Board, 2008. *trends.collegeboard.org.* 2008. 21 November 2010.

Bell, Derrick. "*Brown v. Board of Education* and the Interest Convergence Dilemma." Rpt. in Crenshaw et al. 20–29.

———. *Race, Racism, and American Law.* 4th ed. Gaithersburg, NY: Aspen Law and Business, 2000.

———. "Racial Realism." Rpt. in Crenshaw et al. 302–12.

Berlin, James. *Rhetoric and Reality: Writing Instruction in American Colleges, 1900–1985.* Carbondale: Southern Illinois University Press, 1987.

Bernstein, Susan Naomi. "Teaching and Learning in Texas: Accountability Testing, Language, Race, and Place." *Journal of Basic Writing* 23.1 (2004): 4–24.

Berube, Michael, and Cary Nelson. *Higher Education under Fire: Politics, Economics, and the Crisis of the Humanities.* New York: Routledge, 1995.

Bizzell, Patricia. "'Contact Zones' and English Studies." *College English* 56.2 (1994): 163–69.

Bloom, Allan. *The Closing of the American Mind.* New York: Simon and Schuster, 1988.

Boren, Mark. *Student Resistance: A History of the Unruly Subject.* New York: Routledge, 2001.

Bowen, William G., Martin A. Kurzweil, and Eugene M. Tobin. *Equity and Excellence in American Higher Education.* Charlottesville: University of Virginia Press, 2005.

Brekke, Alice. "The Impact of Testing on One California University Campus: What the EPT Has Done to Us and for Us." *Writing Program Administration* 3.3 (1980): 23–26.

Brown, Roscoe C., Jr. "Testing Black Student Writers." Greenberg et al. 98–108.

Bruch, Patrick, and Richard Marback, eds. *The Hope and the Legacy: The Past, Present, and Future of "Students' Right to Their Own Language."* Cresskill, NY: Hampton Press, 2005.

Bruininks, Robert H. "Transforming the University of Minnesota: President's Recommendations." *Foundational Documents: Report and Recommendations. umn.edu.* 6 May 2005. 24 September 2009.

Calahan, Margaret, and Lana Muraskin. *National Study of Student Support Services. Interim Report: Volume 1, Program Implementation.* Washington, DC: Department of Education, Office of Planning, Budget, and Evaluation, 1994.

Cannon, Garland. "Multidialects: The Student's Right to His Own Language." *CCC* 24.5 (1973): 382–85.

Carey, Nancy, Margaret W. Calahan, Kusuma Cunningham, and Jacqueline Agufa. *A Profile of the Student Support Services Program: 1997–1998 and 1998–1999 with Select Data from 1999–2000.* Washington, DC: U.S. Department of Education, 2004.

Carodine, Keith, Kevin F. Almond, and Katherine K. Gratto. "College Student Athlete Success both In and Out of the Classroom." *New Directions for Student Services* 93 (2001): 19–33.

Carpenter, John. "The Illini Union Sit-In of September 9–10, 1968 and Why It Happened." Master's thesis, University of Illinois at Urbana-Champaign, 1975.

Carter, Deborah J., and Reginald Wilson. *Minorities in Higher Education: 1996–1997. Fifteenth Annual Status Report.* Washington, DC: American Council on Education, 1997.

Chair of Senate Committee on Student English (SCSE). "(Draft) Report and Tentative Plans: Writing Laboratory/Clinic." February 1969. Record series 9/5/33, box 1. University of Illinois archives, Urbana.

———. Letter to Subcommittee on the Recruitment of a Director. 21 January 1969. Record series 9/5/33, box 1. University of Illinois archives, Urbana.

———. Letter to vice-chancellor of academic affairs. N.d. University of Illinois English Department archives, Urbana.

———. Letter to writing lab codirector. 28 March 1969. Record series 9/5/33, box 1. University of Illinois archives, Urbana.

Chancellor of UIUC. Letter to dean of Liberal Arts and Sciences. 22 May 1968. Record series 25/2/17, box 1. University of Illinois archives, Urbana.

Chaney, Bradford. *National Evaluation of Student Support Services: Examination of Student Outcomes After Six Years: Final Report.* Washington, DC: U.S. Department of Education, 2010. *www.ed.gov.* April 2010. 27 November 2010.

Chaney, Bradford, Lana Muraskin, Margaret Calahan, and Rebecca Rak. *National Study of Student Support Services: Third-Year Longitudinal Study Results and Program Implementation Study Update.* Washington, DC: U.S. Department of Education, Office of the Under Secretary, 1997.

Cheatham, Harold E. Introduction. *Cultural Pluralism on Campus.* Ed. Harold E. Cheatham. Lanham, MD: American College Personnel Association, 1991. 1–8.

Cheney, Lynne V. *Academic Freedom.* Ashland, OH: John M. Ashbrook Center for Public Affairs, 1992.

Clark, Marguerite. "The Impact of Higher Education Rankings on Student Access, Choice, and Opportunity." *College and University Ranking Systems: Global Perspectives and American Challenges.* Ed. Institute for Higher Educational Policy. Washington, DC: Institute for Higher Educational Policy, 2007. 35–48. *ihep.org.* 2007. 2 December 2010.

Clark, William G. Response to "The Students' Right to Their Own Language." *CCC* 26.2 (1975): 216–17.

College Board. "Trends in College Pricing 2010." *www.collegeboard.com.* 2010. 27 November 2010.

———. "Trends in Student Aid 2010." *www.collegeboard.com.* 2010. 27 November 2010.

"Comments on the English Qualifying Exam." 22 February 1967. Record series 9/5/33, box 1. University of Illinois archives, Urbana.

Committee on the Use of English (CUE). Minutes. 29 October 1975. Record series 15/1/34, box 14. University of Illinois archives, Urbana.

———. Minutes. 2 December 1975. Record series 15/1/34, box 14. University of Illinois archives, Urbana.

———. Minutes. 15 January 1976. Record series 15/1/34, box 14. University of Illinois archives, Urbana.

———. Minutes. 11 February 1976. Record series 15/1/34, box 14. University of Illinois archives, Urbana.

———. "Report of the State of Student Writing in the College." 10 August 1976. Record series 24/1/35, box 26. University of Illinois archives, Urbana.

Conference on College Composition and Communication (CCCC). "Committee on CCCC Language: Background Statement." Spec. issue of *CCC* 25.3 (1974): 1–18.

———. "Guidelines for the Ethical Conduct of Research in Composition Studies." *ncte.org.* 2003. 27 February 2008.

Connors, Robert. *Composition-Rhetoric: Backgrounds, Theory, and Pedagogy.* Pittsburgh: University of Pittsburgh Press, 1997.

Cook, Bryan J., and Jacqueline E. King. *2007 Status Report on the Pell Grant Program.* June 2007. Washington, DC: American Council on Education, 2007. *acenet.edu.* June 2007. 21 November 2010.

Cooper, Charles R., ed. *The Nature and Measurement of Competency in English.* Urbana: NCTE, 1981.

———. Preface. Cooper, *Nature* vii–xiv.

Coulson, John E., and Clarence Bradford. *Evaluation of the Special Services for Disadvantaged Students (SDSS) Program: Final Report.* Washington, DC: U.S. Department of Education, 1983.

"Course Proposal for Rhetoric 199: Writing Workshop." 17 June 1982. University of Illinois English Department archives, Urbana.

Couturier, Lara, and Alisa F. Cunningham. *Convergence: Trends Threatening to Narrow College Opportunity in America.* Washington, DC: Institute for Higher Education Policy, 2006. *ihep.org.* 2006. 21 November 2010.

Crenshaw, Kimberle. "Introduction." Crenshaw et al. xiii–xxxii.

Crenshaw, Kimberle, Neil Gotanda, Gary Peller, and Kendall Thomas, eds. *Critical Race Theory: The Key Writings That Formed the Movement.* New York: New Press, 1995.

Crew, Louie. "Comment on James Sledd." *College English* 34.4 (1973): 585–87.

Crouch, Mary Kay. "Basic Writing at Cal State Fullerton: The Ongoing Battle to Abolish 'Remediation.'" Greene and McAlexander 123–43.

Crowley, Sharon. *Composition in the University: Historical and Polemical Essays.* Pittsburgh: University of Pittsburgh Press, 1998.

"CUNY Black Male Initiative: Campus Involvement." *www.cuny.edu.* 2010. 27 November 2010.

"CUNY Black Male Initiative: Task Force Report." *www.cuny.edu.* 12 September 2005. 27 November 2010.

Dadak, Angela M. "No ESL Allowed: A Case Exploring University and College Writing Program Practices." Matsuda et al. 94–108.

Daniels, Harvey. "What's New with the SAT?" *English Journal* 63.6 (1974): 11–12.

Davi, Angelique. "In the Service of Writing and Race." *Journal of Basic Writing* 25.1 (2006): 73–95.

Davis, Jerry S., Deborah Nastelli, and Kenneth E. Redd. *National Association of State Scholarship and Grant Programs: 24th Annual Survey Report, 1992–1993 Academic Year.* Pennsylvania: Pennsylvania Higher Education Assistance Agency, 1993.

Davis, Junius, Graham Burkheimer, and Anne Borders-Patterson. *The Impact of Special Services Programs in Higher Education for "Disadvantaged" Students.* Washington, DC: U.S. Department of Health, Education, and Welfare, 1975.

Dean A. "The Role of English in the College Education of Minorities: A Crown Don't Make No King." Conference on College Composition and Communication, Miami, FL. 17 April 1969.

———. Personal interview. 15 April 2002.

Dean B. "The Educational Opportunities Program: A Report on Its Objectives, Problems, and Accomplishments." 19 December 1974. Record series 24/1/1, box 144. University of Illinois archives, Urbana.

———. "EOP Annual Report, 1974–1975." 19 December 1975. Record series 41/1/6, box 49. University of Illinois archives, Urbana.

———. "EOP Annual Report, 1974–1975: Addendum." 19 December 1975. Record series 41/1/6, box 49. University of Illinois archives, Urbana.

———. Memo to head of the English Department. 11 February 1975. University of Illinois English Department archives, Urbana.

Dean of Liberal Arts and Sciences (LAS). Letter to head of the English Department. 25 May 1971. University of Illinois English Department archives, Urbana.

———. Letter to vice-chancellor for academic affairs. 21 October 1974. University of Illinois English Department archives, Urbana.

———. Letter to vice-chancellor for academic affairs. 11 June 1984. University of Illinois English Department archives, Urbana.

———. Letter to vice-chancellor of academic affairs. 18 May 1987. University of Illinois English Department archives, Urbana.

Dean of Office of Minority Student Affairs (OMSA). "Educational Opportunities Program Status Report 1985–86." N.d. University of Illinois English Department archives, Urbana.

———. Personal interview. 27 March 2002.

DeGenaro, William. "Why Basic Writing Professionals on Regional Campuses Need to Know Their Histories." *Open Words: Access and English Studies* 1.1 (2006): 54–68.

"Departmental Response to Internal and External Reviews of EOP." 24 February 1992. University of Illinois English Department archives, Urbana.

Detzner, Daniel, Robert Poch, and David V. Taylor. "Foreword." *The General College Vision: Integrating Intellectual Growth, Multicultural Perspectives, and Student Development.* Ed. Jeanne L. Higbee, Dana B. Lundell, and David R. Arendale. Minneapolis: General College and the Center for Research on Developmental Education and Urban Literacy, 2005. xv–xix.

Director A. "A Glance Before and After." N.d. University of Illinois English Department archives, Urbana.

———. Letter to dean of Liberal Arts and Sciences. 9 December 1968. University of Illinois English Department archives, Urbana.

———. "SEOP Proposal." 28 April 1969. University of Illinois English Department archives, Urbana.

Director B. Memo to the head of the English Department. 17 October 1974. University of Illinois English Department archives, Urbana.

———. "Proposal for Change in the Rhetoric Placement Policy at the Lower Level." January 1974. University of Illinois English Department archives, Urbana.

Director C. "The Directive: Rhetoric 103." Program description. 1976. University of Illinois English Department archives, Urbana.

———. "The Directive: Rhetoric 104." Program description. 1976. University of Illinois English Department archives, Urbana.

———. Letter to director of the EEL. 6 October 1975. University of Illinois English Department archives, Urbana.

———. "To the Rhetoric Teaching Staff." 1976. University of Illinois English Department archives, Urbana.

Director D. "Report on EOP Rhetoric." 26 April 1982. University of Illinois English Department archives, Urbana.

Director E. "To the EOP Rhetoric Review Committees" N.d. University of Illinois English Department archives, Urbana.

———. Personal interview. 1 April 1998.

Director of assessment for the EOP writing lab. "To Rhetoric 103 Instructors." 23 September 1969. University of Illinois English Department archives, Urbana.

Director of rhetoric. Letter to VCAA. 18 February 1982. University of Illinois English Department archives, Urbana.

———. Letter to VCAA. 22 February 1982. University of Illinois English Department archives, Urbana.

Director of the EEL. Memo to "Administrators, Faculty and Students Re: The Expanded Encounter with Learning." N.d. University of Illinois English Department archives, Urbana.

———. Memo to Director B. 15 October 1974. University of Illinois English Department archives, Urbana.

Douglas, George H. *Education without Impact: How Our Universities Fail the Young.* New York: Birch Lane Press, 1992.

Douglass, John Aubrey. *The Conditions for Admission: Access, Equity, and the Social Contract of Public Universities.* Stanford: Stanford University Press, 2007.

Downs, Donald Alexander. *Cornell '69: Liberalism and the Crisis of the American University.* Ithaca: Cornell University Press, 1999.

D'Souza, Dinesh. *Illiberal Education: The Politics of Race and Sex on Campus.* New York: Free Press, 1991.

Duffy, Elizabeth A., and Idana Goldberg. *Crafting a Class: College Admissions and Financial Aid, 1955–1994.* Princeton: Princeton University Press, 1998.

Eaton, Judith S. *The Unfinished Agenda: Higher Education and the 1980s.* New York, MacMillan, 1991.

Egerton, John. *Higher Education for "High Risk" Students.* Atlanta: Southern Education Foundation, 1968.

———. *State Universities and Black Americans: An Inquiry into Desegregation and Equity for Negroes in 100 Public Universities.* Atlanta: Southern Education Foundation, 1969.

Elbow, Peter. *Writing without Teachers.* New York: Oxford University Press, 1973.

Elgin, Suzette Haden. "Why *Newsweek* Can't Tell Us Why Johnny Can't Write." *English Journal* 65.8 (1976): 29–35.

Emig, Janet. *The Composing Processes of Twelfth Graders.* Urbana: NCTE, 1971.

Engle, Jennifer, and Colleen O'Brien. *Demography Is Not Destiny: Increasing the Graduation Rates of Low-Income Students at Large Public Universities.* Washington, DC: Pell Institute. *pellinstitute.org.* N.d. 21 November 2010.

Engle, Jennifer, and Vincent Tinto. *Moving beyond Access: College Success for Low-Income, First-Generation Students.* Washington, DC: Pell Institute. *pellinstitute.org.* N.d. 21 November 2010.

English Department head. Letter to dean of Liberal Arts and Sciences. 25 March 1968. University of Illinois English Department archives, Urbana.

———. Letter to dean of LAS. 22 June 1989. University of Illinois English Department archives, Urbana.

———. Letter to dean of LAS. 27 June 1990. University of Illinois English Department archives, Urbana.

———. Letter to Director D. 4 January 1982. University of Illinois English Department archives, Urbana.

"EOP Ten-Year Enrollment History and Review of Placements." 18 April 1993. University of Illinois English Department archives, Urbana.

Eskey, David. "Reflections on How Much We Don't Need Wild Men, Even Make-Believe Wild Men Who Are Really Professors: Reply to James Sledd." *College English* 36.6 (1975): 703–6.

"Ethnography of the University: Cross-Campus Initiative." University of Illinois at Urbana-Champaign. *illinois.edu.* N.d. 4 February 2010 (no longer available online).

"Ethnography of the University Initiative: From the Directors." University of Illinois at Urbana-Champaign. *illinois.edu.* N.d. 2 December 2010.

"The Expanded Encounter with Learning Program." 1971. Record series 41/1/30, box 3. University of Illinois archives, Urbana.

"External Review of the EOP Rhetoric Program." 22 April 1991. University of Illinois English Department archives, Urbana.

Faggett, Harry Lee. "Instructional Assurance of the Students' Right to Write." *CCC* 24.3 (1973): 295–99.

Farr Whiteman, Marcia. "Dialect Influence in Writing." Farr Whiteman 153–65.

———, ed. *Variation in Writing: Functional and Linguistic-Cultural Differences.* Hillsdale, NJ: Erlbaum, 1981.

Farrell, Thomas J. "IQ and Standard English." *CCC* 34.4 (1983): 470–84.

Fasold, Ralph W., and Roger W. Shuy, eds. *Teaching Standard English in the Inner City.* Washington, DC: Center for Applied Linguistics, 1970.

Fox, Tom. *Defending Access: A Critique of Standards in Higher Education.* Portsmouth, NH: Boynton/Cook, 1999.

"Freshman Rhetoric Staff Bulletin." 15 March 1967. University of Illinois English Department archives, Urbana.

Gandara, Patricia, Gary Orfield, and Catherine L. Horn. *Expanding Opportunity in Higher Education: Leveraging Promise.* Albany: SUNY Press, 2006.

Gay, Pamela. "Rereading Shaughnessy from a Postcolonial Perspective." *Journal of Basic Writing* 12.2 (1993): 29–40.

Genovese, Michael A. *The Nixon Presidency: Power and Politics in Turbulent Times.* New York: Greenwood Press, 1990.

Gibson, Michelle, and Deborah T. Meem. "The Life and Death of a College, a Department, and a Basic Writing Program." Greene and McAlexander 49–70.

Gilyard, Keith. "Basic Writing, Cost Effectiveness, and Ideology." *Journal of Basic Writing* 19.1 (2000): 36–37.

———, ed. *Race, Rhetoric, and Composition*. Portsmouth, NH: Boynton/Cook, 1999.

Giroux, Henry. *Living Dangerously: Multiculturalism and the Politics of Difference*. New York: Peter Lang, 1993.

Gitlin, Todd. *The Twilight of Common Dreams: Why America Is Wracked by Culture Wars*. New York: Metropolitan Books, 1995.

Glau, Greg. "*Stretch* at 10: A Progress Report on Arizona State University's *Stretch* Program." *Journal of Basic Writing* 26.2 (2007): 30–48.

Gleason, Barbara. "Evaluating Writing Programs in Real Time: The Politics of Remediation." *CCC* 51.4 (2000): 560–88.

———. Response in "Symposium on Basic Writing, Conflict and Struggle, and the Legacy of Mina Shaughnessy." *College English* 55.8 (1993): 886–89.

Goggin, Maureen Daly. *Authoring a Discipline: Scholarly Journals and the Post–World War II Emergence of Rhetoric and Composition*. Mahwah, NJ: Lawrence Erlbaum, 2000.

Gordon, Edmund W. *Opportunity Programs for the Disadvantaged in Higher Education*. Washington, DC: American Association of Higher Education, 1975.

———. "Programs and Practices for Minority Group Youth in Higher Education." *Barriers to Higher Education*. Ed. Stephen J. Wright. New York: College Entrance Board, 1971. 109–26.

Grabill, Jeffrey T. *Community Literacy Programs and the Politics of Change*. Albany: SUNY Press, 2001.

Graff, Gerald. *Beyond the Culture Wars: How Teaching the Conflicts Can Revitalize American Education*. New York: W. W. Norton and Company, 1992.

Gray-Rosendale, Laura, Loyola K. Bird, and Judith F. Bullock. "Rethinking the Basic Writing Frontier: Native American Students' Challenge to Our Histories." *Journal of Basic Writing* 22.1 (2003): 71–106.

Greenberg, Karen L. "Competency Testing: What Role Should Teachers of Composition Play?" *CCC* 33.4 (1982): 366–76.

———. "The Politics of Basic Writing." *Journal of Basic Writing* 12.1 (1993): 64–71.

Greenberg, Karen L., Harvey S. Wiener, and Richard A. Donovan, eds. *Writing Assessment: Issues and Strategies*. New York: Longman, 1986.

Greene, Nicole Pipenster. "Basic Writing, Desegregation, and Open Admissions in Southwest Louisiana." Greene and McAlexander 71–100.

Greene, Nicole Pipenster, and Patricia J. McAlexander, eds. *Basic Writing in America: The History of Nine College Programs*. Cresskill, NJ: Hampton, 2008.

Greene, Robert L., and Robert J. Griffore. "The Impact of Standardized Testing on Minority Students." *Journal of Negro Education* 49.3 (1980): 238–52.

Grego, Rhonda, and Nancy Thompson. "Repositioning Remediation: Renegotiating Composition's Work in the Academy." *CCC* 47.1 (1996): 62–84.

———. *Teaching/Writing in Thirdspaces: The Studio Approach*. Carbondale: Southern Illinois University Press, 2008.

Grossberg, Lawrence. *We Gotta Get Out of This Place: Popular Conservatism and Postmodern Culture*. New York: Routledge, 1992.

Grutter v. Bollinger. 539 U.S. 306. U.S. Supreme Court. 2003.

Guralnick, Elissa S. "The New Segregation: A Recent History of EOP at the University of Colorado, Boulder." *College English* 39.8 (1978): 964–74.

Guralnick, Elissa S., and Paul Levitt. "Improving Student Writing: A Case History." *College English* 38.5 (1977): 506–11.

Hairston, Maxine. "Diversity, Ideology, and the Teaching of Writing." *CCC* 43.2 (1992): 179–93.

Harper, Shaun R. "Race, Interest Convergence, and Transfer Outcomes for Black Male Student Athletes." *New Directions for Community Colleges* 147 (2009): 29–37.

Harris, Joseph. "Negotiating the *Contact Zone.*" *Journal of Basic Writing* 14.1 (1995): 27–42.

Hazelkorn, Ellen. "The Impact of League Tables and Ranking Systems on Higher Education Decision Making." *Higher Education Management and Policy* 19.2 (2007): 1–24.

Head A. Letter to dean of LAS. 24 September 1974. University of Illinois English Department archives, Urbana.

Head B. Letter to Director D. 4 January 1982. University of Illinois English Department archives, Urbana.

Heller, Donald E. "Educational Attainment in the States: Are We Progressing toward Equity in 2028?" Marin and Horn 87–109.

Heller, L. G. *The Death of the American University.* New Rochelle, NY: Arlington House, 1973.

Hendrickson, John R. "Responses to CCCC Executive Committee's Resolution 'The Student's Right to His Own Language.'" *CCC* 23.3 (1972): 298–301.

Hendrix, Richard. Foreword. Greenberg et al. vii–ix.

———. "The Status and Politics of Writing Instruction." Farr Whiteman 53–70.

Henze, Brent, Jack Selzer, and Wendy Sharer. *1977: A Cultural Moment in Composition.* West Lafayette, IN: Parlor Press, 2008.

Hirsch, E. D. *Cultural Literacy: What Every American Needs to Know.* New York: Vintage, 1988.

Hoogeveen, Jeffrey L. "The Progressive Faculty/Student Discourse of 1969–1970 and the Emergence of Lincoln University's Writing Program." Moon and Donahue 199–219.

Hoover, Mary Rhodes, and Robert L. Politzer. "Bias in Composition Tests with Suggestions for a Culturally Appropriate Assessment Technique." Farr Whiteman 197–207.

Horner, Bruce. "The 'Birth' of Basic Writing." Horner and Lu 3–29.

———. "Rethinking the 'Sociality' of Error: Teaching Editing as Negotiation." *Rhetoric Review* 11 (1992): 172–99.

Horner, Bruce, and Min-Zhan Lu. "Introduction." Horner and Lu xi–xx.

———, eds. *Representing the "Other": Basic Writers and the Teaching of Basic Writing.* Urbana: NCTE, 1999.

Hower, Thomas R. "Brown University's Anti-Harassment Code: The Case of Douglas A. Hann." Huemann and Church 149–69.

Huemann, Milton, and Thomas W. Church, eds. *Hate Speech on Campus: Cases, Case Studies, and Commentary.* Boston: Northeastern University Press, 1997.

Hunt, Jean M. "To Geneva Smitherman." *College English* 35.6 (1974): 722–25.

Hunter, Paul. "'Waiting for Aristotle': A Moment in the History of the Basic Writing Movement." *College English* 54.8 (1992): 914–27.

Illinois Board of Higher Education (IBHE). "Background on the Study of Remediation." N.d. University of Illinois English Department archives, Urbana.

———. "Update on the Granting of Graduation Credit for Remediation Courses." 13 July 1982. University of Illinois English Department archives, Urbana.

"Information about the English Qualifying Examination." 21 November 1967. University of Illinois English Department archives, Urbana.

Jones, William. "Basic Writing: Pushing against Racism." *Journal of Basic Writing* 12.1 (1993): 72–80.

Kanpol, Barry, and Peter McLaren. "Introduction: Resistance Multiculturalism and the Politics of Difference." *Critical Multiculturalism: Uncommon Voices in a Common Struggle.* Ed. Barry Kanpol and Peter McLaren. Westport, CT: Bergin and Garvey, 1995. 1–18.

Karen, David. "The Politics of Race, Class, and Gender: Access to Higher Education in the United States, 1960–1986." *American Journal of Education* 99.2 (1991): 208–37.

Kimball, Roger. *Tenured Radicals: How Politics Has Corrupted Higher Education.* New York: Harper and Row, 1990.

Kinloch, Valerie Felita. "Revisiting the Promise of *Students' Right to Their Own Language:* Pedagogical Strategies." *CCC* 57.1 (2005): 83–113.

Kirklighter, Christina, Diana Cardenas, and Susan Wolff Murphy, eds. *Teaching Writing with Latino/a Students: Lessons Learned at Hispanic Serving Institutions.* Albany: SUNY Press, 2007.

Kochman, Thomas. "Social Factors in the Consideration of Teaching Standard English." *Florida FL Reporter* 7.1 (1969): 87–88, 157.

Kubota, Ryuko, and Kimberly Abels. "Improving Institutional ESL/EAP Support for International Students: Seeking the Promised Land." Matsuda et al. 75–93.

Kurlaender, Michal, and Erika Felts. "*Bakke* beyond College Access: Investigating Racial/Ethnic Differences in College Composition." Marin and Horn 110–41.

Kynard, Carmen. "'I Want to Be African': In Search of a Black Radical Tradition/African-American-Vernacularized Paradigm for 'Students' Rights to Their Own Language,' Critical Literacy, and 'Class Politics.'" *College English* 69.4 (2007): 356–86.

Kynard, Carmen, and Robert Eddy. "Toward a New Critical Framework: Color-Conscious Political Morality and Pedagogy at Historically Black and Historically White Colleges and Universities." *CCC* 61.1 (2009): 171; W24–44. *ncte.org.* September 2009. 3 March 2010.

LaBelle, Thomas J., and Christopher R. Ward. *Ethnic Studies and Multiculturalism.* Albany: SUNY Press, 1996.

Lalicker, William. "A Basic Introduction to Basic Writing Program Structures: A Baseline and Five Alternatives." *Teaching Developmental Writing: Background Readings.* 3rd ed. Ed. Susan Naomi Bernstein. Boston: Bedford St. Martins, 2007. 15–25.

Lamos, Steve. "Basic Writing, CUNY, and 'Mainstreaming': (De)Racialization Reconsidered." *Journal of Basic Writing* 19.2 (2000): 22–43.

———. "'What's in a Name?': Institutional Critique, Writing Program Archives, and the Problem of Administrator Identity." *College English* 71.4 (2009): 389–414.

Laurence, Patricia. Response in "Symposium on Basic Writing, Conflict and Struggle, and the Legacy of Mina Shaughnessy." *College English* 55.8 (1993): 879–82.

———. "The Vanishing Site of Mina Shaughnessy's Errors and Expectations." *Journal of Basic Writing* 12.2 (1993): 18–28.

Laurence, Patricia, Peter Rondinone, Barbara Gleason, Thomas J. Farrell, Paul Hunter, and Min-Zhan Lu. "Symposium on Basic Writing, Conflict and Struggle, and the Legacy of Mina Shaughnessy." *College English* 55.8 (1993): 879–903.

Lavin, David E., and David Hyllegard. *Changing the Odds: Open Admissions and the Life Chances of the Disadvantaged.* New Haven: Yale University Press, 1996.

Lawrence, Janet, Molly Ott, and Lori Hendricks. "Athletics Reform and Faculty Perceptions." *New Directions for Higher Education* 148 (2009): 73–81.

L'Eplattenier, Barbara, and Lisa Mastrangelo. *Historical Studies of Writing Program Administration: Individuals, Communities, and the Formation of a Discipline.* West Lafayette, IN: Parlor Press, 2004.

Lewis, Shirley. "Practical Aspects of Teaching Composition to Bidialectical Students: The Nairobi Method." Farr Whiteman 189–96.

Lloyd-Jones, Richard. "A View from the Center." *CCC* 29.1 (1978): 24–29.

Lu, Min Zhan. "Conflict and Struggle: The Enemies or Preconditions of Basic Writing?" *College English* 54.8 (1992): 887–913.

———. "Importing 'Science': Neutralizing Basic Writing." Horner and Lu 56–104.

———. "Professing Multiculturalism: The Politics of Style in the Contact Zone." *CCC* 45.4 (1994): 442–58.

———. "Redefining the Legacy of Mina Shaughnessy: A Critique of the Politics of Linguistic Innocence." *Journal of Basic Writing* 10.1 (1991): 26–40. Rpt. in Horner and Lu 3–29.

Lunsford, Andrea. "Cognitive Development and the Basic Writer." *College English* 41.1 (1979): 38–46.

———. "What We Know—and Don't Know—about Remedial Writing." *CCC* 29.1 (1978): 47–52.

Lyons, Scott Richard. "Rhetorical Sovereignty: What Do American Indians Want from Writing?" *CCC* 51.3 (2000): 447–68.

Maher, Jane. "Writing the Life of Mina P. Shaughnessy." *Journal of Basic Writing* 16.1 (1997): 51–63.

Marin, Patricia, and Catherine L. Horn, eds. *Realizing Bakke's Legacy: Affirmative Action, Equal Opportunity, and Access to Higher Education.* Sterling, VA: Stylus, 2008.

Martinez, Aja Y. "Resisting the Empire of Color-Blind Racism." *College English* 71.6 (2009): 584–95.

Matalene, Carolyn B. "Objective Testing: Politics, Problems, Possibilities." *College English* 44.4 (1982): 368–81.

Matsuda, Paul Kei. "Basic Writing and Second Language Writers: Toward an Inclusive Definition." *Journal of Basic Writing* 22.2 (2003): 67–89.

Matsuda, Paul Kei, Christina Ortmeier-Hooper, and Xiaoye You, eds. *The Politics of Second Language Writing: In Search of the Promised Land.* West Lafayette, IN: Parlor Press, 2006.

McCurrie, Matthew Killian. "Measuring Success in Summer Bridge Programs: Retention Efforts and Basic Writing." *Journal of Basic Writing* 28.2 (2009): 28–49.

McDaniel, Reuben R., and James W. McKee. *An Evaluation of Higher Education's Response to Black Students.* Bloomington: Indiana University Press, 1971.

McElroy, Edward J., and Maria Armesto. "TRIO and Upward Bound: History, Programs, and Issues—Past, Present, and Future." *Journal of Negro Education* 67.4 (1998): 373–80.

McMahon, Christopher. "Preserving the Bastion: The Case of the *Dartmouth Review.*" Huemann and Church 192–212.

McNenny, Gerri. "Writing Instruction and the Post-Remedial University: Setting the Scene for the Mainstreaming Debate in Basic Writing." *Mainstreaming Basic Writers: Politics and Pedagogies of Access.* Ed. Gerri McNenny. Mahwah, NJ: Lawrence Erlbaum, 2001. 1–18.

Mellon, John. "Language Competence." Cooper, *Nature* 21–64.

Mendez Newman, Beatrice. "Teaching Writing at Hispanic Serving Institutions." Kirklighter et al. 17–36.

Meyers, Walter E. "And Neither Do the Purists: To Geneva Smitherman." *College English* 35.6 (1974): 725–29.

Miller, Richard. "Fault Lines in the Contact Zone." *College English* 56.4 (1994): 389–408.

Miller, Susan. *Textual Carnivals: The Politics of Composition.* Carbondale: Southern Illinois University Press, 1991.

Moon, Gretchen Flesher. "Locating Composition History." Moon and Donahue 1–13.

Moon, Gretchen Flesher, and Patricia Donahue, eds. *Local Histories: Reading the Archives of Composition.* Pittsburgh, PA: University of Pittsburgh Press, 2007.

Muraskin, Lana, and John Lee, with Abigail Wilner and Watson Scott Swail. *Raising the Graduation Rates of Low-Income College Students.* Washington, DC: Pell Institute for the Study of Opportunity in Higher Education, 2004.

Mutnick, Deborah. "The Strategic Value of Basic Writing." *Journal of Basic Writing* 19.1 (2000): 69–83.

National Council of Teachers of English (NCTE). *Essays on Teaching English as a Second Language and as a Second Dialect.* Urbana: NCTE, 1973.

———. *Language Programs for the Disadvantaged: The Report of the NCTE Task Force on Teaching English to the Disadvantaged.* Urbana: NCTE, 1965.

———. *Nonstandard Dialect.* Urbana: NCTE, 1968.

Nauer, Barbara. "Race and the Comp Teacher Copout." *College English* 36.4 (1974): 493–96.

NCTE liaison to EOP rhetoric program. "Meeting of Subcommittee on the Recruitment of a Director for the Writing Laboratory." 3 January 1969. Record series 9/5/33, box 1. University of Illinois archives, Urbana.

"Notes on Meeting with Dean of Liberal Arts and Sciences." 17 October 1974. University of Illinois English Department archives, Urbana.

Odell, Lee. "Defining and Assessing Competence in Writing." Cooper, *Nature* 95–138.

Office of Minority Student Affairs. "Programs." *illinois.edu.* N.d. 24 September 2009 (no longer available online).

Omi, Michael, and Howard Winant. *Racial Formation in the United States: From the 1960s to the 1990s.* 2nd ed. New York: Routledge, 1994.

O'Neill, Wayne. "The Politics of Bidialecticalism." *College English* 33.4 (1972): 433–38.

Orfield, Gary. Foreword. *Who Should We Help? The Negative Social Consequences of Merit Scholarships.* Ed. Donald E. Heller and Patricia Marin. Cambridge: Harvard University Civil Rights Project, 2002. xi–xii.

Otte, George, and Rebecca Williams-Mlynarczyk. *Basic Writing.* West Lafayette, IN: Parlor Press, 2010.

Pandey, Anita. "A Cyber Step Show: E-Discourse and Literacy at an HBCU." *Critical Inquiry into Language Studies* 2.1 (2005): 35–70.

Parents Involved in Community Schools v. Seattle School District No. 1 et al. 561 U.S. 1. 2007.

Parker, Tara L., and Richard C. Richardson Jr. "Ending Remediation at CUNY: Implications for Access and Excellence." *Journal of Educational Research and Policy Studies* 5.2 (2005): 1–22.

Parks, Stephen. *Class Politics: The Movement for the Students' Right to Their Own Language.* Urbana: NCTE, 1999.

Patthey-Chavez, G. Genevieve, and Constance Gergen. "Culture as an Instructional Resource in the Multiethnic Composition Classroom." *Journal of Basic Writing* 11.1 (1992): 75–96.

Pell Institute for the Study of Opportunity in Higher Education. *www.pellinstitute.org.* November 2010. 27 November 2010.

Perl, Sondra. "The Composing Processes of Unskilled College Writers." *Research in the Teaching of English* 13.4 (1979): 317–36.

———. "A Look at Basic Writers in the Process of Composing." *Basic Writing.* Ed. Lawrence N. Kasden and Daniel R. Hoeber. Urbana: NCTE, 1980. 13–32.

Person, Dawn R., Marcella Benson-Quaziena, and Ann Marie Rogers. "Female Student Athletes and Student Athletes of Color." *New Directions for Student Services* 93 (2001): 55–64.

Pixton, William H. "An Open Letter of Congratulations to the NCTE for the 1974 Resolutions." *College English* 37.1 (1975): 92–94.

———. "Responses to CCCC Executive Committee's Resolution 'The Student's Right to His Own Language.'" *CCC* 23.3 (1972): 298–301.

Poliakoff, Michael. *Cutting Costs: A Trustee's Guide to Tough Economic Times.* Washington, DC: American Council of Trustees and Alumni Institute for Effective Governance, 2010. *www.goacta.org.* 2010. 2 December 2010.

Porter, James E., Patricia Sullivan, Stuart Blythe, Jeffrey T. Grabill, and Libby Miles. "Institutional Critique: A Rhetorical Methodology for Change." *CCC* 51.4 (2000): 610–42.

Powell, Malea. "Rhetorics of Survivance: How American Indians Use Writing." *CCC* 53.3 (2002): 396–434.

Powell, Pegeen Reichert. "Retention and Writing Instruction." *CCC* 60.4 (2009): 664–82.

Pratt, Mary Louise. "Arts of the Contact Zone." *Profession* 9 (1991): 33–40.

Prendergast, Catherine. *Literacy and Racial Justice: The Politics of Learning after Brown v. Board of Education.* Carbondale: Southern Illinois University Press, 2003.

———. "Race: The Absent Presence in Composition Studies." *CCC* 50.1 (1998): 36–53.

President's Commission on Campus Unrest. *Report of the President's Commission on Campus Unrest.* New York: Commerce Clearing House, 1970.

Professor of business and technical writing. Letter to dean of LAS. 23 February 1976. University of Illinois English Department Archives, Urbana.

Ravitch, Diane. "Multiculturalism: E Pluribus Plures." *American Scholar* 59.3 (1990): 337–54.

Reeher, Kenneth R., and Jerry S. Davis. *National Association of State Scholarship and Grant Programs: 20th Annual Survey Report, 1988–1989 Academic Year.* Pennsylvania: Higher Education Assistance Agency, 1989.

Regents of the University of California v. Bakke. 438 U.S. 265. U.S. Supreme Court. 1978.

"Report of Internal Review Committee of the EOP-Rhetoric Program." 7 May 1991. University of Illinois English Department Archives, Urbana.

Renfro, Sally, and Allison Armour-Garb. *Open Admissions and Remedial Education at the City University of New York.* Report Submitted to the Mayor's Advisory Task Force. *www.nyc.gov.* June 1999. 21 November 2010.

Rhetoric 102 instructor. "Race and the University." Rhetoric 102 course syllabus. *www. illinois.edu.* Fall 2008. 4 February 2010.

Rhetoric 102 student. "An Eye Opener: The Bridge Transition Program." Final paper for Rhetoric 102. *www.ideals.illinois.edu.* Fall 2008. 4 February 2010.

Ritter, Kelly. *Before Shaughnessy: Basic Writing at Yale and Harvard, 1920–1960.* Carbondale: Southern Illinois University Press, 2009.

Rondinone, Peter. Response in "Symposium on Basic Writing, Conflict and Struggle, and the Legacy of Mina Shaughnessy." *College English* 55.8 (1993): 883–86.

Rose, Mike. "Standards, Teaching, Learning." *Journal of Basic Writing* 28.2 (2009): 93–102.

Roueche, John E., and Jerry J. Snow. *Overcoming Learning Problems: A Guide to Developmental Education in College.* San Francisco: Jossey-Bass, 1977.

Ruble, Shirley M. "On Students' Right to Their Own Language." *College English* 37.1 (1975): 94–95.

Schlesinger, Arthur M. *The Disuniting of America: Reflections on a Multicultural Society.* New York: W. W. Norton, 1993.

Schmidt, Benno C., Herman Badillo, Jacqueline V. Brady, Heather MacDonald, Manfred Ohrenstein, Richard T. Roberts, and Richard Schwartz. *The City University of New York: An Institution Adrift.* Report of the Mayor's Advisory Task Force on the City University of New York. *www.cuny.edu.* 7 June 1999. 2 February 2010.

Schoem, David, Linda Frankel, Ximena Zuniga, and Edith A. Lewis. "Teaching about Ethnic Identity and Intergroup Relations." *Multicultural Teaching and the University.* Ed. David Schoem, Linda Frankel, Ximena Zuniga, and Edith A. Lewis. Westport, CT: Praeger, 1993. 1–12.

Schulman, Bruce. *Lyndon B. Johnson and American Liberalism: A Brief Biography with Documents.* Boston: Bedford Books of St. Martin's Press, 1995.

Schwartz, Bernard. *Behind* Bakke: *Affirmative Action and the Supreme Court.* New York: New York University Press, 1988.

Seaman, Barrett. *Binge: What Your College Student Won't Tell You.* Hoboken, NJ: Wiley, 2005.

Senate Committee on Student English (SCSE). "Job Description: Research Position in English and Communication." N.d. Record series 9/5/33, box 1. University of Illinois archives, Urbana.

———. Minutes. 7 November 1967. Record series 9/5/33, box 1. University of Illinois archives, Urbana.

———. Minutes. 22 October 1968. Record series 9/5/33, box 1. University of Illinois archives, Urbana.

———. Minutes. 15 September 1969. Record series 9/5/33, box 1. University of Illinois archives, Urbana.

Severino, Carol. "Where the Cultures of Basic Writers and Academia Intersect: Cultivating the Common Ground." *Journal of Basic Writing* 11.1 (1992): 4–15.

Sharp, Linda A., and Holly K. Sheilley. "The Institution's Obligations to Athletes." *New Directions for Higher Education* 142 (2008): 103–13.

Shaughnessy, Mina. *Errors and Expectations.* New York: Oxford University Press, 1977.

———. "The Miserable Truth." *Journal of Basic Writing* 17.2 (1998): 106–12.

———. "Open Admissions and the Disadvantaged Teacher." *CCC* 24.5 (1973): 401–4.

Sheils, Merrill. "Why Johnny Can't Write." *Newsweek* 9 December 1975. 58–65.

Shor, Ira. "Our Apartheid: Writing Instruction and Inequality." *Journal of Basic Writing* 16.1 (1997): 91–104.

Silard, John. "Minority Access to Higher Education" *One Nation Indivisible: The Civil Rights Challenge for the 1990s.* Ed. Reginald C. Govan and William L. Taylor. Washington, DC: Citizens' Commission on Civil Rights, 1989. 168–71.

Sledd, James. "Bi-Dialecticalism: The Linguistics of White Superiority." *College English* 58.9 (1969): 1307–15, 1329.

———. "Doublespeak: Dialectology in the Service of Big Brother." *College English* 33 (1972): 439–56.

———. "Hang Your Clothes on a Hickory Limb: Comment for David Eskey." *College English* 36.6 (1975): 699–703.

Smitherman, Geneva. "CCCC's Role in the Struggle for Language Rights." *CCC* 50.3 (1999): 349–76.

———. "English Teacher, Why You Be Doin' the Thangs You Don't Do." *English Journal* 61.1 (1972): 59–65.

———. "God Don't Never Change: Black English from a Black Perspective." *College English* 34.6 (1973): 828–33.

———. "Soul N' Style." *English Journal* 64.6 (1975): 12–13.

———. *Talkin' and Testifyin': The Language of Black America.* Boston: Houghton Mifflin, 1977.

———. "Toward Educational Linguistics for the First World." *College English* 41.2 (1979): 202–11.

Snyder, Thomas D., Sally A. Dillow, and Charlene M. Hoffman. *Digest of Education Statistics 2008.* Washington, DC: National Center for Education Statistics, 2009. nces.ed.gov. 2009. 21 November 2010.

Soliday, Mary. *The Politics of Remediation: Institutional and Student Needs in Higher Education.* Pittsburgh: University of Pittsburgh Press, 2002.

"Special Education Opportunities Program." N.d. Record series 25/2/17. University of Illinois archives, Urbana.

"Special Educational Opportunity Program Recruitment for Fall Semester 1968." 14 November 1968. Record series 25/2/17. University of Illinois archives, Urbana.

Stanley, Jane. *The Rhetoric of Remediation: Negotiating Entitlement and Access to Higher Education.* Pittsburgh: University of Pittsburgh Press, 2009.

Storch, Jason, and Matthew Ohlson. "Student Services and Student Athletes in Community Colleges." *New Directions for Community Colleges* 147 (2009): 75–84.

Strickland, Donna. "Errors and Interpretations: Toward an Archeology of Basic Writing." *Composition Studies* 26.1 (1998): 21–35.

Student Support Services Program. "Performance and Efficiency Measure Results: 2005–06." *ed.gov.* 6 January 2009. 2 February 2010.

Task Force on the City University of New York Black Male Initiative. "Final Report to the Chancellor." *www.cuny.edu.* 12 September 2005. 4 February 2010.

Tassoni, John Paul. "(Re)membering Basic Writing at a Public Ivy: History for Institutional Redesign." *Journal of Basic Writing* 25.1 (2006): 96–124.

Tassoni, John Paul, and Cynthia Lewiecki-Wilson. "Not Just Anywhere, Anywhen: Mapping Change through Studio Work." *Journal of Basic Writing* 24.1 (2005): 68–92.

Taylor, Hill. "Black Spaces: Examining the Writing Major at an Urban HBCU." *Composition Studies* 35.1 (2007): 99–112.

Thompson, Robert J., and Carmine Scavo. "The Home Front: Domestic Policy in the Bush Years." *Leadership and the Bush Presidency: Prudence or Drift in an Era of Change?* Ed. Ryan J. Barilleaux and Mary E. Stuckey. Westport, CT: Praeger, 1992. 149–64.

Tibbetts, Arn, and Charlene Tibbetts. *What's Happening to American English?* New York: Scribner, 1978.

Tinto, Vincent, and Roger H. Sherman. *The Effectiveness of Secondary and Higher Education Intervention Programs: A Critical Review of the Research.* Washington, DC: Office of Education, Department of Planning, Budget, and Administration, 1974.

Toma, J. Douglas. "The Collegiate Ideal and the Tools of External Relations: The Uses of High-Profile Intercollegiate Athletics." *New Directions for Higher Education* 105 (1999): 81–90.

Traub, James. *City on a Hill: Testing the American Dream at City College.* Reading, MA: Addison-Wesley, 1994.

Trimbur, John. "Literacy and the Discourse of Crisis." *The Politics of Writing Instruction: Postsecondary.* Ed. Richard Bullock, John Trimbur, and Charles Schuster. Portsmouth, NH: Heinemann, 1991. 277–95.

Trimbur, John, Robert G. Wood, Ron Strickland, William H. Thelin, William J. Rouster, Toni Mester, and Maxine Hairston. "Responses to Maxine Hairston, 'Diversity, Ideology, and Teaching Writing' and Reply." *CCC* 44.2 (1993): 248–56.

Troyka, Lynn. "The Phenomenon of Impact: The CUNY Writing Assessment Test." *Writing Program Administration* 8.1–2 (1984): 27–36.

University of Illinois at Urbana-Champaign (UIUC). "EOP Rhetoric Report." N.d. University of Illinois English Department archives, Urbana.

———. *Profile of Students, Faculty, and Staff by Racial/Ethnic Group, Gender, and Disability: University of Illinois Participation and Success, Fall 2009.* Urbana: University Office for Planning and Budgeting. *illinois.edu.* 2009. 21 November 2010.

———. *A Report on the Participation and Success of Underrepresented Students and Staff: Submitted to the Illinois Board of Higher Education, 2000.* Urbana: Office of Planning and Budgeting. *illinois.edu.* September 2000. 21 November 2010.

———. *A Report on the Participation and Success of Underrepresented Students and Staff: Submitted to the Illinois Board of Higher Education, 2001.* Urbana: Office of Equal Opportunity and Access. *illinois.edu.* October 2001. 21 November 2010.

———. *A Report on the Participation and Success of Underrepresented Students and Staff: Submitted to the Illinois Board of Higher Education, 2002.* Urbana: Office of Equal Opportunity and Access. *illinois.edu.* September 2002. 21 November 2010.

———. *A Report on the Participation and Success of Underrepresented Students and Staff: Submitted to the Illinois Board of Higher Education, 2003.* Urbana: Office of Equal Opportunity and Access. *illinois.edu.* November 2003. 21 November 2010.

———. *A Report on the Participation and Success of Underrepresented Students and Staff: Submitted to the Illinois Board of Higher Education, 2004.* Urbana: Office of Equal Opportunity and Access. *illinois.edu.* November 2004. 21 November 2010.

———. *A Report on the Participation and Success of Underrepresented Students and Staff: Submitted to the Illinois Board of Higher Education, 2005.* Urbana: Office of Equal Opportunity and Access. *illinois.edu.* January 2006. 21 November 2010.

———. *A Report on the Participation and Success of Underrepresented Students and Staff: Submitted to the Illinois Board of Higher Education, 2006.* Urbana: Office of Equal Opportunity and Access. *illinois.edu.* January 2007. 21 November 2010.

———. *A Report on the Participation and Success of Underrepresented Students and Staff: Submitted to the Illinois Board of Higher Education, 2007–2008.* Urbana: Office of Equal Opportunity and Access. *illinois.edu.* 2008. 21 November 2010.

———. "Responses to IBHE Questions on Remedial Courses." N.d. University of Illinois English Department archives, Urbana.

———. "Responses to IBHE Questions on Remedial Courses: Attachment 1." N.d. University of Illinois English Department archives, Urbana.

———. *Student Data Book: Fall Term 1993 with a Ten-Year Overview.* Urbana: University Office for Academic Policy Analysis, 1994.

———. "Underrepresented Groups at the University of Illinois: Participation and Success, Fall 1991." Urbana: University of Illinois Office of Planning and Budgeting, 1991.

———. "Underrepresented Groups at the University of Illinois: Participation and Success, Fall 1992." Urbana: University of Illinois Office of Planning and Budgeting, 1992.

———. "Underrepresented Groups at the University of Illinois: Participation and Success, Fall 1993." Urbana: University of Illinois Office of Planning and Budgeting, 1993.

———. "Underrepresented Groups at the University of Illinois: Participation and Success, Fall 1994." Urbana: University of Illinois Office of Planning and Budgeting, 1994.

———. "Underrepresented Groups at the University of Illinois: Participation and Success, Fall 1995." Urbana: University of Illinois Office of Planning and Budgeting, 1995.

———. "Underrepresented Groups at the University of Illinois: Participation and Success, Fall 1996." Urbana: University of Illinois Office of Planning and Budgeting, 1996.

———. "Underrepresented Groups at the University of Illinois: Participation and Success, Fall 1998." Urbana: University of Illinois Office of Planning and Budgeting, 1998.

University of Maryland College Park. "The Nyumburu Black Male Initiative Program: Progressive Leadership in Action." *theblackmaleinitiative.org.* N.d. 27 November 2010.

University System of Georgia. "Welcome to the University System of Georgia's African-American Male Initiative Web Site." *www.usg.edu/aami.* 14 October 2010. 27 November 2010.

U.S. Department of Education (U.S.D.E.). "Student Support Services Program: Funding Status." *ed.gov.* 3 February 2010. 21 November 2010.

———. "TRIO Student Support Services (SSS) Performance and Efficiency Measure Results: 2007–2008." *ed.gov.* N.d. 21 November 2010.

U.S. Department of Education (U.S.D.E.), Office of Higher Educational Programs. "Student Support Services." *ed.gov.* N.d. 24 September 2009.

U.S. Department of Education (U.S.D.E.), Office of Post-Secondary Information. "Statistical Information." *ed.gov.* N.d. 24 September 2009.

Valadez, Concepcion M. "Identity, Power and Writing Skills: The Case of the Hispanic Bilingual Student." Farr Whiteman 167–78.

Vice-chancellor for academic affairs (VCAA). Letter to chair of SCSE. 30 January 1969. Record series 9/5/33, box 1. University of Illinois archives, Urbana.

———. Letter to dean of Liberal Arts and Sciences. 22 January 1975. University of Illinois English Department archives, Urbana.

———. Letter to dean of Liberal Arts and Sciences. 20 June 1990. University of Illinois English Department archives, Urbana.

———. Letter to members of the English Department. 12 October 1981. University of Illinois English Department archives, Urbana.

———. "Remedial Courses." 11 February 1982. University of Illinois English Department archives, Urbana.

———. "Remediation Activities." 12 February 1981. University of Illinois English Department archives, Urbana.

Vice-chancellor for student affairs. "Office of Minority Student Affairs." 10 February 1988. University of Illinois English Department archives, Urbana.

Villanueva, Victor. "Colonial Memory and the Crime of Rhetoric: Pedro Albizu Campos." *College English* 71.6 (2009): 630–38.

———. "On the Rhetoric and Precedents of Racism." *CCC* 50.4 (1999): 645–61.

Wagner, Geoffrey. *The End of Education.* New York: A. S. Barnes and Co., 1976.

———. "On Remediation." *College English* 38.2 (1976): 153–58.

Walker, Samuel. *Hate Speech: The History of an American Controversy.* Lincoln: University of Nebraska Press, 1994.

White, Edward M. "The California State University English Placement Test (EPT)—Purpose and Potential." *Writing Program Administration* 3.3 (1980): 19–23.

———. *Teaching and Assessing Writing: Recent Advances in Understanding, Evaluating, and Improving Student Performance.* San Francisco: Jossey-Bass, 1985.

White, Edward M., and Leon L. Thomas. "Racial Minorities and Writing Skills Assessment in the California State University and Colleges." *College English* 43.3 (1981): 276–83.

Wible, Scott. "Pedagogies of the 'Students' Right' Era: The Language Curriculum Research Group's Project for Linguistic Diversity." *CCC* 57.3 (2006): 442–78.

Wiener, Harvey. "Questions on Basic Skills for the Writing Teacher." *CCC* 28.4 (1977): 321–24.

Williams, Patricia. *The Alchemy of Race and Rights.* Cambridge: Harvard University Press, 1991.

Williamson, Joy Ann. *Black Power on Campus: The University of Illinois, 1965–1975.* Urbana: University of Illinois Press, 2003.

"Working Report for Changes in the Preset EOP Rhetoric Program." N.d. University of Illinois English Department archives, Urbana.

Writing lab codirector. Letter to SCSE chair. 26 March 1969. Record series 9/5/33, box 1. University of Illinois archives, Urbana.

Writing lab staff member. Memo to director of undergraduate studies for the Department of English. 1 October 1974. University of Illinois English Department archives, Urbana.

Yancey, Kathleen Blake. "Looking Back as We Look Forward: Historicizing Writing Assessment as a Rhetorical Act." *CCC* 50.3 (1999): 483–503.

Youdelman, Jeffrey. "Limiting Students: Remedial Writing and the Death of Open Admissions." *College English* 39.5 (1978): 562–72.

Young, Morris. *Minor Re/Visions: Asian American Literacy Narratives as a Rhetoric of Citizenship.* Carbondale: Southern Illinois University Press, 2004.

———. "Native Claims: Cultural Citizenship, Ethnic Expressions, and Rhetorics of Hawaiianness." *College English* 67.1 (2004): 83–101.

Zhang, Yu, and Tsze Chan. *An Interim Report on the Student Support Services Program: 2002–03 and 2003–04, with Select Data from 1998–2002.* March 2007. Washington, DC: U.S. Department of Education, 2007. *ed.gov.* March 2007. 21 November 2010.

Zhang, Yu, Tsze Chan, Margaret Hale, and Rita Kirschstein. *A Profile of the Student Support Services Program: 1998–1999 through 2001–2002.* July 2005. Washington, DC: U.S. Department of Education, 2005. *ed.gov.* July 2005. 21 November 2010.

INDEX

Abels, Kimberly, 168
Academic Writing Program (AWP), UIUC, 15, 145–49, 158–60, 174–75, 189n9, 191n12
Accardi, Steven, 168–69
Adams, Peter Dow, 127
Adler-Kassner, Linda, 8, 14, 176; *The Activist WPA*, 163
admissions, affirmative action and, 151–52. *See also* CUNY: Open Admissions at; open admissions programs
affirmative action, 2, 151–52
African Americans: expressive styles of, 31; student perceptions of high-risk/BW programs, 26; in student population, 1, 25, 124
Allen, Virginia, 183n17; "Teaching Standard English as a Second Dialect," 36–38
Almond, Kevin F., 170
alternative history, 8–13
American Historical Association, 20
American University, 168
Andersen, Paul V., 19
archival research, methodological and ethical considerations for, 18–20
Arizona State University, 166
assessment: competence concerns and, 94–96; criticisms of, 96–97; discussions of, 3; in EOP Rhetoric program, 47–48, 52–53; exams/tests for, 94–95, 99–101; holistic, 97–98, 100, 110, 185n5; race consciousness and, 96–102; racism in, 101; white mainstream standards and, 96–102
athletics programs, 170–72, 191n17
AWP. *See* Academic Writing Program (AWP), UIUC

back-to-basics approach, 57, 58
Bakke, Allan, 86–87
Bakke decision. *See University of California Regents v. Bakke* (1978)

Bartholomae, David, 137; "The Tidy House," 133–36
Basic Educational Opportunity Grants, 25. *See also* Pell Grants
basic writing (BW) movement, 62, 65, 67–68
basic writing (BW) programs. *See* high-risk/ basic writing (BW) programs; race-conscious basic writing programs
Basic Writing in America (Greene and McAlexander), 4, 10
Bell, Derrick, 6–8, 28, 88, 161–62, 179n6
Benson-Quaziena, Marcella, 171
Bentley College, 190n12
bidialecticalism: competence concerns and, 103; concept of, 35–36; and EOP Rhetoric program, 46–48, 51–52, 54; as limit on race consciousness, 36–40, 55; popularity of, 36; and Standard English, 35–40
Bizzell, Patricia, 126
black colleges and universities, 22–23
Black Cultural Sensibility, 31
Black English Vernacular (BEV), 12, 31
Black Idiom (BI), 31
Black Male Initiative (BMI), CUNY, 172–73, 191n18
Bloom, Allan, *The Closing of the American Mind*, 118–19
BMI. *See* Black Male Initiative (BMI), CUNY
Borough of Manhattan Community College, 12
Bowen, William, 191n12
Brooklyn College, 12
Brown, Roscoe C., Jr., "Testing Black Student Writers," 97–99
Brown University, 117
Brown v. Board of Education (1954), 7, 64
Bruch, Patrick, 33
Bruffee, Kenneth, 128
BW programs. *See* high-risk/basic writing (BW) programs

California, 152

California State University system, English Placement Test (EPT), 3, 94–95, 99–102

California State University–Fullerton, 4, 156

Carodine, Keith, 170

CCC. See College Composition and Communication

CCCC. *See* Conference on College Composition and Communication

CCNY. *See* City College of New York

CE. See College English

Center for Applied Linguistics, *Teaching Standard English in the Inner City*, 36

Chicago Tribune (newspaper), 16

Chronicle of Higher Education (newspaper), 152

City College of New York (CCNY), 9–10, 122–23, 131

City University of New York (CUNY): Black Male Initiative (BMI), 172–73, 191n18; College Preparatory Initiative (CPI), 122; fiscal crisis and, 59; Freshman Skills Assessment Tests (FSAT), 91, 122; high-risk/BW programs at, 4, 9–10, 156; minority access and support within, 24; Open Admissions at, 4, 10, 24, 26, 59, 63, 89–90, 122–23, 125, 131, 153, 184n2; placement assessment at, 91, 122–23, 153, 184n4; Search for Education, Elevation, and Knowledge (SEEK) program, 89–90; Writing Assessment Test (WAT), 3, 94–95, 99

Civil Rights Movement, 21

Clark, William G., "In Response to the 'Students' Right to Their Own Language'," 38–39

College Board, 99

College Composition and Communication (CCC) [journal], 15, 94, 99

College English (CE) [journal], 15, 62, 63, 64, 127, 131

Colley, W. B., 62

color-blind approaches: *Bakke* decision and, 86–87; cognitivist, 66–69; disciplinary/institutional responses to, 61–70, 83–84; EEL program and, 80–84; in EOP Rhetoric program, 72–76, 113–14, 139–49; in high-risk/BW programs, 15, 179n2; and interest divergence, 69–70, 83–84; principles of, 58; by progressive-leaning scholars, 136; at UIUC, 45; to writing instruction, 17–18

Columbia College, 166

Columbia University, 21

community colleges, 186n11. *See also* two-year institutions

competence, 86–116; bidialecticalism and, 103; and disciplinary reconvergence, 102–3; EOP Rhetoric program and, 103–15; and interest reconvergence, 92–102, 114–16

composition discipline: color blindness in, 61–70; competence concerns in, 102–3; current situation in, 156–58; interest convergence/divergence in, 39, 102–3, 137, 156–58; legacy of 1960s-era high-risk/BW programs in, 125–36; race consciousness in, 35, 61–69; responses of, to high-risk/BW programs, 3, 5–8, 15–18, 31. *See also* freshman composition; writing instruction

Conference on College Composition and Communication (CCCC), 19, 189n8. *See also* "Students' Right to Their Own Language" (SRTOL) [CCCC]

Connerly, Ward, 152

conservatism: EOP Rhetoric program critiqued from standpoint of, 139–41; high-risk/BW programs critiqued from standpoint of, 118–19, 131–33

contact zones, 121, 133–34

Cooper, Charles R., *The Nature and Measurement of Competency in English*, 94

Cornell University, 21

Couturier, Lara, 153, 155

Crenshaw, Kimberle, 58

critical race theory, 6–7

culture wars, 117–50; composition discipline and, 125–36; and EOP Rhetoric program, 137–49; and interest redivergence, 124–25, 137, 150; and multiculturalism, 118–22

Cunningham, Alisa, 153, 155

CUNY. *See* City University of New York

Dadak, Angela M., 168

Daniels, Harvey, "What's New with the SAT?," 62–63

Dartmouth Conference, 30
Dartmouth Review (journal), 117
Davi, Angelique, 190n12
Davila, Bethany, 168–69
desegregation, 6–7
Digest of Educational Statistics, 25, 182n6
discipline, of composition. *See* composition discipline
discrimination, 77–79. *See also* racism; reverse racism/discrimination
Donovan, Richard A., *Writing Assessment* (with Wiener and Donovan), 94
drill, as teaching method, 37, 44–45, 47–48, 51–52
Duffy, Elizabeth A., 89, 90–91

Eaton, Judith, 92
Educational Opportunity Programs (EOPs), 2, 64–65. *See also* EOP Rhetoric program, UIUC
Educational Testing Service (ETS), 62
EEL. *See* EOP Rhetoric program, UIUC: Expanded Encounter with Learning
egalitarianism, 5, 7–8, 14
Egerton, John, 27
Elbow, Peter, *Writing without Teachers*, 30
Emig, Janet, *The Composing Processes of Twelfth Graders*, 30
Engle, Jennifer, 164–65, 191n14
English as a Second Language (ESL) programs, 168–70
English Journal, 30
EOP Rhetoric program, UIUC: assessment in, 47–48, 52–53; assessments of, 109–12, 141–43; budget of, 43, 71, 140–41, 145; color-blind approach in, 72–76, 113–14, 139–49; competence concerns and, 103–15; contrasting viewpoints in, 44–55; critiques of, 139–45; culture wars and, 137–49; defense of, 105–12; documentation of, 183n19; dual structure of (1980s), 114; Expanded Encounter with Learning (EEL), 77–84; IBHE and, 103–15, 186n13; institutional analysis using, 3, 15–18; interest convergence/divergence and, 53–54, 83–84, 149; and literacy crisis, 70–76; origins of, 15, 41–42, 181n20; race consciousness and, 16–17, 42–55, 103–15, 138–39; racial composition of,

140, 143–44, 146–47, 181n17; racialization of, 16–18, 181n19; reconfiguration of, 142–49; Standard English in, 46–55, 111; student-instructor ratio in, 15–16; termination of, 15, 145; white mainstream and, 111–12; writing lab of, 42–55, 76–83
errors: EOP Rhetoric program and, 111–12; in Standard English usage, 18, 67–69, 74–76
ethics, in research, 19
Evaluation of the Special Services for Disadvantaged Students (SDSS) Program, 90
excellence: integration opposed to, 10, 182n7; maintenance of, 26; pressures for, 14, 151–53, 156, 160, 164, 168

Fanon, Frantz, 31
Farr Whitman, Marcia, *Variation in Writing*, 94, 186n6
Farrell, Thomas, 128; "IQ and Standard English," 12
federal financial support, 25, 60
financial aid. *See* federal financial support; student financial aid
Florida FL Reporter (journal), 36
Fourteenth Amendment, 88
Fox, Tom, 5
freshman composition, 29. *See also* composition discipline; writing instruction

gatekeeping functions, 29, 45–46, 95
Giroux, Henry, *Living Dangerously*, 120
Glau, Greg, 166
Gleason, Barbara, 4
Goggin, Maureen Daly, 15
Goldberg, Idana, 89, 91
Goldstein, Matthew, 173
Gordon, Edmund W., 27
graduation rates, 164–67
Graff, Gerald, *Beyond the Culture Wars*, 119–21
Gratto, Katherine K., 170
Greenberg, Karen, 137; *Writing Assessment* (with Wiener and Donovan), 94
Greene, Nicole Pipenster, 151, 153, 180n11; "Basic Writing, Desegregation, and Open Admissions in Southwestern Louisiana," 12–13; *Basic Writing in America* (with Patricia McAlexander), 4, 10

Grego, Rhonda, *Teaching/Writing in Third Spaces* (with Nancy Thompson), 156–58
Grutter v. Bollinger (2003), 152, 189n3
Guralnick, Elissa, "The New Segregation," 64–65

Hairston, Maxine, 126
Harper, Shaun R., 172, 191n17
Harrison, Myrna, 180n13
Harvard University, 88, 93, 185n2
Heller, Donald E., 189n3
Hendrix, Richard, "The Status and Politics of Writing Instruction," 96–97
Henze, Brent, 18
hidden archives, 18–19
higher education: African American population in, 1; costs of, 152; racial crisis in, 22–23; racialization of, 174–75
high-risk/basic writing (BW) programs: African-American students' perceptions of, 27; *Bakke* decision and, 89; change effected by, 26–28; color-blind approaches to, 179n2; cost of, 2; criticisms of, 4, 125, 131–36; debates over legacy of 1960s-era, 125–36; disciplinary/institutional responses to, 3, 5–8, 15–18, 31; future of, 152–53, 155, 162–63, 167; limitations on, 5, 25–26; literacy crisis and, 58–59, 62, 84–85; origins of, 2, 23–28; politics and, 132–34; prevalence of, 2; purpose of, 2, 124; race-based placement in, 16, 64–65, 72–74, 79–80; race-conscious approaches to, 30–35, 127–31, 134–36, 163–76, 179n2, 180n11; rejection of, 61, 63–65, 116, 156–58; renaissance of, 116; story-changing and, 163–76; terminology concerning, 179n2, 182n10; theories of, 6–8. *See also* race-conscious basic writing programs
holistic assessment, 97–98, 100, 110, 185n5
Hopwood v. Texas (1996), 152
Horner, Bruce, 182n7
Hunt, Jean M., 30, 38
Hyllegard, David, 21, 24, 59

IBHE. *See* Illinois Board of Higher Education

identity politics, 120
Illinois Board of Higher Education (IBHE), 103–15, 186n13
The Impact of Special Services Programs in Higher Education for "Disadvantaged" Students, 59
institutional critique, 8–9, 11–13
integration, academic excellence opposed to, 10, 182n7
interest convergence/divergence: and color-blind approaches, 69–70, 83–84; competence concerns and, 92–102, 114–16; in composition discipline, 39, 102–3, 137; culture wars and, 124–25, 137, 150; defined, 7; and EOP Rhetoric program, 53–54; and high-risk/BW programs, 7–8, 13–14, 162–63; institutional dynamics of, 53–54, 83–84, 149, 155–56, 158–60; limits of, 93–102; literacy crisis and, 58–61; race consciousness and, 155–56; racial crisis and, 27–28, 54–55; story-changing and, 163–76; theoretical value of, 13–14
international students, 168

Jackson State College, 22
Jones, William, "Basic Writing," 129–30
Journal of Basic Writing (*JBW*), 3, 15, 94

Kent State University, 22
King, Martin Luther, 42
Kubota, Ryuko, 168
Kurzweil, Martin, 191n12
Kynard, Carmen, 180n14

LaBelle, Thomas J., 1
Language Curriculum Research Group (LCRG), 12
Laurence, Patricia, 131–32, 188n13
Lavin, David E., 21, 24, 59
Lewiecki-Wilson, Cynthia, 189n8
literacy crisis: causes of, 57–58, 71; and changing attitudes, 56–61; disciplinary/institutional responses to, 61–70; and high-risk/BW programs, 58–59, 62, 84–85; and interest divergence, 58–61; K–12 teachers blamed for, 71; popularization of, 57, 59, 61–62, 66; remedies for, 57; at UIUC, 70–76

Lloyd-Jones, Richard, 61–62, 180n13
Lu, Min Zhan: "Conflict and Struggle,"
127–29, 131–32; "The Politics of Style in
the Contact Zone," 128

mainstream. *See* white mainstream
Marback, Richard, 33
Matsuda, Paul Kei, 169
McAlexander, Patricia, 151, 153, 180n11; *Basic
in America* (with Nicole Pipenster
Greene), 4, 10
McCurrie, Matthew Killian, 166
McDaniel, Reuben R., Jr., 26–27
McKee, James W., 26–27
McNenny, Gerri, 126
methodology in research, 19–20
Mlynarczyk, Rebecca, *Basic Writing* (with
George Otte), 167
Moon, Gretchen Flescher, 8
multiculturalism, 118–22, 126
Mutnick, Deborah, 5, 190n12

National Commission on the Reform of
Secondary Education, 73
National Council of Teachers of English
(NCTE), 43, 63; *Language Programs for
the Disadvantaged*, 36; *Nonstandard Dia-
lect*, 36
National Study of Student Support Services,
123
National Testing Network in Writing
(NTNW), 94
NCTE. *See* National Council of Teachers of
English (NCTE)
New York City Board of Higher Education,
26
New York Times (newspaper), 73

O'Brien, Colleen, 164–65, 191n14
Ohlson, Matthew, 171
Ohmann, Richard, 62
Omi, Michael, 11, 56
open admissions programs, 2, 4, 27. *See also*
City University of New York (CUNY):
Open Admissions at
open enrollment, 2
Otte, George, *Basic Writing* (with Rebecca
Mlynarczyk), 167

*Parents Involved in Community Schools v.
Seattle School District No. 1* (2007), 152
Parker, Tara L., 153–54
Parks, Stephen, 180n11; *Class Politics*, 9,
180n14
Pell Grants, 25, 60, 154
Pell Institute for the Study of Opportunity
in Higher Education, 167, 191n14
Person, Dawn R., 171
politics: conservative criticism of higher
education, 57–59, 61, 63–64, 119, 131–32;
high-risk/BW programs and, 59, 61,
132–34; multiculturalism and, 119–21,
126; progressive critique of higher education, 119, 133–36; writing instruction
and, 57–58
Polliakoff, Michael, 152
Porter, James E., 8
Powell, Pegeen Reichert, 164
Pratt, Mary Louise, 133; "Arts of the Contact Zone," 120–21
predominantly black colleges and universities, 22–23
Prendergast, Catherine, 5–6, 185n2
President's Commission on Campus Unrest,
22–23, 25
progressive-leaning scholars: critiques of
EOP Rhetoric program by, 141–45; critiques of higher education politics by,
119, 133–36; critiques of high-risk/BW
programs by, 133–36; critiques of multiculturalism by, 119–20
Proposition 209 (California), 152
protests and demonstrations, 1
Purdue University, 118

race: in higher education, 174–75; interest
convergence/divergence framework and,
14; role of, in social structure, 11; of student population, 1, 25, 60, 182n6
race consciousness: *Bakke* decision and,
89; BMI and, 191n18; and college
placement, 87–89, 91–93; in composition discipline, 35; CUNY and,
89–90; disciplinary/institutional responses to, 61–69; EEL program and,
77–82, 185n13; EOP Rhetoric program
and, 16–17, 42–55, 103–15, 138–39;

race consciousness (*cont.*)
  high-risk/BW programs and, 30–35,
    127–31, 134–36, 163–76, 179n2, 180n11;
    limitations on, 36–40, 55, 116; limits of
    institutional, 46–48; rejection of, 63–70,
    72, 75–76, 155–56 (*see also* color-blind
    approaches); revival of, 89–90, 92–93,
    172–75; in scholarship, 11–12; in SRTOL,
    33–35, 182n15; SSS and, 90; tenets of,
    32–33; at UIUC, 42–55, 138, 173–75;
    white mainstream and, 56, 96–102; writ-
    ing instruction and, 17, 34, 179n5. *See
    also* race-conscious basic writing pro-
    grams; racism
race theory, 11
race-conscious basic writing programs
    (RCBW): effectiveness of, 164–67; other
    programs/initiatives supported by,
    167–72; and racial justice, 190n12; re-
    vival of, 172–75; story-changing strate-
    gies concerning, 163–76; universal
    service of, 190n12
racial crisis: interest convergence and, 27–28,
    54–55; perceptions of, 21–22; at UIUC, 42
racial justice, 6–7, 190n12
racism: in assessment, 101; campus incidents
    of, 117–18; campus unrest in response to,
    22; and EOP Rhetoric program, 16;
    high-risk/BW programs and, 129–30;
    standards as expression of, 5. *See also*
    discrimination; race consciousness; re-
    verse racism/discrimination; white
    racism
Ramsey, Paul, 98
reading, 34
reform: effectiveness of, 161–62; egalitarian
    impetus for, 5, 9, 14; historical perspec-
    tive on, 8–13, 161–62, 176–77; limita-
    tions on, 5, 10–13, 161; literacy crisis
    attributed to, 57–58; standards and, 5–6
remediation: back-to-basics approach to,
    63–64, 72–75; definition of, 186n10;
    high-risk/BW programs viewed as, 4, 10,
    48–50, 52; provision of, 41; rejection of,
    13; at UIUC, 45, 47–50, 103–5, 113,
    186n11
retention rates, 164–67
reverse racism/discrimination, 56, 64–65
Richardson, Richard C., Jr., 153–54

Roberts, John, 152
Rogers, Ann Marie, 171
Rose, Mike, 6, 179n5
Rutgers University: Academic Foundations
    Department, 129–30; Educational Op-
    portunity Fund (EOF) Program, 129–30

scribal fluency, 98
SCSE. *See* University of Illinois at Urbana-
    Champaign (UIUC): Senate Committee
    on Student English
Selzer, Jack, 18
service activities, 25–26
Sharer, Wendy, 18
Shaughnessy, Mina, 9–10, 65–69, 94, 128,
    131, 132, 182n10; *Errors and Expectations*,
    3, 67–68; "The Miserable Truth," 65–67
Sheils, Merrill, "Why Johnny Can't Write,"
    57–58, 62, 71
Sherman, Roger M., *The Effectiveness of
    Secondary and Higher Education Inter-
    vention Programs*, 184n5
Shor, Ira, 189n8
Sledd, James, 179n5; "Bidialecticalism," 39
Smith College, 118
Smitherman, Geneva, 2–3, 33, 182n12;
    "CCCC's Role in the Struggle for Lan-
    guage Rights," 11–12; "God Don't Never
    Change," 30–32, 38; "Soul N' Style"
    journal column, 30; *Talkin' and Testifyin'*,
    3, 30, 39
Soliday, Mary, 180n11; *The Politics of Reme-
    diation*, 9–10
South Carolina State College, 21–22
special assistance programs, 103–4
special services. *See* Student Support Ser-
    vices (SSS) program
SRTOL. *See* "Students' Right to Their Own
    Language"
SSS programs. *See* Student Support Services
    (SSS) program
Standard English: alternatives to, 9; assess-
    ment of, 62–63; bidialecticalism and,
    35–40; cognitive capacity and, 12; cri-
    tique of, 12; in EOP Rhetoric program,
    46–55, 111; errors regarding, 18, 67–69,
    74–76; impact of appeals to, 5–6; lit-
    eracy crisis and, 57; race-conscious ap-
    proaches to, 179n5; student errors

regarding, 67–69. *See also* white mainstream

standards: college placement and, 90–91; critique/questioning of, 6, 12, 28, 32–33, 63; in EOP Rhetoric program, 47–55; impact of, on high-risk/BW programs, 5–6, 10–13; and SSS programs, 60; white mainstream, 5–6, 9, 25–28, 37–39, 96–102

Stanford University, 118

Sternglass, Marilyn, 123

Storch, Jason, 170–71

story-changing, 8, 14, 163–76, 190n12

Stretch program, Arizona State University, 166

Strickland, Donna, 127

student financial aid, 92, 154–55

Student Support Services (SSS) program: assessments of, 59–60, 123, 154; companion programs to, 182n3; coverage of, 2; criticisms of, 125; development of, 24–25, 185n3; federal funding for, 25, 60, 123–24; growth of, 154; merit-based aid and, 91, 124; race consciousness and, 90

students: international, 168; racial composition of, 1, 25, 60, 124, 153–55, 158–60, 182n6

"Students' Right to Their Own Language" (SRTOL) [CCCC], 3; class and, 9, 180n11; impact of, 11, 38; literacy crisis attributed to, 57; opening sentences of, 29; origins of, 11, 33, 180n13, 182n13; race and, 9, 180n11; race consciousness in, 33–35, 182n15; undermining of, 9, 11–12

Studio program, University of South Carolina, 156–58, 189n8

Summer Bridge program, Columbia College, 166

Supplemental Educational Opportunity Grants, 25

support services. *See* Student Support Services (SSS) program

Talent Search, 182n3

Tassoni, John Paul, 18, 189n8

Taylor, Hill, 190n12

Test of Standard Written English (TSWE), 62–63, 99–100

Texas, 152

Thomas, Leon L., "Racial Minorities and Writing Skills Assessment" (with Edward M. White), 99–102

Thompson, Nancy, *Teaching/Writing in Third Spaces* (with Rhonda Grego), 156–58

Tibbetts, Arn and Charlene, *What's Wrong with American English*, 62

Tinto, Vincent, 164; *The Effectiveness of Secondary and Higher Education Intervention Programs* (with Roger M. Sherman), 184n5

Tobin, Eugene, 191n12

Toma, J. Douglas, 170

traditional teaching: critique of, 33–34; preservation of, 25, 28. *See also* drill

Traub, James, *City on a Hill*, 122, 187n4

TRIO programs, 2, 182n3

two-year institutions, 124, 151, 154–55, 191n17. *See also* community colleges

UIUC. *See* University of Illinois at Urbana-Champaign

University of California Regents v. Bakke (1978), 85–89, 92–93, 98, 185n1, 185n2

University of California–Davis, 86–87

University of Cincinnati, 4, 156

University of Colorado–Boulder, 64, 171

University of Illinois at Urbana-Champaign (UIUC), 15, 41–42; autonomy of, 186n13; Bridge/Transition, 174–75, 192n20; Committee on the Use of English (CUE), 71–72; English Qualifying Exam (EQE), 45–46, 183n21; Ethnography of the University Initiative (EUI), 174–75; interest divergence at, 158–60; and literacy crisis, 70–76; minority enrollments at, 158–60; Office of Minority Student Affairs (OMSA), 181n20; placement at, 103–15, 138; President's Award Program (PAP), 138; race consciousness at, 42–55, 138, 173–75; Rhetoric 199 (Special Options Rhetoric), 113–14; Rhetoric 200 course, 45; Senate Committee on Student English (SCSE), 43–53, 76, 78, 183n19. *See also* Academic Writing Program (AWP), UIUC; EOP Rhetoric program, UIUC

University of Louisiana-Lafayette (ULL), 4, 12–13, 156

University of Michigan, 118
University of Minnesota, 4, 156
University of North Carolina–Chapel Hill, 168
University of South Carolina (USC), 156–58
University of Wisconsin, 118
Upward Bound, 2, 182n3
USC. *See* University of South Carolina

Wagner, Geoffrey, 184n7; *The End of Education*, 63; "On Remediation," 63–64
Ward, Christopher R., 1
White, Edward M.: "Racial Minorities and Writing Skills Assessment" (with Leon L. Thomas), 99–102; *Teaching and Assessing Writing*, 94
white mainstream: *Bakke* decision and, 88–89, 93; color-blind approaches as supportive of, 58; and EOP Rhetoric program, 111–12; financial aid policies and, 92; interests of, 6–8, 125; maintaining power/status of, 5–6, 9, 25–28, 35–40, 48–55, 96–102; race-conscious spaces within, 190n12; and racial justice, 93; and SRTOL, 9. *See also* Standard English; standards

white racism, power and influence of, 14, 22–23, 161–62, 177
Wible, Scott, "Pedagogies of the Students' Right Era," 12
Wiener, Harvey, *Writing Assessment* (with Greenberg and Donovan), 94
Williams, Darnel, 180n13
Williams, Patricia, 134–36; *The Alchemy of Race and Rights*, 135
Williamson, Joy Ann, 16–17
Winant, Howard, 11, 56
Winterowd, Ross, 180n13
writing instruction: bidialecticalism and, 37; cognitive approach to, 66–69; color-blind approaches to, 17–18; as error correction, 18, 50, 67–69, 74–76; race-conscious approaches to, 17, 34, 179n5; scholarship and, 29–30; SRTOL recommendations on, 34. *See also* composition discipline; freshman composition
writing process, 66–67

Yancey, Kathleen Blake, 186n5
Youdleman, Jeoffrey, 70